W9-AFH-431

OPEN FORUM

Fund for an OPEN Society

Volume 2/Number 2   February, 1979

REPORTLAND

The Official Journal of the Greater Portland Convention and Visitors Association, Inc.

PORTLAND'S CONVENTIONS BOOKED TO DATE EXCEED $107 MILLION

$107 million! That's the current estimated economic value of Portland's convention business for the years 1979 through 1986. David L. Heini, Executive Director of Greater Portland Convention and Visitors Association reported after analyzing the organization's records on October 31st.

Heini said that GPCVA's records as of that date showed 817 international, national, regional and state conventions included in the bookings, with a total delegate attendance estimated at more than 425,000 persons, for the eight-year period.

During the four-month period from July 1st through October 31st, 1979, a total of 121 new conventions was added to GPCVA's calendar, adding more than 60,000 delegates to the rolls of conference visitors who will be journeying to Portland for future meetings. The new convention listings for the four-month period have an estimated economic value to the community of $15.1 million.

Heini noted that the statistics cited herein are not the year-end report, but constitute an interim progress report, to which will be added new bookings obtained during the coming months.

PORTLAND'S WINNING TEAM

These Portland representatives successfully bid for the 1983 Fall Board session of the National Association of Home Builders. The City of Roses will host the expected 3,000 delegates for six days in September of 1983. Standing in front of GPCVA's booth at NAHB's '79 Fall Board Meeting in Atlanta are, from left to right, are Tony Raiter, GPCVA; Dick Edwards, President of the Home Builders Assn. of Metro Portland; Jim Goodrich, Executive Vice President of the Metro chapter; Paul Corso of Northwest Natural Gas Co., Albany, the team's "Paul Bunyan;" Patsy Rogers, Atlanta model; and Jim Meehan, GPCVA's Director of Sales. The 1983 site decision, determined by floor vote of attending delegates, was overwhelmingly in Portland's favor over Anaheim and Reno.

Travel Writers Publicizing Portland

John Bedford, travel writer for the Rotherham (England) Advertiser and Sheffield Morning Telegraph, and who is an Associate Member of the Guild of British Newspaper Editors, wrote to Tony Raiter, Director of Tourism for GPCVA: "I am appreciative of your assurance in your recent letter that I can count on you as my Portland contact for future work in making your spectacular city more familiar to the British than it is at the moment. My visit was

far too short but perhaps we can put that right at some future date. I expect my current articles mentioning some of the delights of Portland to be in print in the next few weeks and will see that you get clippings.

Jack Butters, free-lance writer from Lindfield, New South Wales, Australia, whose articles appear in Signpost, a new travel magazine, two leading women's magazines, Woman's World and Woman's Day, Australian Financial

Review, and is editor of Travel Trade Destination, wrote to report that his articles were nearing completion and when published, clippings thereof would be mailed to GPCVA.

His closing comment was: "Meantime, thanks again for all your assistance. The penalty for being so helpful to me is that you're likely to win me back again."

... A. Leon Higginbotham, Jr.

... the essence of the day's experience captured in Judge Higginbotham's statement that spoke of ... which I think gave a mes... conference and dreams which ... Hastie.

... m in the land with its back
... ull.
... and strains sometimes the
... d
... who claim this dream for

... we know they must atone
... common like sunlight and

... for lack of substance any

... no race or color.
... ocked secure in any one

... embattled with its back

... for one it must be saved

Dream of Freedom,
by Langston Hughes

... sage of Bill Hastie and
... mmitment: to save the
... be saved for all "

EDITING YOUR
NEWSLETTER

A Guide to Writing, Design and Production
Second Edition

Mark Beach

Coast to Coast Books
2934 N.E. 16th Avenue
Portland, Oregon 97212

Acknowledgements

First edition

Seven newsletter editors read large portions of this book while still in rough draft: **Joyce Astrup** and **Gail Workman,** Columbia River Girl Scout Council; **Elizabeth Buehler,** Oregon Historical Society; **Adrian Greek,** Positive Action Center; **Marie Taber,** Irvington Community Council; **Elizabeth Tilbury,** Greenpeace of Oregon; **Jack Webster,** Oregon Bass and Panfishing Club. Their helpful criticism constantly kept me focused on the needs of practicing editors.

Three others also gave extensive comments on early drafts: **Harry Stein, Carl Warren** and **Jerry Stewart.**

Some portions of the book required comment from specialists such as **Jack Stewart,** Gestetner Corp.; **Frank Spencer,** Western Paper; **Hal Fitzke,** A.B. Dick Co.; **Don Johnson,** Portland Community College; **Gavin Bjork,** Portland State University; **Kenneth Hauer,** U.S. Postal Service; **Bill Gilchrist,** Cooper Mountain Art Forms; and **Susan Page.** All gave generously of their expertise and experience.

The University of Wisconsin Extension Service and the Warren Paper Company both granted permission to reproduce copyrighted materials.

The contributions of my wife **Kathleen Ryan** show up on every page. She was the most careful and severe critic of rough draft; she always came up with just one more photograph or drawing; she helped mold all the parts together during the challenging process of layout. I deeply appreciate the effort she put into the project.

Second edition

Dozens of people made comments about the first edition which shaped my thinking about the second. I especially want to thank **Polly Pattison, Carl Vandermuelen, Steve Shepro, Sheridan Barre** and **Sol Morrison.**

For permission to use copyrighted materials, I want to thank Charles Scribner's Sons Publishers, Watson-Guptill Publications, Van Nostrand Reinhold Company, Oxford University Press, Universal Press Syndicate, Edwin Newman, International Association of Business Communicators, Georgia-Pacific Company and Graphic Products Corp.

Cover design: **Verni Moore,** Portland OR
Typesetting: **Qualitype** and **Matthew Tiger,** Portland OR
Printed in the USA by **Publishers Press,** Salt Lake City UT

Contents

Introduction

This book is for newsletter editors with little training in writing, editing, graphics, design or printing. I have assumed readers will be either volunteers or employees for whom the newsletter job is one among their many duties.

In writing this book I had two goals in mind. First, I wanted to help you make a better newsletter. Second, I wanted to help you keep costs low. To meet those goals, I organized the material around twelve basic questions faced by every editor.

- Do I need a newsletter?
- What are the goals of my newsletter?
- Who is my audience?
- What is my job as editor?
- How much time should I spend on each issue?
- How do I define and gather news?
- How do I write and edit for clear, interesting prose?
- What regular features should I include?
- How do I make effective headlines?
- How do I use photographs, drawings and graphic aids?
- How do I do layout and pasteup?
- How do I get the best print job at the lowest cost?

Local and personal circumstances will shape your responses to these questions. Each editor will have a unique set of answers. Your own answers will help you with two tasks all editors have in common: making a production schedule and creating a budget. There are forms at the end of this book to help with both.

To make this book more useful I included a number of features suggested by newsletter editors who read rough drafts. Most of the sample forms are typed rather than typeset so they appear just as they were first used. Some information is presented in the form of short quotations from editors. All examples are from newsletters which actually came into someone's home or office. Finally, I did most of the typing, layout and pasteup myself so I would constantly keep in mind the typical editor's job.

The guidelines, techniques and examples in this book were drawn from editing experiences in a wide range of organizations: business, political, hobby, fraternal, educational, religious, labor, agricultural and social service. Furthermore, while the book is specifically designed for newsletter editors, most of its information will also help in making fliers, brochures, bulletins and other small publications.

No newsletter is perfect. Neither is any book. If you find mistakes in this book or have suggestions for making it better, please let me know. Write in care of the publisher. Of course, if you like the book and find it helpful, I would like to hear about that, too.

The first newspaper in the United States was founded in 1704 and called *The Boston News Letter.* The colonies were growing fast. Commercial news such as ship arrivals could no longer travel efficiently by word of mouth.

Editor John Campbell had to be as versatile as his counterparts in the 1980s: he gathered information, wrote articles, fit copy, supervised printing and maintained address lists. He was also aware—even then, almost four centuries ago—of how much readers liked his personal approach. The words community and communication have the same ancient origin. Newsletters help knit people together into communities of common interests.

The *Boston News Letter* was a business venture requiring careful crafting. Newsletters today involve the same blend of practical and artistic skills. As editor of a newsletter, you probably control the entire literary, visual and manufacturing process. I hope this book helps make your work effective. Equally important, I hope your task proves satisfying: that each issue leaves you with a sense of creative fulfillment. That feeling is your right in any job and your special opportunity as a newsletter editor.

Getting Ready

When I teach a workshop on newsletter editing participants are always surprised at the first question of the day: Does your organization really need a newsletter? Editors typically assume newsletters are needed to link leaders and members. The assumption is usually accurate—usually, but not always.

A newsletter is one medium of communication. Here the words "one medium" are important. The goal is communication. A newsletter is simply one way to reach a goal. Other methods of sending messages might be more effective, less expensive, or both.

Setting goals

To assess your communications needs, you should consider two factors: the purposes of your message and the nature of your audiences. The factors are related to each other. Only some purposes will apply to the specific audience you have in mind. No audience will prove receptive to every purpose.

Purposes can usually be described in a word or two. Here is a list of examples. Doubtless you can add more based on your knowledge of your own group.

teach	advertise
inform	solicit
announce	praise
motivate	persuade
entertain	impress
explain	illustrate
recruit	interpret
report	inspire
analyze	define
clarify	justify

Your audiences can also be described on a list. Like a good list of purposes, the audience list should be highly specific. For example, your organization might want to communicate with the following types of people:

- its own members.
- prospective members.
- members or leaders of similar groups.
- government officials, elected or appointed.
- key civic, industry, or other leaders.
- radio, TV, newspaper and other journalists.
- staff of national organizations of which you are a part.
- teachers in local schools and colleges.

When purposes and audiences are combined the result is a statement of communication goals. The statement should be quite explicit, for it is a guide to the methods your group uses to get across its messages. If the statement is vague, it will not serve its function of providing standards for selection from among possible media.

A good statement of communication goals has phrases such as the following:

- to persuade our members to contribute money and recruit new members.
- to advertise to our members services and goods offered by merchants who believe in our cause.
- to impress local and state legislators with the seriousness and soundness of our organization.
- to inform local radio and TV news editors of our activities so they will send out reporters and photographers.
- to interpret our views about property taxes to executives of local financial institutions.

- to teach and inspire our members by explaining the meaning of Bible stories.
- to report and illustrate to our members techniques which will help them do their jobs better.
- to announce activities of our group to leaders of similar organizations.
- to provide our members a convenient schedule of forthcoming events.
- to convince prospective members to join our organization.

Not all these goals are suitable for a newsletter. For example, a newsletter may be too slow and impersonal to get media people to cover your events. News releases delivered in person would probably work better. A newsletter might persuade your members to contribute money but not get them into action for recruiting. Motivation for recruitment might be done better face-to-face by the membership committee. Local executives might welcome some interpretation of your views on taxes but might not sort through your newsletter to find it. An occasional letter from your president directed specifically at executives would probably get more attention.

A clear, complete and specific statement of communication goals has several advantages for both you and your organization. It defines the functions of the newsletter and other methods of sending messages. Thus it also helps define your job as editor. A goals statement provides some basis for budgeting: it is a start toward answers for questions about frequency, length, quality, quantity and distribution of your newsletter. Finally, and perhaps most important, a goals statement is the beginning of evaluation.

"Management thinks this is their newsletter, but I feel I'm really working for 500 employees. They're the ones who want to know what's happening. Often I feel caught between the two when I have to cut a story. I'm lucky I have a good boss to keep the president out of my hair."

Evaluation

Editors are often frustrated because they lack clear standards of success. Sometimes all they hear is, "The last issue was great" or "I wish the last issue had been more interesting." But what made that last issue either interesting or dull? You cannot repeat the process or correct mistakes without more detailed criticism.

Goals for newsletters can be written so evaluation is built in. You simply ask, "What would happen if we met a particular goal?" When you get an answer, you add it on to the goal. Here are examples:

- The newsletter should explain to our members our stand on key issues **so less time is spent at meetings interpreting decisions already made.**
- The newsletter should be a timely reminder to our members of important committee meetings **so meetings begin on time and with a quorum.**
- The newsletter should stimulate enough interest in joining our organization **so at least five prospective members attend each monthly meeting.**
- The newsletter should be sufficiently entertaining **that readers begin reporting funny experiences they have had on the job.**

Five key questions

You can build a process by which goals are developed and their attainment evaluated. That process should be suited to your own organization. It might be as simple as holding a few conversations with your president or supervisor or as complicated as sponsoring a membership retreat. It might involve only one or two other people, a small group, or a large setting. It might take only an hour or might stretch out over several months.

Whatever the process best for you and your group, you should have five results in mind—the answers to five key questions about how you do your job.
- What goals am I expected to reach?
- What are the criteria of success?
- What is my job definition?
- Who gives me supervision and advice?
- What is my budget?

Defining your job

Let's assume you have started to answer questions about goals and criteria. What about your job definition? What do the words "to edit" mean to you and your organization?

Here is a rather short list of words describing activities which might go along with your job.

write	maintain addresses
interview	run equipment
read	repair equipment
summarize	buy paper
criticize	contract printing
rewrite	select type styles
research	keep accounts
type	solicit advertisements
photograph	coordinate volunteers
design	write checks
pasteup	fill out forms
draw	carry boxes
fold	photocopy labels
staple	scale photographs

Not *every* editor does all these tasks. On the other hand, most editors could add a few words to the list. Furthermore, experienced editors know there are aspects of the job not represented on the list at all. These aspects could be called political and exist within every organization. They concern your control over content, design and money. The internal politics also stem from how you work with key staff, officers and readers.

You can get a good start on defining your job by thinking of your responsibilities in five categories.

- ► literary/journalistic
- ► secretarial/clerical
- ► artistic/aesthetic
- ► administrative/financial
- ► administrative/political

With these categories in mind you are in a good position to work with a person or group to get supervision and advice. If you have no one to perform these functions, you should take steps now to fill the gap. Every editor needs some outside points of view on questions involving content, style and design. Every editor needs help from other people or units in the organization. Every editor needs someone to help deal with higher level officials or bodies which make policy.

Most successful editors, even if they have an individual supervisor, like to work with a small group which meets occasionally just to discuss how things are going. A newsletter committee with no job other than to advise and review can be a welcome source of support for work which is often poorly understood. By knowing what it actually takes to write, design and print a quality product at modest cost, the committee can help make your work both more efficient and more pleasant. It can also suggest sources of help and new approaches which might not occur to you on your own.

Writing a budget and getting it accepted is one of the most important tasks of a newsletter committee. Obviously the job should be done in close consultation with you. Just as obviously, the committee acting as advocate may be more effective than you when it comes to interpreting financial needs and competing for funds within the organization.

Planning information

You and your advisory committee need some information from people such as staff, colleagues, members and—most important—readers. One editor used a survey asking reader opinion about content and soliciting volunteers for specific newsletter tasks. By urging everyone at his group's annual convention to answer his questions, he got a lot of people involved as well as learned valuable information.

Whatever process you use to gather planning data, you need help to answer three major questions:

1. What should be the goals of my newsletter?
2. What support and help can I expect?
3. What duties and freedoms do I have as editor?

Whether you use a written survey, informal discussions, focus groups, or a meeting with management, you probably will not get direct answers to these questions. Your planning process will simply yield information upon which answers can be based. It's your job, working with your supervisor or editorial committee, to shape answers. Furthermore, a survey or other formal process is only one source of guidance for defining goals and duties. Traditions, habits, opportunities, prior commitments and dozens of other factors will also influence how you approach your work.

Your time and money

Newsletters are edited by volunteers, employees and freelancers. Regardless of category, every editor faces two questions about the task:

1. How much time should it take to produce this newsletter?
2. How should I be compensated for my work?

Neither question has an answer suited to every situation, for both depend upon your experience, budget, working conditions and job definition as editor. There are, however, guidelines to help you and your supervisors shape answers you will all find workable.

Time

Let's assume you are the typical editor who takes the newsletter from start to finish: you collect and write stories, plan text and visuals, do layout and pasteup, and supervise production and distribution. Let's also assume you have learned the ropes: you know your organization and service people, you have answered basic questions such as timing, length and format, and you have produced four or five issues. In other words, you have settled into the job.

Making these assumptions, how many hours work should each issue take? Here are some guidelines based upon the nature of your newsletter.
—One sheet, two sides, your own typing or word processing, print in-house or quick printer:
ten to twelve hours.
—Four pages (11x17 sheet, two sides), your manuscript to word processer or typesetter, commercial printing:
twenty-five to thirty hours.
—Eight pages, typeset, commercial printing (is more than double the work of four pages):
sixty-five to seventy hours.
—Add second ink color and, presumably, more complicated graphics, pasteup and printing:
increase times by twenty percent.
—Add supervisor who ignores deadlines, checks every word, insists upon last minute changes, requires you at every staff meeting, and writes deadly prose far over space allotment:
double times.

Money

As a **volunteer,** no one pays you for the skilled services you contribute. You are, however, entitled to a reasonable budget and clear set of expectations. You also deserve to work relatively free from hassles and with appreciation for your gift of time.

As an **employee,** your situation is complicated. To make it more simple for purposes of this discussion, let's make two assumptions: 1) you know roughly how many hours your newsletter should take and 2) you want payment appropriate to your skills as editor, artist and production manager.

If you are trained in a field such as graphics or public relations, you already have a rough idea what is the going rate in your area for people with your background and experience. You can get more data from professional organizations such as IABC and CASE, many of which do yearly salary surveys.

If you are trained in some other field such as secretarial work, you can look at your salary in one of two ways:

1) Decide the boss defines your job, go for an appropriate allocation of time, and don't worry about how editing affects your salary.

2) Decide whether being editor should increase your salary. If you like this approach, start by gathering three kinds of data: a) hourly fees in your area for services you are doing such as writing and paste up, b) contract fees from local freelancers to produce newsletters similar to yours and c) salaries for people with full-time public relations jobs that focus on printed products.

You must make sense of this income information based upon your own situation. Frequently the fact-finding points to only one conclusion: you deserve more than you are getting for editorial work. Of course, the research might show you are being paid too much: that your other skills have a higher market value than editorial work. If that's your case, perhaps it is time to give up the newsletter job.

As a **freelancer,** your situation regarding payment is more complicated than for either a volunteer or employee. Here are eleven key points to remember:

1. Work with your client on a precise job definition. Go through this book to make a list of every possible activity so you both know exactly what your fee includes.

2. After computing how many hours the job will take, add at least twenty-five percent for unexpected approvals, missed appointments and general hassle.

3. Once you settle on your job definition, help your client develop a realistic budget for everything else. That gives you an idea of where to set your fee and helps your client understand total costs.

4. Start-up time is very high. If you are developing a newsletter, not simply taking over one already set up, the first issue may take triple the hours of a routine issue; the second and third issues double.

5. Charge a fee per issue, month or year. Hourly rates make both parties nervous.

6. Bill your expenses, including travel, to keep your fees low.

7. When setting fees, remember fringe benefits. You're paying your own pension fund, insurance and other goodies, which employers usually buy or match. Set your fee based upon salaries for comparable work, then add twenty to twenty-five percent.

8. Remember overhead. If you were an employee, you would not have to pay for heat, lights, office space or equipment from your salary.

9. Watch for the start-and-switch game: you do all the development work, then the secretary takes over when the going gets easy. Protect yourself with a long contract, high initial fee, or termination penalty.

10. Build a production cycle for each client. It's the only way to keep the jobs both separated and on track. And there's a bonus: carefully integrating three or four newsletters might mean you could contract them all through one typesetter and printer. Take advantage of quantity prices to save money for your clients and earn money for yourself.

11. Learn supply systems to increase your profits. If you broker services (art, typesetting, printing) or materials (paper), mark up the costs. Twenty percent is common.

A word to the boss

Every newsletter editor—whether volunteer, employee or freelancer—needs effective supervision. If you are the boss, good newsletter management has six aspects.

1. **Designate only one person.** Committees don't produce good newsletters.

2. **Set goals.** Be clear about why you want a newsletter.

3. **Plan evaluation.** Give your editor clear criteria to know whether goals are being met.

4. **Form a budget.** Tell your editor how much money is available.

5. **Give freedom.** Expect your editor to learn the job and do it well; stay out of issue by issue decisions about content, format and art.

6. **Be a good example.** Keep your editor informed; honor deadlines and space agreements; read each issue promptly upon publication.

Employee or freelancer?

Should you assign the newsletter to an employee or hire a freelance writer/producer? Here are some arguments on both sides of that question.

Your own employee already knows your organization and—equally important—is known by others. Your own editor has easy, usually informal access to information and may already be on your payroll. On the other hand, your employee probably is not trained in writing, graphics and printing, thus may turn out an amateur product using too much time and money. Moreover, your employee doubtless will have several tasks in addition to editing, thus making newsletter costs difficult to determine and job definitions hard to keep clear.

A freelancer is presumably a skilled professional, thus might put out your newsletter faster, cheaper and better than doing it in-house. On the other hand, your relationship will be less personal: more formal appointments and dealing by phone. Moreover, the newsletter itself might seem a bit formula rather than special for you. With a freelancer you have a tight job definition and know exactly what your dollar buys.

Hiring a freelancer

Hiring freelance newsletter editing is like buying most other business services. Start by deciding what you want to accomplish. Read the material on these pages about goals, evaluation and being an editor. Be prepared to answer the freelancer's legitimate questions about purposes and budget. The freelancer should translate your concepts into an interesting, useful newsletter—but it's your job to have the concepts in the first place.

What if you get serious about freelance services? What next?

1. Get candidates as you would for any other job. And don't just go to your local ad agency: most areas have dozens of individuals who can do a fine job for less money. A notice sent to typesetters, writers clubs and typing services will turn up leads.

2. Ask for samples. Look at writing and design work the candidate does for others. Styles vary greatly. If your chemistries don't match, keep looking.

3. Get references, then follow up. Ask other clients if they were happy with what they got.

4. Expect a businesslike arrangement: clear lists of duties, deadlines, fees and payment terms.

The right freelancer can give you a fine newsletter and, as a bonus, free your regular employees for work they were trained for.

What's in a name?

A good newsletter name has three qualities: accuracy, liveliness and good taste. Few editors have problems with accuracy and even fewer with good taste. Liveliness, however, often seems elusive. A solid, serviceable name may also sound flat, but renaming risks a new title too cute or ridiculous.

Most newsletter names are built around a key word suggesting communication. Here's a list of terms most commonly used.

topics	post	viewpoint
alert	gram	outlook
focus	forecast	guide
times	survey	facts
log	review	interchange
notes	report	update
list	spotlight	intercom
news	scope	light
wire	bulletin	tab
line	ink	resources
advisory	trends	journal

Older publications tend to use such words in straightforward fashion: *Hilltop School Bulletin; Franklin Real Estate Review; St. Mary's Report.* Titles such as these work well. Readers know what to expect and no one can claim bad taste.

Newsletters of more recent origin often play on communication terms to get upbeat titles. A hospital may use *Housecalls, Check-up, Making Rounds, Vital Signs,* or *Stethoscope.* Financial institutions choose names such as *Bank Notes* and *General Ledger.* Sometimes the names fit perfectly with content, as *Babbling Bookworms* (reviews books for children), *Newsounds* (Bell Association for the Deaf), and *Ruff Times* (financial analysis edited by Howard Ruff). Even initials can sometimes fit into a title, such as *ARTAFacts* from American Retail Travel Agents.

There are plenty of good names not using words about communication. Who would be unsure what to expect from *Metal Collecting, Consumer Trends, Venture Capital,* or *Hospital Purchasing*? Titles such as these do fine for newsletters that often reach people unfamiliar with your organization or message. If your publication is for an in-group, however, you might find one of those rare, perfect names such as *Write in There* (World Pen Pals), *The Log* (California Carvers' Guild), or *The Merry-Go-Round* (National Carousel Association). Titles can also play on jargon, such as *Thruput* for computer programmers and *Point Blank* for gun owners.

What if you need a name and are fresh out of ideas? Where do you look for inspiration? Any pile of newsletters may get you started, but for thousands of ideas look through one of the three standard directories. Your public library may have the *National Directory of Newsletters and Reporting Services (Gale* Research Company), the *Newsletter Yearbook Directory* (Newsletter Clearinghouse), or "Internal Publications," volume five of *Working Press of the Nation* (National Research Bureau). The Gale Research set is strong on newsletters for organizations and associations; the Newsletter Clearinghouse book is best for subscription (commercial) publications; the NRB volume lists newsletters in business, industry and government. All three sources together include names and descriptions of approximately ten thousand newsletters.

"The hardest part about getting started was deciding on a name. I mean, what do you call a newsletter for a bunch of people who sell real estate?

"We had all kinds of suggestions. Most were too cute—names like Property Pointers and Turf Topics. Some were just blah. Who wants to be called just Newsletter of the Evans Realty Company? Finally some one said we're searching for a name just like we're always looking for listings, so why not call it Title Search.

"That's how we got our name."

Age of personal communication

In the early 1970's, Ray Hiebert, then Dean of Journalism at the University of Maryland, said the age of mass communication was over and the future belonged to personal communication. This certainly fits many newsletters. In magazines and newspapers, the editor does not intrude except on the editorial page. In fact, there are often strong objections when a newspaper appears to editorialize in news columns. A newsletter editor, however, considers editorializing part of the job.

First among modern editors, Willard Kiplinger set the current style in 1923. He used the news as a jumping off place to tell his readers the significance of events and trends. Even today the title *Kiplinger Washington Letter* deliberately omits the word "news." Willard's son Austin writes about the news rather than simply reporting it.

Most newsletter editors base their work on a personal style of editorial commentary. Many pride themselves on giving inside information written with a certainty not found in the daily press. And because editors are experts in narrow fields, they know more than a generalized reporter can take time to learn. That is why more general media often quote newsletters as sources of stories: editors become authorities asked to interpret, counsel and often predict.

In addition to authoritative tone, readers like newsletters because they are brief and tightly focused. Specialization is especially important. It wasn't television alone that killed the two giant magazines *Life* and *Look*: readers felt they were too general. Even the TV industry itself, with the growth of satellites and cable, is developing narrowcasting in addition to broadcasting.

Many newsletters are popular because they refine the success formula of *Reader's Digest:* they selectively digest trade journals or other publications in a highly special field. Other newsletters seem to fill the void left when long letters between relatives and friends went out of style—the kind of chatty letter that brought the family together to read out loud. Like popular talk show hosts, editors sound off on everything from politics to cooking, invite comments from readers, and get into arguments. Their pages are alive with strong personality.

Newsletter style is so popular—and effective—that some publishers incorporate newsletters within their magazines. *U.S. News and World Report* contains five one-page newsletters, each designed to appear typewritten. Research about *Business Week* shows their newsletter pages "Personal Business" attract more readers than the rest of the magazine.

Whether staffed by a board of editors or just one person, newsletters are the personalized journalism of which Dean Hiebert spoke.

(Adapted from *Publishing Newsletters* by Howard Penn Hudson, Charles Scribner's Sons Publishers, 1982. Mr. Hudson is editor of *Newsletter on Newsletters* and an authority on newsletters operated for profit.)

"Talk about your politics!

"The night before my first issue was due at the printer our president comes over with a hand-written, three page report. I was up to my ears in rubber cement and he's insisting I type his mess and put it on page one.

"Was I ever surprised! I tried to explain my position and get him to wait 'til next month, but he wouldn't back down. He ended up leaving my house with his letter on top of a box of files and pasteup supplies—and the need for a new editor. Was HE ever surprised!"

Public relations

Newsletter editors often are a one-person public relations staff. If you're in that category—or even if a newsletter is your only task—you can make your newsletter do double duty as a public relations medium. The first duty is to use the newsletter itself for PR; the second is to reach other media via your newsletter.

From the standpoint of public relations, newsletters have four special strengths.

1. **Timely information.** The informal look of newsletters makes them seem always up-to-date.

2. **Inside information.** Because audiences are so tightly targeted and writing so personal, newsletters often seem better sources than more general media.

3. **Trustworthy information.** Newsletters usually carry no advertizing and are often strongly opinionated. Editors protect their integrity.

4. **Specialized information.** Often a newsletter is the only source on a topic—or at least the only source not buried in some academic library.

How can you as editor take best advantage of these strengths? In particular, how can you get people in other media to use your newsletter as a source of information? Here are ten ways.

1. Don't hesitate. Newspaper and TV reporters want to know what your organization is doing — and they want you to tell them. That's how they get most of their "news."

2. Get a media list: a name-and-phone number guide to TV and radio stations, newspapers and magazines, and PR people for regular events such as trade shows. If the media themselves don't have one, try a Chamber of Commerce, coalition of neighborhood groups, political party headquarters, or ecumenical church offices. If all else fails, ask an advertising agency.

3. Meet the key people. Find out who covers news in your field, then learn their interests, deadlines and preferred formats. Let them get to know you, too, so they'll call when they need information.

4. Make your newsletter personal. Mail a copy individually addressed to a key contact; circle the items you want that person to notice; attach a short note with greetings and your phone number.

5. Keep other newsletters in mind. Most editors are eager for news. Your story to the right five hundred readers might be more effective than randomly telecast to 20,000 viewers.

6. Write well. Reporters and editors are happy to use your prose if it's good. When you write quotable prose, you control the message directly to the audience.

7. Run some stories specifically for PR. A good editorial or summary of policy might be picked up as a forceful statement of your organization's views. Tell your contacts they are free to use the story and be sure to ask for credit to your newsletter.

8. When you get coverage, especially in print, feature the fact in your own newsletter. Exposure in public media makes you more credible to your own readers.

9. Think beyond standard media. Good public relations includes reaching out to leaders in other businesses or agencies, legislators, and others you want to impress, inform, or convince.

10. Teach your associates to think PR. Ask fellow workers to suggest people you should keep informed. Urge them to point out activities or plans which, although routine to insiders, might interest outsiders.

"Food Facts is supposed to deal with the co-op movement here in the western part of the state. Well, a lot of us in the movement feel very strongly about environmental issues. I'm one of them. I wrote an editorial opposing the freeway extension to Fernwood Park.

"At the annual meeting of our regional board there was a group just waiting for my report. They said they were with me a hundred percent on the freeway question, but I should stick to food news in the paper. They didn't want Facts as a forum for anyone's private cause."

Building Content

Editors often don't know what readers want. Editors' supervisors usually share the uncertainty. Both may labor under the old stereotype of newsletters with little more than birth notices and bowling scores. Neither may recognize that candid information helps readers be more productive, committed and effective.

Your organization may be a small school or large factory, a rural church or urban neighborhood, a local club or international association. Whatever your size and purposes, your readers are far better educated and more thoughtful than just a few years ago. Sure they want to know about retirements and awards and the softball schedule, but their top priorities lie with data which materially affect their lives.

What evidence says an effective newsletter typically has serious content? Newsletters themselves form one answer. Samples from all over the country, from every type of organization, showing every grade of skill in writing and design, reflecting every level of budget, all show an increasing tendency toward sophisticated news and analysis. Other evidence comes from the phenomenal spread of newsletters as a medium—and especially of newsletters published for profit. Thousands of readers are paying well for serious information in newsletters affecting their economic, political and personal lives.

The professionalization of editors via organizations, training and accrediting procedures offers more evidence that serious writing can succeed. Organizations for editors in the fields of education, association management, business and hospital public relations offer training, awards and, of course, their own newsletters. These professional editors give top priority to topics such as morale, productivity and economics.

Almost ten thousand editors belong to the International Association of Business Communicators. In 1981, IABC surveyed 45,000 employees to learn about reader interest. The survey covered forty businesses in eight industrial categories and asked about seventeen topics. Results showed employees rate information in the following order.

Rank	Subject
1	Organization's plan
2	Personnel policies and practices
3	Productivity improvement
4	Job-related information
5	Job-advancement opportunities
6	Effect of external events on my job
7	Organization's competitive position
8	News of other departments/divisions
9	How my job fits overall organization
10	How organization uses its profits
11	Organization stand on current issues
12	Organization community involvement
13	Personnel changes/promotions
14	Financial results
15	Advertizing promotions/plans
16	Stories about other employees
17	Personal news (birthdays, etc.)

Clearly employees want to know about plans and the effect of such things as government regulations, consumer patterns and economic forces. Other research and experience points in the same direction: newsletter readers want to be treated like the literate audience they are.

Two dozen ideas

1. The new supervisor or leader. What are long-range hopes or goals? How does new role affect relations with old friends? What is best part of new job—and part of old job missed the most?

2. Parenting. How do demands of your organization or company affect being a parent? What help available and activities offered for families? Are there services/opportunities for children of employees?

3. Suggestion program. What is an effective suggestion? Getting management to listen, then act. Life history of a suggestion that brought results. What rewards good suggestions bring.

4. Who's in school. What opportunities and support company has for workshops or courses. How training benefits both organization and individual. What developments or trends require more training.

5. Stress. Symptoms of stress in fellow workers, supervisors and yourself. How stress related to safety and productivity. What help is available and how to seek it in nonthreatening ways.

6. New department or committee. Why it formed, what it does, who's in charge, when, where and how it's all happening. Most important, how it fits into the overall plan.

7. Jargon. Prime examples of jargon in your field or industry. "Before" and "after" examples of jargon translated into English. Reader suggestions or contest to rewrite common jargon into readable prose.

8. Trends. Long range trends in economy, politics, society, or your own field. How are they likely to affect your operation? What plans by management or leadership to cope or take advantage of trends.

9. Tours. Do we give tours? If so, of what and to whom? Why offer tours? Who's in charge and how are arrangements made? How about tours for employees, including visits to related nearby industry?

10. Emergency services. What types of emergencies might occur in our setting? How are we prepared to handle? Are there hotlines: local and in-group or plant? Our response to community emergencies?

11. Design for safety. How safety is a planned condition. Who plans it and how. Drawings of floor plans for good traffic patterns. Good signs and other visual aids. Protective devices and clothing.

12. Cutting costs. What management/leadership views as waste or chance to be more efficient. Worker/member ways to cut costs in everyday operations. Economic pressure and how to respond.

13. Annual reports. Before report, readers could suggest visuals and content. After report, newsletter to summarize report and feature outstanding visuals. Why annual reports necessary and who gets ours.

14. Crisis communication. What do we consider a crisis? Who should be informed and who will issue official comment/instructions? How to check-in during crisis: hotlines, telephone chains, radio news.

15. Energy saving. Results of energy audit. Who's doing what to save energy? How much energy we spend and in what form. Long range planning to spend less money and use less energy.

16. Quality control. What do we regard as quality? How are quality standards established and monitored? Are we getting the quality we want? New machines or techniques to raise quality.

17. Company giving. Who gets charitable and political donations and for how much? Who decides amounts or shares? How we work with United Way and similar community agencies.

18. Board of control. Who are our directors/trustees/board members? How does someone get on the board and what do they do? How often do they meet, where and what reports made.

19. Break time. Series of features on how various people spend time during short work breaks: eating, recreation, athletics, reading, napping, meetings. Most unusual activity or snack on break.

20. Internships and apprentices. How young people break in. What we do to help employees working with newcomers. Is quality and number of newcomers sufficient to meet standards and demands?

21. Deductions. Step-by-step through a paycheck to explain F.I.C.A., pensions, insurance and other deductions. Which are required and which options? How payroll department or computers work.

22. Long distance friends. People who have dealt with each other for years by phone or letter only. How they "met" and what your person does. Arrange their first meeting and cover the story.

23. Speaker programs. What schools or other outside groups want to learn about us or from our employees. What suport we give to members/workers invited to speak and who are our popular speakers.

24. New working conditions. Trends such as job sharing, off site work, staggered hours, and four day week. How trends might fit with our operation and what plans we are developing.

Where's the border?

This book is full of rules and guidelines. It is also, however, a book urging you to be creative and to use common sense with design.

My page design calls for the bold border you've seen thus far. Here is an exception—the first of several. This fine article about church newsletters came from *Newsletter Forum*, a newsletter for editors. The article already looked fine in their format: why change it to fit mine?

Here's How To Put Out

By Ronald Farrar

"We aren't communicating."
What a cliche!
Well, we **aren't** communicating. Not at work, at school, at home — and especially not at church. There are no perfect bridges across the communications gap — especially within a busy church congregation — but there are some means by which communications can be sharply improved. One of these is a weekly newsletter.

Many of you are 'way ahead of us in that you've been publishing church newsletters for years. For those who aren't however, these nuts-and-bolts ideas, the product of an experience at the Oxford-University United Methodist Church, may help.

> *Don't try to be too professional. . .the value of the newsletter is in content — not in slickness of paper or cuteness of design.*

A. Make a commitment. In our case, this was easy. The pastor, the Rev. Lavelle Woodrick, strongly felt the need for a weekly newsletter; he recruited the editor — who then helped recruit other volunteer staff members — and he got approval from the administrative board for the project.

B. Determine the objectives. Here is what we hoped our newsletter might attempt:

1. To inform congregation members about their church — services, problems, goals, organizations.

2. To call attention to, and provide recognition for, outstanding performance by individuals and groups within the church — and to encourage more such achievements.

3. To help unify the congregation by focusing on common goals, priorities and accomplishments.

4. To promote the worship service for the following Sunday.

5. To overcome criticism regarding the church by paying special attention to activities and procedures which might be misunderstood or might cause criticism.

6. To provide a regular means of communication with **all** members of the congregation — not merely those who attend worship services each Sunday.

7. To make known to all members of the congregation the special opportunities that exist in the church for worship and service.

8. To expand the ministry by providing an additional outlet, or forum, for the minister or a layman who wants to reach the congregation in a different way.

9. To provide a systematic means of information-gathering about the church and all its activities. Two such uses that might be made of this information are (a) to identify events and activities for publicity in local news media, and (b) for later use as part of church records and history.

C. Develop news sources. The newsletter can be only as good as the information it delivers. The pastor — the prime news source — can't do it all. Every effort should be made to develop a network of reporters from throughout the various sub-groups in the congregation. With proper encouragement, news can come from such possibilities as:

1. Pastoral messages.

2. A brief promotion, or "tease," regarding the sermon topic for the Sunday ahead.

a Church Newsletter
—Bookman Medium, 24 pt

3. Sunday school classes — study topics, promotions socials, unusual events.

4. The choir — especially new members, soloists, a mention of the anthem to come Sunday, spotlight on musical background of individual choir members.

5. Methodist Youth Fellowship, and related youth activities.

6. News of Scouts, Cubs and other organizations that may have church sponsorship or support.

7. Civic activities, such as the Red Cross Blood Drive, etc., that may use church facilities on occasion.

8. Profiles of new church members, families, newcomers, transfers, as they unite with the congregation.

9. Promotion, and explanation, of special events related to Advent, Epiphany, Pentecost, etc.

10. Financial information — collections, budget data, progress reports on how outstanding obligations are being met.

11. Reports from commissions, boards, quarterly conferences and other official bodies.

12. Announcements of special events to be at the church, such as weddings, visiting choral groups, etc.

13. Obituaries of church members — in more detail than can be provided in the Sunday bulletin, from the pulpit, or in the local press.

> *The main job is to get on with it: if we had waited until we had pre-solved all our problems we might never have got out the first issue.*

14. Birthdays of church members; perhaps even wedding anniversaries, births, other news of interest to families.

15. Reports from circle groups, which concern women especially.

16. Reports from college student members of the congregation who are away at school.

17. Items from other congregations, or news from the church nationally or internationally.

18. Reports from missionaries we help sponsor abroad.

19. Items which might be generated from parishioners — such as questions of general interest asked of the minister.

20. Bible verses or other brief devotional items which may be especially appropriate during a given week.

21. Consciousness-raising announcements, such as news from shut-ins, or those in the hospital or nursing homes, etc.

22. Regular features from senior citizen groups, call-a-friend and related activities.

23. Human interest items from church members (unusual travel, family reunions, other personal mentions). Most editors learned this a long time ago: Names make news.

24. Guest editorials — from members of the congregation, as well as messages from the Ministerial Alliance, District Superintendent or Bishop, or others who may be interested in reaching the congregation.

25. Exerpted material — clippings from the **Advocate, Upper Room,** etc. — of direct interest.

26. Feature stories about unusually colorful members of the congregation — older people, perhaps, who can recall unique moments in the history of the local church.

D. Develop a schedule. In a typical week, the newsletter might be produced in this fashion:

Sunday, Monday — Items are developed by correspondents and reporters as well as the pastor and church secretary. These items are drafted in finished form — e.g., names spelled correctly, facts checked for accuracy, no loose ends, etc., — and dropped into a special newsletter mailbox at the church.

Tuesday — Newsletter editor rewrites, edits, prepares copy for printing.

Wednesday — retyping (either by church secretary or — as in our case — by volunteer typist), onto stencil for mimeographing, or camera-ready copy for offset, depending on production method you prefer. Copy to printer.

Thursday — Finished newsletters addressed, sorted for mailing, delivered to postoffice before noon, if possible.

Friday — Newsletter should arrive in homes of church members.

E. Involve as many people as possible. Every Sunday School group, every board or commission, every church-related activity should designate a newsletter reporter. The pastor is the major source, obviously, but he needs plenty of help. Our newsletter has a staff of seven — which means we can rotate editors to prevent overworking any one person.

F Publish every week if you can. Habit is a powerful force — in reading patterns as in almost everything else — and you'll want to get the congregation accustomed to looking forward to the newsletter prior to the services each Sunday. Also, it's much easier, once you're geared up, to develop a weekly routine than to publish a newsletter on an irregular basis. Don't worry about having enough news: There'll be more than you can handle anyway.

G. Don't try to be too professional. Because we operate with volunteer help and a low budget, we've had to adopt a plain, and rather homely format. However, the value of the newsletter is in content — not in slickness of paper or cuteness of design.

H. Evaluate. And, if necessary, modify. We changed printing and addressing systems in the first few weeks. Probably we will change format and some other things before long. The main job is to get on with it. If we had waited until we had pre-solved all our problems we might never have got out the first issue.

I. Enjoy. Producing a newsletter is fun! The staff knows (before anyone else) what's going on, and publishing a tiny newspaper every week brings us in contact with fellow churchgoers we may not have got to know otherwise.

—Optima Roman, 10 on 10½

Ron Farrar is director of the College of Communications at the University of Kentucky. His article on church newsletters was written as a result of an experience at the Oxford-University United Methodist Church which he attended while chairman of the Department of Journalism at the University of Mississippi.

"Most of us in the journalism schools aren't nearly as well informed — nor are we informing our students — about newsletters as much as we should," Farrar writes. "Perhaps The Newsletter Forum will spur us to involve newsletters in our curriculum far more prominently."

Gathering news

It would be great to have a staff of dependable, skilled reporters. For most editors, that is a dream which never comes true. Sure, you will get lots of promises and some cooperation. As the deadline for each issue approaches, however, you will probably end up relying mostly on yourself for the information you need.

Here are some tips to avoid last-minute confrontations with blank paper.

► Keep an accurate, up-to-date list of key names and phone numbers. Make the rounds by phone a few days before your copy deadline.

► Have a standing appointment with key officers and staff a week or so before every deadline. Get their ideas about what the next issue should include.

► Get yourself on mailing lists for materials you might summarize or use for tips. How about legislative reports, environmental impact statements and lists from sources such as the Government Printing Office?

► Ask to be sent copies of newsletters from groups similar to yours. They will be full of ideas for design as well as content.

► Start a clipping file from newspapers and magazines. If the clippings do not lead to a story, at least they may produce a filler to replace a last minute deletion.

► Tell your readers about your need for news.

► Be sure your masthead is in every issue. As you do your job and participate in your group, build in ways for people to help you.

At the right is a short form one editor used to gather news. He printed copies on 5 x 8 index cards and made sure they were handed out at every committee and staff meeting. To press the point—and get more news—he mailed one every month to every officer and board member.

Would you take just ONE MINUTE at this meeting to help with the next issue of _Patterns_. Simply check any items you'd be willing to have me call to discuss.

_____ Outstanding quilt you have seen.

_____ History of a particular design.

_____ Quilt designs used to decorate other items.

_____ New methods or materials.

_____ Quilt-related travel plans by anyone in the club.

_____ Honors to anyone in the club.

_____ Special activities planned.

_____ New book or article.

_____ Sources for quilting materials.

_____ Teaching techniques.

_____ Display techniques.

_____ Classes or demonstrations.

_____ Persons I should interview.

Please write any other ideas.

Thank you.   George Becker
              381 9956

name   phone number   address

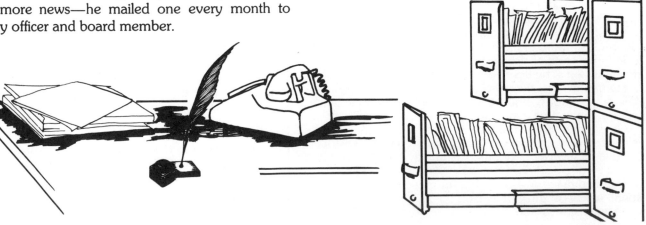

Doing interviews

Interviews can make your newsletter highly personal at the same time they get across information. Readers like them. As an added bonus, much of your copy is written by the person you interview. You simply edit and present the material.

Editors often overlook interviews as a chance to put readers in touch with a person they might never meet. The interview situation also gives you a chance to be a "member of the press" and possibly talk with someone otherwise inaccessible.

Here are a few guidelines for effective interviews.

Before

- Write down what questions you would like answered. Limit the list only to "must information" and tailor it to your readers' interests.
- Make an appointment. Usually some neutral ground such as a restaurant is the best place to meet. Stay away from the telephone—yours or your subject's.
- When you make the appointment, tell your subject information you need and how much time you want.
- Ask for a photo to run with the story. If you plan to take a photographer to the interview, be sure to check if it's OK with your subject.

"Month after month I struggled with every issue. Finally my term as editor was over and I was having lunch with my replacement. I heard myself giving two simple rules for doing newsletters in half the time.

"First, be organized. Make a plan, then stick to it. Visualize the whole issue with a map. Second, avoid perfection. Don't think every sentence or drawing has to be a work of art. You'll never make it, but you sure can eat up a lot of hours trying.

"I was astonished to hear myself give such good, simple advice—and embarrassed that I'd never followed it myself."

- Ask your subject for a resume, biography sheet or press clipping you can read in advance. This will save you both time by getting you past the introductory questions about things such as birthplace and education. It may also suggest discussion topics which would not otherwise occur during the inteview.

During

- Get there early. Be ready to offer greetings and introduce anyone else involved.
- Confirm any time limits, taboo subjects and other administrative details.
- Ask your questions. You are in charge and should guide the conversation. That doesn't mean being rigid but merely keeping the discussion on track.
- Get specifics. If someone is quoted, get the full name and title. If there are references to written materials, get correct titles. Take time to check details while your subject is still with you.
- Watch as well as listen. Expressions, posture and gestures signal feelings behind the answers.
- Ask for the best way to contact your subject to confirm or clarify anything just before publication.
- Finish with personal amenities, especially a genuine thank you.

After

- Write your notes immediately after the interview. Don't let those quotations or observations slip away in the rush of other business.
- If you are uncertain about anything, call your subject to verify. This is the time to be sure you have all the quotations written accurately.
- When writing, put the questions and answers in context. Say something about the physical setting, how you felt, how your subject seemed to feel, and what your subject did as well as said. Put personality around the quoted words.

Inexperienced interviewers often doubt their ability to recall quotations and wonder if they should use a tape recorder. For short discussions, typical for newsletter work, the machine is not needed. If you go over your notes right after the conversation, you can translate your personal shorthand into full, accurate sentences.

Managing reporters

How often have you wondered how to get people to write material completely, accurately and on time? Probably as often as you have put together an issue of your newsletter. There is always someone who absolutely promised to have something ready but who just didn't make it.

You have a right to feel angry. On the other hand, the experience should also lead to some questions only you can answer.

- ▶ Did you make your needs clear? What did you expect in terms of length, content and deadline?
- ▶ Did you pressure someone into feeling uncomfortable? Some people are willing to gather information but feel afraid to put it into words which will appear in print.
- ▶ Did you offer the rewards of authorship: reasonable control over content and dependable by-lines?

Whether your writers work for free or on some payroll, they are all essentially volunteers. Writing for the newsletter is not their primary responsibility and probably not even a major duty. Their main job is probably to make some other part of the organization function. You need their help because they have access to information. Keeping in mind their volunteer status will help you stay sensitive to what is reasonable to expect.

One approach to working with volunteer reporters is to decide which you want most, participation or dependability. It is almost impossible to have both. To get participation, you must set up conditions which encourage people to contribute. And you must give up some control. To get dependability, you need to take control—and do most of the work yourself.

An editor of a newsletter for a sailing club solved many of her problems by circulating copies of a simple set of directions. Her guidelines made everyone's work easier and led to a better publication.

Tips to TELLTALES

- Write your story. Don't just send a flier or minutes of your meeting. If you can't write it out, phone it to me at 384 5879 or tell me on the dock.

- Be accurate. Check your facts.

- Be specific. Give full names, not just last or nicknames; days of the week as well as dates; addresses as well as place names.

- Edit. Then edit again. Take out all unnecessary words. We all would rather be sailing.

- Give a contact: the name and phone number for details.

- Put a large question mark and arrow showing anything I should check - anything you are not sure about.

- Send photographs or drawings if you can. Art makes interest.

- Suggest anyone I can call for details, update, more art or a related story.

- Send me the story right away and certainly by the monthly deadline:

Second friday

Thanks for your help.

Jane

Jane Scheaffer

Handling advertising

"We used to get a lot of hassle from neighborhood merchants. They thought they should get free display ads just because they paid dues to the organization. After awhile I just gave up and quit the editing job.

"The new editor really handled the situation well. First he got the advisory committee to rule against all display advertising. Then he made a list of all merchant members. He prints the list in every issue and sets it off in a nice box with the headline Support Local Business.

"Who could argue with that?"

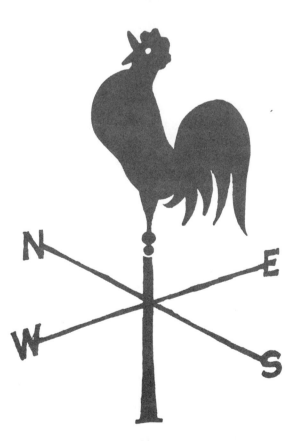

All newsletters advertise. Indeed, advertising may be their most important function. Pages are filled with notices of meetings, requests for donations and lists of special needs and events. Most of this material relates to sponsoring organizations, but often other interests are also represented.

Advertising is usually divided into two categories: display and classified. Display ads are the ones with pictures and often set apart in boxes or by border design. Classified ads are simply notices arranged (classified) into groups and given topical headings.

Advertising has a number of advantages.

► It keeps your readers informed.
► It provides material for fillers.
► It helps get things your group needs: volunteers, donations, attendance and other forms of support.
► It helps personalize the publication.
► It creates reader interest.

There may also be disadvantages.

► You may end up with too much material.
► People or groups whose ads you cut may feel offended.
► Some readers may not like people or groups represented by particular ads. They may think you are serving special interests.

If you want to carry ads for **anything** not sponsored by your organization, it is a good idea to work out a policy with your advisory committee or supervisor. As a minimum the policy should deal with your editorial control over content and whether anyone will have to pay. Most editors who accept ads insist upon copy in writing so they are not responsible for listing a wrong date, place or cost.

Most editors do not like to charge for space. Billing and collection is too much bother. Free classifieds to members and the honor system for small fees from display advertisers work pretty well.

Writing well

Writing may seem the hardest part of newsletter work. Wanting good prose stimulates foreboding memories of misplaced modifiers and dangling participles. Sometimes the whole idea of putting words on paper leads to paralysis of hand and brain.

Most writers, no matter how professional or experienced, have those feelings. The malady is known as Writer's Block. Writers themselves have spent millions of hours seeking a cure. Most of that search, however, has seemingly been an excuse to avoid writing. Furthermore, it has led nowhere.

Writer's Block has only one known cure—a simple formula passed through the centuries from ancient scribes: a deadline measured in hours rather than days. This cure, while effective, is often painful. Writers working under pressure from imminent deadlines tend to be waspish with friends, associates and spouses. Moreover, deadlines for newsletter editors usually bring worries about production as well as prose.

While a tight deadline is the only certain cure for Writer's Block, there are several methods of prevention. All require constant application of the four principles of good writing.

Four principles

Writing is work.

Editors often think good writing comes naturally as a gift which some have and others lack. On the contrary, writing is a learned skill and requires constant practice. Most good writers—and all great ones—write, rewrite, then rewrite again. The very best may go through six or eight drafts before being satisfied.

Good writing reflects natural speaking.

When you talk, you use plain language, concrete words and common images. You speak directly to the listener with words interesting because they carry your personality. Newsletter writing must be as simple and direct as speaking. Prose which is fancy or formal only ends up confusing most readers.

Read aloud some of your own writing. If you react "I never talk that way," go back and rewrite. You don't need the slang and shorthand of everyday speech, but you do need the straightforward words used in talking.

Simple writing is especially important in a newsletter because it is such a personal medium. Readers want a sense of your personality as editor. Successful newsletters make readers feel they are hearing—not reading—inside information prepared just for them.

Readers are impatient.

Your job is to get information to your readers before they get your newsletter to the wastebasket. Success depends upon your ability to compete with housework, spouses, hobbies, television, occupations, children and sleep. Competition is especially keen for the many newsletters arriving unsolicited or as "benefits" of membership.

Design and graphics help you compete, but neither overcome the effects of bad writing. Keep sentences, paragraphs and stories short. You might try a guideline such as: sentence maximum fifteen words; paragraph maximum five sentences; story maximum five paragraphs. Short items also cut costs on preparation, printing and postage.

Set goals.

Just as with your newsletter as a whole, each story, each paragraph, even each sentence should have a purpose. Look again at the list on page two. Any of those words, and more you supply, might fit a particular story. Don't begin the story until you have at least one word to describe your reason for writing it.

Proper goals say how you want readers to feel or what you want readers to do. Thus goals help you keep readers clearly in mind so your words don't stray from the effect you seek. And notice the list on page two does not include the word "communicate." Although a common goal, the word says nothing about reader thought or action. It's simply not useful.

"The last editor we had lasted about two issues. She had New York Times standards and was just way out of line.

"People write for a newsletter like ours because they like to tell their friends what's happening and they like to see themselves in print. When some one cuts up their work or ignores it, they feel insulted. And they tell everyone else how they're feeling.

"It hurts an organization more to have alienated members than to print bad grammar."

Ten ways to improve writing

Be specific.

When you talk with a friend, your words usually refer to things which can be sensed. Your ideas and stories have heat, weight, color and sound. Concrete words form images and examples. When language gets general and abstract, it grows dull and vague.

General: The annual convention was well attended.

Specific: Eighty-five people came to the convention.

General: Members will have an opportunity to give feedback.

Specific: Say what you think by writing to the Executive Director before Friday.

General: Financial considerations negatively impacted our sales effort.

Specific: Last quarter sales fell by eighteen percent because our best customer went bankrupt.

Jargon words and specific words are natural enemies. Use jargon only if you want to fill space without conveying meaning. Otherwise, jargon is vague and, by definition, limited. In either case, it defeats the purposes of writing by cutting you off from your readers.

Use simple words.

You rarely need complicated language to tell a story—even a complicated story. Everyday words will usually do the job.

Why write assist when you mean help?
Why write obtain when you mean get?

Change	to
ascertain	discover, find out
attempt	try
communicate	say, write, tell
facilitate	help, ease
implement	do
indicate	show, point out
insufficient	not enough
numerous	many
personnel	people, workers, staff
terminate	end

And don't use "utilize."

Use strong verbs.

Verbs are the guts of language, making other words work. Weak verbs make dead prose. With strong verbs your writing will sparkle with life.

Strong verbs link directly to the five senses—touch, sight, smell, sound, and taste—and to familiar emotions. They are short and personal: run, fight, love, say. And strong verbs tend to couple with other short, strong words: drove in, pulled out, bent over.

Weak verbs seem abstract and impersonal. They tend to be long words: employ, postpone, construct. Moreover, weak verbs attract heavy adverbs: frequently employ, constantly postponing, tediously constructing.

Weak verb	Strong verb
inform	tell, say
reduce	cut
indicate	show
modify	change
endeavor	try
desire	want

Use action.

Readers want to know who or what is the subject of the sentence, then what happened. Action builds interest. To get it, simply begin a sentence with the subject and follow with a strong verb.

Change to: A candidate will be Ellen James. Ellen James said she would run.

Change to: The Lincoln School auditorium was the site where members congregated. Members met in the auditorium of Lincoln School.

Notice most forms of the verb "to be" produce drab sentences. To perk up your writing, find strong verb replacements for "is," "be," "was," and "were." Those replacements will almost force you to start sentences with their subjects.

Use pronouns.

Pronouns help purge ponderous prose. Little words such as "he," "she" and "they" relieve readers from two or three word phrases repeated, it seems, after each comma. After naming people and places,

Change to: The sales manager informed the audit task force that projections were encouraging a reduction in personnel. She told them some people would be fired because of falling profits.

Don't hesitate to use the first person pronouns "I" and "we." Get rid of those cumbersome phrases such as "Your editor thinks. . ." and "The committee decided. . . ." If you think something, let readers know in clear, simple terms just as if you were speaking directly to them.

Keep down the nouns.

While verbs are the guts of language, nouns are the fat. Nouns plant themselves in sentences so firmly the most brutal editor has trouble slicing them out.

To make language move easily from thought to thought, use nouns sparingly. Especially watch for:

Noun clusters—sentence fattening goodies such as "cost impact considerations" (price) and "schedule stretchout adjustment" (delay).

Noun clusters begin with a wish to sound formal and weighty. The director of maintenance, for example, feels "implementation of corrective action" will be taken more seriously than "stopping the leak."

Pompous words—grammatical globules such as "of the order of magnitude" (about), "paradigm" (model), and "in view of the foregoing" (so).

Pompous words are usually abstract. Like noun clusters, they grow wherever writers try to dress up prose with the language of science.

Prepositional phrases—cellulite layers such as "as a result of" (because), "in excess of" (more), and "in the amount of" (for).

Sentences laden with prepositions pad the distance from one idea to the next. Their flab absorbs meaning and encourages sloppy writing.

Use direct questions.

What do readers want to know? If you have an answer, you've gone a long way toward defining goals for your newsletter. Use the same logic for features and stories: write two or three questions, then print them as part of the article.

Using questions strengthens writing in two ways. First, questions force you to focus on your audience: exactly what do you want them to know. Second, questions help readers be efficient: they appreciate your guidance through the material.

A question format is especially useful for touchy or personal topics. Why is a printed interview so effective? Because the writer brings readers together with a person they want to meet or having information they want to hear. Interviewers ask questions on behalf of readers, then print both questions and answers. The technique can work just as well for other kinds of articles.

Delete "that."

Why pick on such a common and apparently useful word? Because that is a word that clutters language and that encourages people that are not careful writers to string out ideas that should be broken into sentences that could be shorter. That's why!

Cross out "that" every time it appears in your last newsletter. No exceptions. Now read the material aloud and replace the "that" only in sentences making no sense without it. Perhaps one sentence in ten will get its "that" back.

Use contractions.

Yes, I know English teachers say contractions don't belong in good writing. They're wrong. At least, they're wrong when it comes to newsletters.

Remember successful newsletters reflect editors' personalities. Few editors converse without contractions, but most turn a spoken "won't" into a written will not. The two word version sounds slightly more formal, thus more distant and less personal. You needn't pepper your prose with contractions; neither should you avoid one where it sounds right.

Write tight.

This is the summary rule and the hardest to define. Avoid clutter. Cut every useless word. Juggle phrases and sentences until they fit precisely together.

Change	All aspects of the situation should be taken into careful consideration prior to the implementation of corrective action.
to	Don't change anything until you've checked it thoroughly.

Clutter depersonalizes. Who could believe there's a living, breathing person making such prose?

Clutter promotes mistakes. When writing isn't clear, readers can't be blamed if they don't get the message.

Clutter hides responsibility. It's easy to dodge responsibility when messages are vague: no one knows what anyone said, so no one is accountable.

Read again this advice to write tight, substituting jargon for clutter. Regardless of topic, writing strewn with jargon is usually good for only one purpose: to boost its author's ego. Newsletters of all media must be free from jargon.

O Facilitative New World!

MY TURN/EDWIN NEWMAN

When I look at the future, I flinch. Many people do, of course, for a variety of reasons. My reason is the expectation, more and more confidently expressed, that the future will be the Age of Information. Already, we are told, an impressive percentage (estimates vary) of those who work no longer grow things or make things or sell things. They engage, instead, in "information transfer." And this, we are assured, is a mere beginning. Which is why I flinch. Much of the information transferred to us now, on paper, is not worth having. Will the world be a better place when, on computer print-outs or flashing word processors, we receive the following?

"It is recommended that the focus, scope and purpose be clearly delineated and understood. Then, with the existing resources, the restructuring of the developmental process will be guided by the central concepts of the previously stated management philosophy. Specific functional and administrative activities, service outputs, and staff capacity development will be defined as real need demands are anticipated or identified. Armed with this real need information, a working management tool can be more accurately designed through the use of the proposed management model."

Human Resources: That paragraph (part of a memorandum that won its author a promotion in the human-resources department of a middle-size state) occupied people, otherwise known as human resources, who might better have been employed doing almost anything else. The Information Age will make it easier to pump out such stuff and circulate it to full-fledged information receivers. Real need knowledge, I imagine it will be called.

Even now, before the Information Age has fully dawned, we may chance upon this:

"For the purpose of communication, some of the dimensions of organizational health are listed. The listed dimensions are only a sampling of indicators which can be considered. Each is a job environmental condition created or not created by management which when present indicates with a high degree of predictability that productive work is underway."

O brave new world, that has such information in't! But hold! There is more, the dimensions of organizational health themselves:

"Clarity and acceptability of agency goals by staff.

"Distortion-free vertical and hori-

The nation is drowning in effusions about setting 'meaningful, priority-based objectives.'

---

zontal communication both formal and informal.

"Adequate distribution of influence within the organization through the decentralization of program authority.

"Cohesiveness of staff within and across program boundaries."

Still receiving?

How many Americans on public and private payrolls already spend their time writing—or as they would prefer to say, conceptualizing—this sort of thing, and how many spend time reading it? The nation is drowning in it, in effusions about setting "meaningful, priority-based objectives" and about "the personal and corporate building of physical, psychological and organizational environments that best facilitate the process of innovation and project management." When this gabble appears on paper, the copies can be thrown away. The original, more likely to be saved, at least by its author, may rot. In a computer data bank, it will be with us, such is the magic of "information retrieval" and "electronic memory systems," forever.

Parameters: We have, today, otherwise blameless citizens who will sit at a typewriter and produce this: "I am reluctant to limit myself to specific titles as they tend to limit the parameters that often encompass a number of areas that for one reason or another have a natural interface."

Limited parameters and natural interfaces rub shoulders with linear and nonlinear model fitting, negative/positive reinforcement concepts, nonevent feedback mechanisms, cognitive mapping, axial rules and neuro-linguistic programing.

All of this we have, and more. What will we get when cathode-ray-tube keyboards are everywhere, hooked into a mighty network of foolish discourse, and when computers can talk to one another? I don't go as far as Kingsley Amis's Lucky Jim, who decided at an early age that there was no point in acquiring new information because it pushed out an equivalent amount of information he already had, leaving him just where he started. As the new electronic marvels buzz away furiously, some of what they do will have value. But, as an inevitable accompaniment, they will preserve what ought to be torn up, discarded, cast aside or should never have been born.

As a child, my daughter had a ready answer when urged to eat something because it was good for her. "Eat it," she would reply, "your own self." To prophets of the information explosion, I say roughly the same thing. Leave me out of it. Transfer—and receive—that information your own self.

Newman, a commentator for NBC News, is the author of "Strictly Speaking" and "A Civil Tongue."

Writing without bias

Good writing means avoiding slurs and stereotypes based upon sex, race or age. Inoffensive prose is often difficult to achieve, for old language patterns die hard. Rewards, however, are worth the effort. Readers will appreciate your work, therefore read your newsletter more completely. And, from the standpoint of writing as a craft, surmounting stereotypes is highly satisfying because it is so strenuous. Here are some guidelines and examples.

Use parallel language. If males in your story are men, females should be women, not girls or ladies. Gentlemen may accompany ladies and boys go with girls, but "man and wife" should be "husband and wife."

Grant equal respect. Physical traits (beauty, strength) and stereotypes (intuition, judgment) are usually irrelevant. So are titles indicating sex.

NO — Mrs. Rogers, who can still wear her college skirts, takes over as president next month.

YES — Ann Rogers takes over as president next month.

NO — Standing next to her handsome husband John, Carol Simon unveiled drawings of Simon Industry's headquarters building.

YES — Accompanied by her husband John, ...

NO — John Rogers and Mrs. Allen planned last year's annual picnic.

YES — John Rogers and Sally Allen . . . .
  or — Rogers and Allen . . . .

A married, divorced or widowed woman may use her husband's name, her given name, or both. Ask which she prefers. Company or publication policy may require titles for first and subsequent references. Be consistent.

NO — Sam Purdy and Julia Brown were promoted. Purdy joined the firm in 1965 and Julia in 1972.

YES — Sam Purdy and Julia Brown were promoted. Purdy joined the firm in 1965 and Brown in 1972.
  or — Sam joined . . . and Julia . . .
  or — Mr. Purdy . . . and Ms. Brown . . .

Use generic titles and descriptions. Usually it's unnecessary to identify a person by sex. Moreover, you seldom need to replace "man" with the cumbersome "person."

Avoid	Use instead
authoress	author
businessman	business leader, executive, broker, entrepreneur, merchant, industrialist
chairman	leader, moderator, director, head, presiding officer, coordinator
co-ed	student
common man	ordinary people, the average person
housewife	homemaker, consumer, customer, shopper
manned	staffed
mankind	humanity, people
man-sized job	big job, enormous task
middleman	intermediary, go-between, liaison
repairman	service representative or (specifically) plumber, electrician or carpenter
righthand man	assistant, key aid
salesman	agent, clerk, representative
spokesman	diplomat, representative
workman	worker

There is no place for terms such as the better half, the fair sex, girl Friday, libber, old wives' tale, or the old man (for husband). In addition, you must look beyond specific words to the tone of an entire story.

NO — Story about woman who keeps up with housekeeping despite recent promotion to department head.

OK — Stick to business. You wouldn't describe how a man manages yardwork despite job promotions.

NO — Stereotyping outside interests: women with needlecraft and men as volunteer firefighters.

OK — Balance articles with men who cook or volunteer in hospitals and women who fish or rebuild cars.

NO — Special women's interest sections with recipes, household hints and fashion news.

OK — Men also need information about cooking, cleaning and grooming.

Be careful with pronouns. Half the population is women, but you don't have to use half your space writing "he/she." Tight writing is harder, but also more interesting.

NO — A careful housewife keeps XYZ soap near her laundry.

YES — A careful housekeeper uses XYZ laundry soap.

NO — When a salesman is properly trained, he will keep management informed of his prospects.

YES — Properly trained sales reps keep management informed about prospects.

NO — Each employee completes time sheets at the end of his shift.

YES — Each employee completes a time sheet at the end of a shift.

NO — The average parent wants more park facilities for his children and more after school activities for her teenagers.

YES — The average parent wants more park facilities for children and more afterschool activities for teenagers.

Avoid qualifiers which reinforce stereotypes. Qualifiers suggest exceptions to rules, thus may convey bias.

Does this sentence	**convey this stereotype?**
– A well-groomed student, Jones is our first black intern.	– Most Blacks or students are poorly groomed.
– Bob Hernandez, an energetic worker,...	– Most Chicanos are lazy.
– No quiet job for her, Betty Wong wants to be president.	– Most Asians or women are shy or non-assertive.

Don't identify by irrelevant category. Do readers really need to know sex, race, age or ethnic group? Only if the information relates to the story.

Would you write	Jerry Brown, noted White governor. . . . ?
Then why write	Julian Bond, noted Black legislator. . . . ?
Would you write	Sally, an outgoing White woman. . . . ?
Then why write	Mary, an outgoing Black woman. . . . ?
Would you write	Allen Jones, first English American to hold the post. . . . ?
Then why write	Allen Oka, first Japanese American to hold the post. . . . ?

Most people assume language simply expresses thought: that ideas occur first, then are put into words. In this theory, language is neutral. Words merely convey information.

Research during the last forty years shows the opposite is also true. Language forms thought as well as conveys it. Word patterns and meanings define how people view their world.

Racism, sexism, and agism are each modes of thinking created in part by language. Writing free from slurs and stereotypes will not alone end discrimination against groups. Inoffensive prose will, however, help readers build thought patterns suited to a society based upon individual freedom and responsibility.

(Adapted from *Without Bias: A Guidebook to Nondiscriminatory Communication,* by International Association of Business Communicators and published in 1982 by John Wiley & Sons.)

Copyright laws

What is a copyright?

A copyright is a monopoly granted by the government to people who create literary products. Technically it means only the author has the right to copy—or to allow someone else to copy.

The monopoly has two limits. First, it covers only the expression of an idea (the actual book, play, or newsletter), not the idea itself. Second, it has a specific time limit.

How long does a copyright last?

A copyright owned by a person lasts fifty years after the person's death. (Following death, the person's estate owns it.) Copyrights owned by companies or organizations are good for seventy-five years following publication of the material.

Different rules apply for material copyrighted before 1978. Before that year copyrights were granted only for periods of twenty-eight years. Owners could get one twenty-eight-year extension—a total of fifty-six years. That means anything published before 1922 and many things published before 1950 are in the public domain.

What's the public domain?

The public has free access to material not protected by copyrights—whose copyrights have expired or were never secured in the first place. You may reprint unprotected prose, art or photographs without infringing on a copyright.

Specifically, what rights are protected?

Copyright owners have five rights to the material they own.
1) to reproduce (for example, to photocopy).
2) to distribute copies to the public in any fashion (that is, to "publish").
3) to prepare derivative works (such as a movie based upon a novel).
4) to perform (a song or play).
5) to display (a painting or photograph).

How do I know if something is copyrighted?

Look for the symbol ©, which should appear within the phrase Copyright © (date) (name of owner). For a newsletter or magazine, the phrase would normally appear as part of the masthead; for a book, on the back of its title page. In these cases, the phrase protects all material within the publication.

Copyright might also apply to a specific article, photograph or drawing. In that case, the phrase would normally appear as a footnote to the article or as part of the caption for visuals.

In Canada, no phrase is necessary. Simply assume that anything published later than 1950 is under copyright.

What if I want to print something under copyright?

You have two choices: 1) ask for permission or 2) publish under the fair use provisions (in Canada called fair dealing provisions).

How do I ask for permission?

The person or business owning the copyright may grant you a license to use the material in one of the five ways described in question four. Get permission by writing a letter describing what you want to use and telling about your newsletter. Be sure to say whether you are profit or non-profit and that you will use whatever credit line the copyright owner wishes. Attach a photocopy of the material you want to use to be sure everyone is clear.

Publishers usually handle copyright requests for authors. Thus the letter can be addressed to the publisher, even though an individual author is legally the copyright holder.

The copyright owner is entitled to charge for using the material. In practice, you will usually get permission at no cost. If your newsletter is for commercial gain, however, you may have to pay a fee.

What about fair use (in Canada fair dealing)?

The copyright law says you may publish small portions of copyrighted materials without permission under specific circumstances. The most common are when you quote for the purpose of commenting or teaching about the material. You may also quote when describing the material as news. There are no rules about how long the quotations may be or how many you may use. Two or three excerpts of fifty words each should normally be no problem; neither should reproduction of one photograph or drawing.

The line between fair dealing and infringement does not exist in legislation. Only a court draws that line when considering an individual situation.

Can photos and drawings be copyrighted?

Yes, definitely! A photographer or artist is the creator of a work just like an author or composer. All the rules apply to them, too.

How do I know if photographs or drawings are protected?

Original photographs should have copyright information stamped on the back or attached. Rights to photos and art appearing in publications may be owned by the publisher, author or photographer/artist. Generally speaking, someone owns rights to everything. If in doubt, ask the publisher.

What about clip art?

Clip art books and files are deliberately published without copyright so anyone is free to reproduce the images.

What if I just ignore the copyright?

That's a question of ethics as well as law. From a legal standpoint, the chances of getting sued for putting material into the ordinary newsletter are close to zero. The copyright owner would probably never even know you lifted the material. From an ethical standpoint, however, you have used someone else's property without permission. In the case of professional writers, artists or photographers, you have also deprived them of a chance to earn their living from the materials they worked to create.

What if I want to copyright my newsletter?

Simple! Just put the copyright phrase in the masthead or some other prominent place. The phrase has three elements: 1) the word "copyright" or symbol © 2) the date, and 3) name of the owner. For example, I own the copyright to this book, so my phrase is Copyright 1982 by Mark Beach.

Any publication with the phrase is legally protected. Note that means any publication without the phrase is not protected. And because each issue of your newsletter is a publication, each issue should carry the phrase.

For official copyright registration, file forms available from the Copyright Office of the Library of Congress, Washington, D.C. 20559. Filing adds no rights beyond those you get by simply using the phrase, but filing does prove the exact date your copyright took effect.

In Canada procedures are even easier. All published works are automatically copyrighted. You need neither phrase nor registration. It is important to note, however, that the automatic protection is for Canada only. If you want protection in the U.S. and other countries requiring the phrase, then follow the U.S. rules. They will not harm you in Canada and they'll protect you elsewhere.

Canada also has official registration procedures with benefits similar to those in the U.S. For forms and information, write Copyright and Industrial Design Branch, Bureau of Intellectual Property, Dept. of Consumer and Corporate Affairs, Ottawa/Hull, K1A OE1.

I only want to copyright my title.

Sorry, copyright laws and agreements don't give monopolies to names and titles. Anyone can use your title for their newsletter. You can, however, register your name as a trademark under that whole different set of laws. And you also can copyright your nameplate as a piece of art to protect your title in its specific visual form.

What if I don't get a copyright?

Then your words are in the public domain: anyone may use them for any purpose. In the case of most newsletters, that's good. Editors like their information used elsewere. Newsletters written for profit, however, should be protected.

What about copyrighting back issues?

Sorry, you're out of luck. The opportunity to copyright ended when you published without notice.

As editor, I'm the writer, but I work for someone else. Who owns the copyright?

Your employer. This is true even if you are a freelance writer under contract for just one article or to produce a whole newsletter. It's also true if you're a freelance photographer or artist. To own the copyright for yourself, you must establish ownership as part of a written contract with your employer. In other words, copyright ownership is negotiable just like any other property right.

What if several people create materials?

Then several people may own the copyright just as they could own any other property.

What if I use someone else's material and get caught. What can they do?

They could go to court to stop you from publishing your newsletter or to destroy copies of the particular issue. They could also seek a fine for violations and also damages. They could also try to put you in jail.

Whether or not anyone actually would do any of these things is a matter of business as well as law. Only the rare case would prove worth the effort.

How do I deal with contributors to my newsletter?

Most won't even think about copyright. If they do, don't argue. The standard arrangement is you have their permission for one-time use; they retain rights for any other uses.

Headlines

Nothing has more effect on the overall tone of a newsletter than its headlines. A nameplate appears only on page one, but heads show throughout. Moreover, readers tend unconsciously to compare your headlines to those written by professionals for newspapers. Readers are accustomed to effective heads and, without appreciating the skill required, expect yours to work as well.

Headlines are advertising. They grab your reader's attention and draw them into the story. Heads also classify the story. When you decide how bold to make headlines and where to place them on the pages, you have told readers what stories to consider most important. Finally, headlines are prominent in design. Good heads enhance the page; poor ones detract.

Because headlines are so important, I have allocated the topic a lot of space in this book. On this page, I discuss how to write them. Pages 42 and 43 show ways to make headlines, while page 95 deals with heads as elements of design.

"When I decided to quit my PR job and go freelance, I didn't realize how often I would have to shift gears. One client wants a slick image, another prefers seeming folksy; one wants lots of names mentioned, another none. Sometimes I feel I have to change my whole personality on route to the next appointment."

Writing effective headlines

Good headlines have their own grammer—linguistic rules shared among newspapers, magazines and newsletters. Fortunately for newsletter editors, rules for headline writing are quite similar to those for story writing.

1. **Active voice.** Put the subject first, then the verb. Write *New branch sets record*, not *Record set by new branch.*

2. **Present tense.** Even though most stories are about past events, the present tense gives headlines punch. Write *Gomez wins honors*, not *Gomez won honors.* Show the future with infinitives: *Gomez to win honors.*

3. **Short words.** Even more important for headlines than body copy. The panel or group acted, not the committee. Write *Road work to start*, not *Highway plan to be implemented.*

4. **One thought.** Get the most important idea or information from the story. Write *Picnic best ever*, not *Record attendance at best ever picnic.*

5. **Abbreviations only for titles.** *Chung Mfg. Co. to merge* is OK, but not *Two mfg. cos. to merge.* Abbreviate titles such as president only before a name.

6. **Capture the whole story.** Write *Professor says weather changing*, not merely *Weather changing.* If your readers know the professor, write *Martoni says weather changing.*

7. **Write line for line.** Be aware of letter size and column width to know how phrases will divide. *Group set to/renew drive* reads wrong. Try *Group votes/to renew drive.*

8. **Avoid standing heads.** *Roberts answers critics* is much more interesting than *President's message.* *Doctor says DMSO cures migrain* is much more likely to get attention than *Monthly medical tip.*

9. **Be impartial.** If the senator merely suggested changes, don't make her lash committee action or challenge senate leadership.

10. **Don't be cute.** Leave puns, rhymes and alliterations to the poets. Certainly you can have fun, but your first job is getting across a clear message.

Making the Parts

Typing

For good looks and readability, typing is the first key stage of newsletter production. The work is typically done in a home or small office without professional equipment or typists. Even hunting and pecking on an old machine, however, can result in a good product. The work must be done carefully and following a few simple rules.

- Decide on your margins and spacing ahead of time. Once you have selected a format, stick with it.
- Clean the keys or typeface before final typing. Ask at a typewriter shop for materials suited to your machine.
- If you are typing for photocopy or offset, use a carbon, film or mylar ribbon. Avoid cloth ribbons. If the film ribbons do not come pre-wound for your machine, wind some yourself. Buy a ribbon of the right width for your machine and wind it onto your spool. The extra effort pays off.
- Use high quality, white paper with a second sheet rolled in as backing. Your goal is sharp letters in high contrast.
- Do not use erasable bond paper. It smears.
- Make corrections with a liquid opaquing solution or (with film ribbon) lift-off tape. Correction tapes of the white carbon variety tend to let the letters show through.
- Try to use an electric typewriter. All printing and copy processes only heighten the effect of uneven key pressure characteristic of manual machines. Electric typing is especially important if you are hand-cutting a stencil for mimeograph.

Typing flush right

Here is a simple way to make your typing come out ✓flush right. ✓Type// your first line to full column width as I have done here. ✓Consider that/ width✓maximum✓for the rest✓of the/// lines. ✓Finish each line✓with ✓one/// slash✓for✓each remaining space✓or/// letter. Then go back over each line to check where you can✓add✓spaces,// one✓extra✓space for each slash✓at/// the end. ✓Finally,✓retype the copy// with the additional spaces put in.

Here is a simple way to make your typing come out flush right. Type your first line to full column width as I have done here. Consider that width maximum for the rest of the lines. Finish each line with one slash for each remaining space or letter. Then go back over each line to check where you can add spaces, one extra space for each slash at the end. Finally, retype the copy with the additional spaces put in.

Improve your typing

This paragraph is typed on a manual, portable typewriter--the kind often dusted off when it's time to work on a newsletter. It is very difficult, especially for an inexpienced typist, to hit the letters evenly and make the lines straight. Furthermore, cloth ribbons seem the rule for machines such as this.

Now I've switched to an old, key-type electric. There is some improvement, but the machine is showing its age and my lack of skill at making proper adjustments. Also, it has elite type and a cloth ribbon. The paragraph just doesn't look good: not the way I want to represent my organization through its newsletters.

I've cleaned the type face and, just as important, switched to a film ribbon. The cleaning job was easy; the ribbon change somewhat harder. Film ribbons are not made for this machine. I had to buy one for another machine and use the automatic rewind to wind it onto the old spool. The same thing could be done with the manual typewriter, although the ribbon transfer would have to be done slowly by hand.

Ah, that's much better! This is a fairly new, element type machine. It is properly adjusted and, as the ultimate bit of magic, has a built-in correction key. Furthermore, I can easily switch type faces and sizes, allowing for more variety in my copy. I can concentrate on the words, no longer having to fight the typewriter.

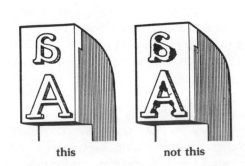

this   not this

Proportional spacing

For many years IBM made Executive model typewriters with spacing individually suited to each letter and symbol. The forward space bar and back space key on those machines move along the lines in tiny units, allowing for precise justification. Furthermore, those machines were among the first exclusively designed for carbon ribbons.

If you have access to one of those old machines, you might try using it for final copy. They are complicated and often frustrating to use, but their product can be very pleasing.

Here are examples of copy typed with standard spacing and proportional spacing.

```
     A standard typewriter gives
equal space to every letter re-
gardless of shape or size.  The
result is copy which looks like
typing,  not printing.   A pro-
portional spacing typewriter, on
the other hand, allocates space
to  each letter appropriate  to
the shape of the  letter.   The
result  is  copy neatly put to-
gether - like printing.
```

```
     Proportional typewriters produce
nice copy,  but  there  is  a  price to
pay.  Most have fixed character  font
styles and sizes.  Standard typewrit-
ers with replacable elements  (type
balls) offer flexibility unmatched by
proportional spacing machines.  The
flexibility,  however,is only possible
because all characters are allocated
equal space.
```

"Some one in our club whom I'd never even met sure made my job a hundred percent easier. She called one night to say the office where she worked was turning in its Selectric typewriters and getting text editors. Would I like one of the old Selectrics complete with a set of elements?

"Would I like one! Where do I sign up? I got our budget committee to cough up the trade-in value of the typewriter as payment. My new friend's boss donated the elements, which were worthless to her anyway, and took a tax writeoff. We even got a box of ribbons and correction tapes.

"Everyone came out a winner on that deal."

Word processing

Most information in this book is about time-tested methods using familiar equipment and materials. This section is different. It is about the world of electronic devices rapidly becoming common features in offices and homes. If you have the good fortune to have one of these machines—or to get access to one—your editing job can become far easier and more creative than you may have thought possible.

In word processing, electronic memories form the links between machines. For example, you could enter words into memory using a standard-format keyboard. Each stroke of the key would produce a magnetic result just as each sound does when you make a tape recording. Words would be stored in the machine itself or on soft copy such as a disk, tape or card.

Memory systems

Individual office machines have traditionally been tied together by what word processing advocates call hard copy—pieces of paper as either rough draft or finished copy. Hard copy has been used to move from one stage of printing to the next—from typewriter to typesetter, for example, or from typesetter to offset printer.

To understand word processing systems, begin by thinking of hard copy as a way of storing information. The pieces of paper preserve information either to be filed or to be moved from one machine to the next. The essence of word processing is that the memory system is electronic rather than on paper. Until the final product is ready to be printed, information can be stored magnetically on a tape, disk or card.

Magnetic information storage is as common as your nearest tape recorder. Whether cassette or eight track, the tapes store words and music and play them at your command. Your tapes are a memory system.

In word processing, electronic memories are the links between machines. For example, you could enter ideas into memory by using a standard typewriter keyboard. Each stroke of a key would produce a magnetic result just as each sound does when you make a tape recording.

Text editing

Few people can write ideas in finished prose the first time through. Almost everyone needs to edit material to be sure it is complete, accurate and clear.

Traditionally, editing has been done on hard copy. We write or type words on paper, look at the paper and make changes.

In the new world of word processing, rough drafts are displayed electronically instead of being put on paper. The display may be one line at a time on a lighted bar or whole paragraphs or even pages at a time on a tube like a TV picture tube. Usually the material gets from the keyboard to the display by way of a short-term memory wired into the machine.

You are probably already familiar with these display media just as you are with memory systems. The lighted bar mechanism is called an LED (light emitting diode) and is common on pocket calculators, wrist watches and clock radios. The tube is called a CRT (cathode ray tube) and is found in medical laboratories, auto shops and other places where data are presented for analysis.

When your rough copy is displayed, you can make changes just as you would by hand on a piece of paper. You can correct typing mistakes and add or delete words. Corrections are made by moving a cursor until it is under the material to be changed, then simply entering the change via the keyboard. The cursor is the little line displayed and moved exactly as the indicator on many electronic TV games.

The machine at which these operations take place is called a text editor. It has a standard typing keyboard plus many additional features including a memory system and electronic display. The memory stores both the material you type in and fixed instructions which you can call up at the touch of a key.

Text editors are rapidly replacing typewriters as the most basic piece of office word processing equipment. The marvel of these new machines is that they allow for changes in format as well as individual words. On most machines a push of a key will adjust column widths and type sizes. The new format will be displayed, allowing you to check for proper hyphenating and overall effect. This electronic wizardry is all possible because text editors are built around micro computors similar to those used for computer games.

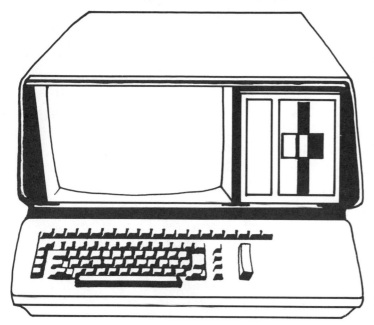

The typical text editor has a keyboard, display tube and slot (upper right) to insert memory disks or cards.

When you finish typing, the words you entered into memory can be printed out in a variety of ways.

- The typewriter itself could act as printer.
- There could be a separate machine with a printing device much like a typewriter element.
- Your words could be transmitted to a phototypesetter and transformed into camera-ready copy.
- Your words could be transmitted to a photocopier and pages produced in whatever numbers you need.
- Material could go electronically into a scanner to produce stencils or offset masters.

All of this could happen without ever handling a piece of paper until the final copy is printed. Moreover, it can happen at very high speeds because the words are printed on paper from memory rather than from a keyboard. The printer is driven by the machine, not the human operator.

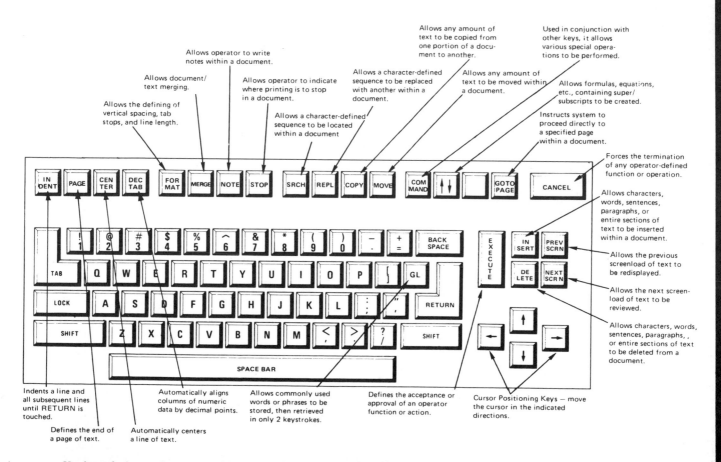

Keyboard shows the range of functions and commands typical of text editors. Drawing courtesy of Wang Laboratories, Inc.

31

Additional functions

Word processing systems begin with a variety of ways to enter information and end with a variety of ways to print final copy. It is this variety of both input and output which gives word processing its flexibility.

You already know rough copy and instructions for corrections and format can be entered from a keyboard or via a memory device. Words can also be entered into memory and display from a machine called an OCR (optical character reader). An OCR looks something like a photocopy machine: paper is placed on a piece of glass or fed into a slot. The OCR "reads" what is on the paper by transforming the characters into electronic impulses for display or storage.

As of this writing, material for an OCR must be typed using a special type face and rigid specifications for margins and spacing. These requirements, however, will relax considerably during the next few years. Shortly OCRs will accept typing from any standard machine.

Once material has been arranged into final form on the display medium, flexibility for output is even greater than for input. Currently the printing units, either as part of a text editor or as separate mechanisms, are common features of word processing systems. At a push of a few keys all material is recalled from memory and typed, often at speeds over 500 words per minute. On-line phototypesetting is also currently possible, although the equipment is less common than printers because of its high cost. On-line photocopy machines are just coming onto the market, while on-line stencil and negative scanners are still in the future.

There is another aspect of word processing which is technologically possible now and may become common during the 1980s: optical scanning, memory, display and formatting of halftones and other line art. Just imagine seeing a picture on a CRT along with your text, then being able to adjust the shapes of picture and text together to produce one unified whole. When you were done, everything would appear on the tube exactly as you wanted it on your newsletter page. The output phase would then give you complete camera-ready copy, photocopies, stencils or offset masters ready to reproduce. Both layout and pasteup would be done electronically, totally eliminating the equipment, supplies and time they now require.

"Our newsletter is always full of tables. My boss wants a table showing monthly sales, a table showing estimated market growth, a table showing wholesale price increases. Next month she'll probably want a table showing typical use of vacation time. There's a table for everything.

"It used to be really boring to type all that stuff. It has to be set up in exactly the right columns and lots of the information is repeated from month to month. Our new text editor has made the job easy and almost fun.

"Three months ago I put all the basic data and format instructions into the memory system. Now when it's newsletter time I just display the standard tables one by one on the tube, erase the top line and add the new bottom line, and push the button. The printer puts out perfect tables all set to paste down on our camera-ready copy."

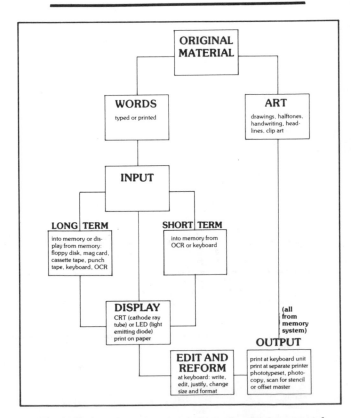

Flow chart shows the steps through which material could be taken in a word processing system.

Word processing terms

Software is the key to word processing. It is the computer programs: the packages of instructions that make machines perform specific operations when commanded from a keyboard.

Software comes in the form of a disk or other memory device and is electronically transferred into machine memory at the start of daily operations. For newsletter work an editor would use a word processing package for general text editing. With a large mailing list, the editor might also have a package which merges and sorts addresses and prints labels. If the editor is like me, the software inventory will include a spelling proofreader.

Hundreds of companies with names such as Micropol, Lifeboat, and Structured Systems make thousands of computer programs with names such as Wordstar, QSORT and NAD. If it takes you a full year to begin understanding how it all fits together, you are probably about average.

Machines **interface** one another when they work together. For example, an OCR might interface with a CRT text editor but not with an older LED memory typewriter. Interfacing can be done via software memory or actually wiring machines into each other.

The **menu** is a set of instructions entered from software into machine memory. The operator selects a specific instruction from the menu and presses the correct keys ordering the machine to carry out the function.

Standalone systems will perform all desired functions from within themselves and their memory software. When they are set up to receive outside help, for example from a main frame computer, it's called **time sharing.**

Disks look something like the old 45 rpm records and are the most popular storage medium for word processing. They come in two sizes — 5 1/4 inch and 8 inch — and are placed in a disk drive which reads their information into machine memory.

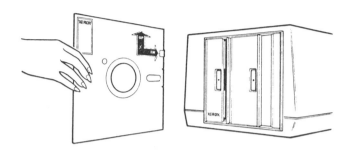

Disk ready for insertion into a dual disk drive.

Print wheels, sometimes called **daisy wheels,** are fonts about three inches across and look like small sunbursts. They allow for much higher speed printing than ball-shaped fonts.

```
>f1<>h/11< This OCR-B print wheel
makes copy ready for an optical
character reading machine to feed
directly into the memory of a
typesetter. Instructions between
>   <  tell typesetting machines
which font and point size to use,
in this case 11 point Souvenir
for text in this book. I could
switch to 12 point italic bold by
entering instruction >f4<>h/12<.
```

Letter quality printout on OCR-B with typesetting font and point size instructions entered at the word processor keyboard.

```
- - - - - - - - - - - - - - - - - - - - - - - - - - - - - - - - -
    A  =  WORK ON A DOCUMENT FILE        |  H = run a program... for:
    B  =  change disk drives             |       checking disk space, copying a
    C  =  delete a file                  |       disk & seeing B drive directory
    D  =  turn directory off (ON)        |  ESC key  =  restart software
    E  =  edit a program                 |  HELP key  =  change help level
    F  =  print a file                   |  CTRL (-)  =  scroll directory down
    G  =  rename a file                  |  CTRL (=)  =  scroll directory up
- - - - - - - - - - - - - - - - - - - - - - - - - - - - - - - - -
            You may touch any key shown above.
- - - - - - - - - - - - - - - - - - - - - - - - - - - - - - - - -

DIRECTORY of disk A:
   BDIR.COM   PIP.COM    STAT.COM   XWS.COM    WSMSGS.OVR    WSOVLYI.OVR
```

Sample menu as it appears on the CRT of Xerox 820 text editor. Disk A holds the word processing program.

Typesetting

Most printed material has been typeset. The term comes from the earliest printing processes which literally required characters, letters, punctuation and spaces to be individually set in place. Today typesetters set characters via keyboards quite like those on typewriters. Letters and marks are stored on film or disks and transmitted photographically or by laser onto sheets ready for printing.

Whether you produce your newsletter by mimeograph, photocopy or offset printing, you should consider typesetting. Even if you decide against it, weighing pros and cons will help you and your organization be more clear about what kind of newsletter you want.

Advantages of typesetting

Space efficiency. Typeset characters are proportionally spaced, saving paper, printing and postage. Typeset letters are also easier to read than typewritten, thus can be printed smaller.

Clear letters. The average typesetting machine can make better camera-ready copy than the best typewriter or word processor printer. Letters have denser blacks and sharper edges, thus reproduce better with any printing process.

Well-spaced, even lines. Typesetters do better than typewriters or printers in keeping lines straight and uniformly separated.

Variety of types and sizes. Even the most versatile typewriter or printer is no match for typesetting. A merely average typesetter might offer fifty styles; a well stocked shop several hundred. And most styles can easily be adjusted for size and distance between letters and lines.

Quality image. Typeset material looks important and professional. Typewritten and letter quality printed copy seems hasty and temporary by comparison.

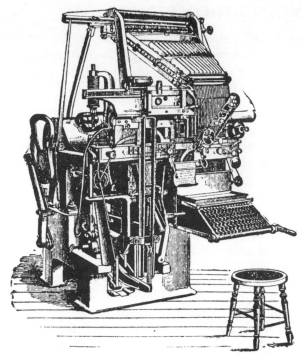

This Nineteenth Century typesetting machine is pictured in a steel engraving. The engravings are good sources of graphics.

Disadvantages of typesetting

Cost. Typesetting requires more skill and much more expensive equipment than typing. Expect to pay well for the service.

Time. Having material typeset will normally add several days to your production schedule.

Bother. Some typesetters pick up and deliver. With most, however, you take the copy to their place of business and get it when the job is done. In either case, dealing with another person in the production process makes the whole matter more complicated and increases chances of mistakes.

Overdone image. If your organization wants to be known as a homey group of volunteers operating on a shoestring, typeset copy may look too slick and professional.

♈ ♉ ♊ ♋ ♌ ♍ ♒ ♎ ♐ **Variety of symbols** 🚌 ☎ 🚤 + − = × ÷

< > ≨ ≩ ≤ ≥ ∼ ≈ · ≠ ≠ ⎯ ✕ ♏ ♍ ® © ◇▫□ △□○◆●■

∫ √ ∅ ∞ π ∈ ♯ ∶ ° ′ ▲ ◀ ▶ ▼⇅ → ← ⟨⟮⟘⟩⟯⟫ ¹²³⁴⁵⁶⁷⁸⁹⁰/₁₂₃₄₅₆₇₈₉₀

αβγδεζηθικλμνξοπρστυφχψω ΓΔΘΛΞΠΣΥΦΨΩ∂

< > ≤ ≥ √ ‾ + − = × ÷ ± ∓ ≦ ≧ ∼ ≈ ≃ ∫ " ∴ {} ☆ ★ ‡ ® ©

Choosing styles and sizes

If you've decided on typesetting, how do you decide among the hundreds of choices about styles, sizes, line lengths and spacings? Here are some simple guidelines based on research and experience.

1. Readers like familiar faces. You're not limited to the small number of old standbys, but don't get too experimental, either. The far out faces are for advertizing, not body copy or most headlines.

Roy Paul Nelson, in his book *Publication Design,* calls seven faces the "you can't go wrong types." Those seven are: Baskerville, Bodoni, Caslon, Clarendon, Garamond, Helvetica and Times Roman. Each has a separate personality, but one of the seven probably would suit your newsletter.

Familiar types are also standard, which means you can change typesetters without changing type faces.

2. Serif faces are more readable than non-serifs. Serifs help the eye move easily along the line.

3. Choose a point size and line measure resulting in about one and a half alphabets per line. Counting all letters, marks and spaces, the ideal line length is about forty characters. Thirty-five to fifty-five is OK; less than thirty or more than sixty show significant drops in readability.

If you bend this rule, bend on the side of narrowness.

4. Set flush right for serious, solid tone; ragged right for a more upbeat feeling. Ragged right does not seem to affect readability, so it is a matter of image or taste. Ragged right has more white space, thus requires more column inches than justified. Always set body copy flush left.

5. Use both upper and lower case as in standard writing. All capital lines are hard to read, even if they are headlines. Lower case letters are easier to read because they are more easily distinguished from one another. Caps also take about a third more space than lower case letters.

6. Use one point more leading than point size of type: e.g., 11-point type on 12-point leading. If you must go to a long line measure—more than sixty characters—increase space between lines by going to two point leading: e.g., 11 on 13.

7. Variety within a face is fine; variety among faces for the same publication can make the page seem a hodgepodge. After very careful thought you might pick a headline face different from body type, but differences should end there. Headlines may be of different sizes, but should be all in the same face.

Readability is based largely on contrast. Each variation in type size or style reduces contrast, thus makes reading more difficult.

8. Use a face which makes a nice pattern in your newsletter. Depending upon your format, some faces might make your pages look too light or dark, too grey or spotty.

9. Avoid reverses for body copy and use italics sparingly. Both slow readers down.

10. Choose type which comes in a variety of styles such as bold, semi-bold and italic. Variety leads to flexibility for things such as headlines and captions as well as body copy itself.

ITC Garamond Light Condensed

ABCDEFGHIJKLMNOPQRSTUVWXYZ

ITC Garamond Light

abcdefghijklmnopqrstuvwxyz
ABCDEFGHIJKLMNOPQRSTUVWXYZ
1234567890 .,;:'"&!?$

ITC Garamond Light Italic

abcdefghijklmnopqrstuvwxyz
ABCDEFGHIJKLMNOPQRSTUVWXYZ
1234567890 .,;:'"&!?$

ITC Garamond Book

abcdefghijklmnopqrstuvwxyz
ABCDEFGHIJKLMNOPQRSTUVWXYZ
1234567890 .,;:'"&!?$

ITC Garamond Book Italic

abcdefghijklmnopqrstuvwxyz
ABCDEFGHIJKLMNOPQRSTUVWXYZ
1234567890 .,;:'"&!?$

ITC Garamond Bold

abcdefghijklmnopqrstuvwxyz
ABCDEFGHIJKLMNOPQRSTUVWXYZ
1234567890 .,;:'"&!?$

Typesetting terms

Body and display type. These terms refer to size, not face or style. Body type is up through 12 points, display 14 points and larger. Body type is sometimes called text type.

Markup. Page 41 shows copy on which corrections have been made. The copy has been marked up: instructions for the typesetter or printer have been added.

Galley proof. Type set individually by hand was put into a frame called a galley. When the setting job was finished, one copy was printed: the galley proof. Final corrections were made on that copy. With modern typeset material, the galley proof is a photocopy of typeset sheets.

Column inch. This is the basic measure for how much space an item will take in your newsletter. A column inch is as wide as your columns and one inch deep (vertical). When you know your type size, style and leading, you can translate your word count into typeset column inches.

Character count. Figure one character to be one letter, symbol or space. A ten pitch typewriter gives ten characters per inch.

With typeset copy, different type sizes and styles give different numbers of characters per inch. Knowing your character count for typesetting means you can accurately figure your total column inches. This book, for example, averages fifty characters per line. By setting my ten pitch typewriter for five inch lines, I could gauge how many column inches my typed copy would be after it was typeset.

Copy fitting or casting off. How many characters or words will fit your format? Considering headlines, body copy and art, how will a particular issue lay out? Answering these questions requires copyfitting (sometimes called casting off). See page 94 for details on how this job is done.

Measure. The width of one line in a column is the measure. This book has a 20 pica measure.

Flush. Type is set flush when the lines begin or end over one another in perfect alignment. A typewriter automatically types flush left; flush right margins must be computed on the machine one at a time. With typesetting and most word processors, you automatically get margins which are flush both left and right. Copy which is not flush is called ragged. Unjustified typing is ragged right.

Justify. When type is set both flush left and flush right, it's justified.

Justified	Ragged Right
MARGIN MARGIN	MARGIN MARGIN
This text is set justified. Notice that each line has been set to the full width, that the typesetter hyphenates where necessary, and that the space between words varies. Justified copy is used for many typesetting applications.	This demonstrates ragged right text. Notice that hyphenation is rarely used in ragged right copy and that all interword spaces are the same width. Ragged right is a very popular style of typesetting.
Ragged Center	Ragged Left
MARGIN MARGIN	MARGIN MARGIN
This copy is set ragged center. Each line is automatically centered, and all interword spaces are the same width. It is extremely simple to set text ragged center.	This copy is set ragged left, the opposite of the ragged right copy above. Notice that the left margin is ragged, and that the right margin is flush. Like ragged right, ragged left copy is easy to access.

Gutter. The gutters of your newsletter are the spaces between its columns of type. Sometimes a fine line is run down the gutter, especially when it is very narrow. In a book the inside space between type and spine is also called the gutter.

Pica. A pica is a linear measure equalling one-sixth of an inch. Typesetting machines are designed to measure column width in picas instead of inches. If your typesetter insists on expressing column width in picas, simply remember there are six picas to the inch.

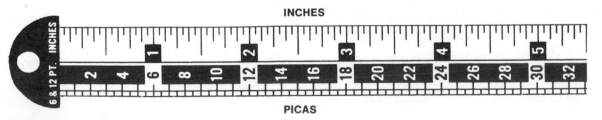

Point. Here is the most important printer's measure. One point is 1/72 of an inch. Thus twelve points equal one pica.

Both type size and leading are measured in points. For size of type, the measure refers to height. For leading, the measure refers to distance between lines. This book, for example, is set in eleven point type with thirteen point leading. The headlines are in 18, 24, or 36 points.

Point Size

6	abcdefghijklmnopqrstuvwxyzabcdefghijklmnopqrstuvwxyzabcd
7	abcdefghijklmnopqrstuvwxyzabcdefghijklmnopqrstuvv
8	abcdefghijklmnopqrstuvwxyzabcdefghijklmnop
9	abcdefghijklmnopqrstuvwxyzabcdefghijkl
10	abcdefghijklmnopqrstuvwxyzabcdefgh
11	abcdefghijklmnopqrstuvwxyzabcd
12	abcdefghijklmnopqrstuvwxyzab
14	abcdefghijklmnopqrstuvwxyz
16	abcdefghijklmnopqrstuvw
18	abcdefghijklmnopqrstu
24	abcdefghijklmnop
30	abcdefghijklm
36	abcdefghijk
48	abcdefgh
60	abcdef

Here are some examples of common type sizes:

six point: This is six point type. This is six point type. This is six point type. Th

eight point: This is eight point type. This is eight point type.

ten point: This is ten point type. This is ten point ty

twelve point: This is twelve point type. This i

Notice that type size refers only to height of letters. The point size does not refer to the width or boldness of letters. Different type faces may all be the same size when measured in points, but also be wider or darker than each other. For example, the following lines are all in ten point type.

Helios Bold Italic

ABCDEFGHIJKLMNOPQRSTUVWXYZ&
abcdefghijklmnopqrstuvwxyz
1234567890(.,:;!?''—/$-%)

Helios Bold Condensed

ABCDEFGHIJKLMNOPQRSTUVWXYZ&
abcdefghijklmnopqrstuvwxyz
1234567890(.,:;!?"—/$-%)

Helios

ABCDEFGHIJKLMNOPQRSTUVWXYZ
abcdefghijklmnopqrstuvwxy

Helios Italic

ABCDEFGHIJKLMNOPQRSTUVWXYZ&
abcdefghijklmnopqrstuvwxyz
1234567890(.,:;!?''—/$-%)

Helios Bold

ABCDEFGHIJKLMNOPQRSTUVWXYZ&
abcdefghijklmnopqrstuvwxyz
1234567890(.,:;!?''—/$-%)

Although the type sizes are technically the same in each sentence, some lines are longer than others. For any given type style, you must know its number of characters per inch (or pica) in addition to its size in points.

Reverse. Printing is usually done dark letters on light background. Black on white is most common. Contrast and drama, however, can be heightened by printing light on dark—by reversing.

Printers make reverses by spreading ink over the background. The light paper shows through to make letters and art.

Although the type sizes are technically t

Although the type sizes are technically

Although the type sizes are technically

Although the type sizes are technica

Although the type sizes are technically

The five lines above are reversed.

Serif. Serifs are tiny lines or hooks added to letters as artistic touches. Serif type faces, also known as Roman, have the decorations. Sans serif faces, also known as Gothic, are plain.

In the eight examples of faces on page 39, four are serif styles and four Gothic. Two of each style were typeset and two typewritten.

Run around. No, this is not what you are getting from your typesetter when asked if you want eleven point Gothic set in twenty pica columns with thirteen points of leading. The term simply refers to setting some type in a column width more narrow than your standard so the block of type will fit neatly next to a photo, drawing or box. Some photos, especially those with light sky in the upper portions, need borders to help define them on the page. A fine line border drawn

just outside the edge of a photo can make it seem matted in a frame. Put borders around photos as you would any other art, using the techniques described on pages 58 and 59.

Leading. The word is pronounced like the metal lead because it originally referred to lead strips placed between lines of type to separate the lines. Today it simply refers to the space between lines. More leading means more space.

Writing has always been a form of art as well as communication. Cave paintings, hieroglyphics and ideograms all expressed creativity and content. Scribes were designers, not mere copyists. Sculptors writing on stone used crosswise cuts to end lines on letters. The ancient decorations led to serifs on modern type.

Set solid (no leading)

Writing has always been a form of art as well as communication. Cave paintings, hieroglyphics and ideograms all expressed creativity and content. Scribes were designers, not mere copyists. Sculptors writing on stone used crosswise cuts to end lines on letters. The ancient decorations led to serifs on modern type.

Set with two points leading (11 on 13)

Rates and business practices

Some typesetters charge by the hour, others by the page. Some keyboard rapidly, others slowly. Some are accurate, others sloppy. Some have the latest machines, others are out of date. In other words, it's very difficult to compare costs.

The best way to select a typesetter is to pick three or four shops conveniently located and with people you like. Take about five pages of typed, marked-up manuscript into each shop. Give each shop the same sheet of specifications, ask each to set your work, then compare price and quality. Once you've made your choice, stay with it for at least a year. Taking time to build a good working relationship will pay off in quality and efficient service.

Like most services, typesetters like repeat business. If you have a shop you like, don't hesitate to negotiate a contract for a year or two. Your newsletter comes out regularly, so you can anticipate your typesetting needs well in advance. You should get lower prices in return for work brought on a dependable schedule. This is another example of how careful planning and firm production schedules are your most effective ways to cut costs.

Eight type faces

Writing has always been a form of art as well as communication. Cave paintings, hieroglyphics, and ideograms all expressed both creativity and content. Scribes were designers, not mere copyists.

Like ancient writing, modern typography is art. Furthermore, today's typewriters and typesetting machines are very versatile. Thus whole publications, such as newsletters, can be made pleasing to both eye and mind.

Writing has always been a form of art as well as communication. Cave paintings, hieroglyphics, and ideograms all expressed both creativity and content. Scribes were designers, not mere copyists.

Like ancient writing, modern typography is art. Furthermore, today's typewriters and typesetting machines are very versatile. Thus whole publications, such as newsletters, can be made pleasing to both eye and mind.

Writing has always been a form of art as well as communication. Cave paintings, hieroglyphics, and ideograms all expressed both creativity and content. Scribes were designers, not mere copyists.

Like ancient writing, modern typography is art. Furthermore, today's typewriters and typesetting machines are very versatile. Thus whole publications, such as newsletters, can be made pleasing to both eye and mind.

Writing has always been a form of art as well as communication. Cave paintings, hieroglyphics, and ideograms all expressed both creativity and content. Scribes were designers, not mere copyists.

Like ancient writing, modern typography is art. Furthermore, today's typewriters and typesetting machines are very versatile. Thus whole publications, such as newsletters, can be made pleasing to both eye and mind.

Writing has always been a form of art as well as communication. Cave paintings, hieroglyphics, and ideograms all expressed both creativity and content. Scribes were designers, not mere copyists.

Like ancient writing, modern typography is art. Furthermore, today's typewriters and typesetting machines are very versatile. Thus whole publications, such as newsletters, can be made pleasing to both eye and mind.

Writing has always been a form of art as well as communication. Cave paintings, hieroglyphics, and ideograms all expressed both creativity and content. Scribes were designers, not mere copyists.

Like ancient writing, modern typography is art. Furthermore, today's typewriters and typesetting machines are very versatile. Thus whole publications, such as newsletters, can be made pleasing to both eye and mind.

Writing has always been a form of art as well as communication. Cave paintings, hieroglyphics, and ideograms all expressed both creativity and content. Scribes were designers, not mere copyists.

Like ancient writing, modern typography is art. Furthermore, today's typewriters and typesetting machines are very versatile. Thus whole publications, such as newsletters, can be made pleasing to both eye and mind.

Writing has always been a form of art as well as communication. Cave paintings, hieroglyphics, and ideograms all expressed both creativity and content. Scribes were designers, not mere copyists.

Like ancient writing, modern typography is art. Furthermore, today's typewriters and typesetting machines are very versatile. Thus whole publications, such as newsletters, can be made pleasing to both eye and mind.

Check list for typesetting

If your newsletter will be typeset, there are ten points to keep in mind to insure high quality at a fair price.

- Insist upon seeing samples of work. Like any other service, typesetting varies in quality. Look especially carefully at how clear are the letters, how even are the right margins, and how straight are the lines. If the work looks sloppy, go on to the next shop.

- Get bids. Costs vary as much as quality. Tell the typesetter, how many pages each issue will be and how often your newsletter comes out, then compare prices. You may get the best price from an independent typesetter or from one associated with your printer. Check costs at both types of shops.

- Before signing anything, agree on firm deadlines. Typesetters work on tight schedules and usually have more than one job going at a time. They have a right to receive your copy on the day you promise. You have the same right from them. Late typesetting can throw off your printing schedule and make your newsletter obsolete before the ink is dry.

- Get a demonstration of what the typesetting machine can do. Learning about equipment in your typesetter's shop can give you ideas about layout and graphics. For example, ask to see the range of signs and symbols. Find out if the machine will do odd point sizes such as seventeen. Some machines will also do lines and other graphics for borders and boxes.

- Use a typesetter whose machines have off-line memories such as disks. Capacity to call your material back to a display screen makes corrections fast and less costly. Permanent electronic memories are also good for storing material only used occasionally: membership forms, calendars, policy statements and seasonal greetings.

- Consider a shop with an optical character reader. At this writing these machines are rare in commercial shops, but finding one can be worth the search. They enable you to keyboard material yourself, then have it read directly into memory for setting. You save the cost of additional keyboarding—by far the largest expense of typesetting.

- Ask your typesetter for advice about printing, use of photographs and graphics, and layout. Your typesetter is part of the printing trade and probably can help you in more ways than simply making good copy. For example, most typesetters have books and catalogues full of clip art for graphics.

- Once you have decided on type face and style, learn how many characters there are per inch of line and how many lines per inch of column. With that knowledge you can estimate the size of typeset blocks by doing a word count of your typed copy.

- Consider having your typesetter do pasteup as well. Most typesetting services are equipped with light tables and materials to turn out camera-ready copy. While pasteup would mean additional costs, the savings in time and effort might be worth it.

- Give your typesetter clean, finished copy typed double-spaced with no errors. The typesetter's job is to duplicate your prose exactly. Corrections after the job is done will just cost you more time and money.

- Proofread everything your typesetter does and build in time for corrections. Remember the typesetter is working at a keyboard essentially the same as a typewriter. Mistakes will slip in.

your proofreading symbols

- Use standard proofreading symbols to give your typesetter instructions for changes. Here are some examples of the more common symbols and how they can be used. You will find more proofing symbols on a page near the back of most dictionaries.

Proofreading symbols are like handwriting: each user has an individual style. Because there is no single right way to draw the symbols or insert them into copy, you and your typesetter should compare techniques to be sure you understand each other.

Marking up copy

∧	insert
two∧	insert period
tw∧o	insert letter
two⌄	insert punctuation
two?/	insert?
ℓ	delete
twoℓ	delete period
twoℓ	delete letter
two̶ℓ	delete word
t̲w̲o̲	upper case letter
/Two	lower case letter
(two)	make into number
②	make into word
tⱺa	separate
tw◡o	close up
toᴗw	transpose
two]	move right
[two	move left
two	put in italics
t̶w̶o̶ℓ …..	do not change: let it stand
¶	new paragraph
no ¶	no new paragraph
two	put in bold type

Futura bold 12 pt. 14 pt. leading, 20 pica columns.

Modern Typesetting ← 18 pt.

The term "typesetting is as old as printing itself. Individual letters and spaces, however, are no longer set as they were centuries ago. The modern typesetter works at a keyboard much like that of a typewriter The machine holds letter and symbols on a heavy strip of film. light flashes through the film onto photosensitive paper.

Most typesetting machines have a tube much like a tv picture tube to display material typed. The display is made before words are photographed so the operator can proofread copy and make corrections. ← no ¶

After a correction is made, the machine will rejustify the line and, if necessary, the whole paragraph. ¶ Computer assisted typesetting machines allow for experimentation with type styles and sizes, column widths and leading. For example, what if you know you want your newsletter set in two columns of 30 picas of Helvitica but are uncertain about how large you want the type face?/ Text could be entered into the machine's memory, then the machine instructed to print in 10, 11 and 12 points. You would quickly have an an example of exactly how your copy would look.

41

Headlines

Making headlines work graphically often seems as hard as writing them in the first place. A few guidelines, however, make the job fairly easy.

1. Choose one type style and stick with it. Going from bold to italic is OK, but don't switch from Baskerville to Helvetica. Stay in the same family of type.

2. Pick a fairly standard typeface. You don't necessarily have to match body copy, but stay close. Oracle heads with Helios body might look nice, whereas Old English or Zapf would look out of place.

3. Use a type with bold letters having little space between them. Some styles even come in condensed so you get the most out of your column width. Be careful, though. Some condensed styles are too skinny in relation to their height. Stick with characters having good proportions.

4. Make major heads plenty big—30 or 36 point—then set guidelines for one or two lesser sizes such as 24 and 18. Use point size to help signify the story's importance.

5. Print headlines downstyle: in upper and lower case just as you would any other sentence. All caps is much harder to read and takes more space. Downstyle also allows the ascenders and descenders of lower case letters to create whitespace between lines, making heads look lively.

6. Plan heads to start flush left. Starting every time at the left margin keeps copyfitting uncomplicated and gives readers a dependable pattern.

Making headlines

There are six ways to make headlines. Three are free, two inexpensive and one moderate. If done very carefully, any will yield high quality.

Hand lettering. A good artist can draw heads freehand or by tracing printed material. For a more special look, use calligraphy. Hand-done heads compatible with your nameplate or logo can look very distinctive.

Words cut from other publications. Most magazines and catalogs are printed in the same typeface throughout and from issue to issue. An evening with a stack of old copies will yield a large supply of words and letters. Cut them out to file for use when you compose your newsletter.

There's nothing quite like $\boxed{100\% \text{ wool}}$ **when it comes to comfort, warmth, and protection.**

There's nothing like protection.

When using this source, look for material printed in sharp black on glossy white paper. Most quality magazines and catalogs do fine, but newspaper copy gives poor results. And remember that words too large for your newsletter can be inexpensively reduced on many photocopy machines. Page 96 tells about this technique.

Typewritten. Typewriters are the most efficient source of free headlines—and the most frequently abused. Typewritten heads must be made and placed with extra care. Placement is described on page 95.

If you have a typewriter with changeable fonts (type ball or print wheel) and want to get serious about making headlines, buy a font just for that purpose. Most suppliers carry elements or wheels with display and bold types. If you buy a display face, be sure the font has both upper and lower case letters. Many have upper case only.

IBM ORATOR Type is a large, sans-serif type style. Its bold, legib

---

IBM PRESENTOR Type is a large, upper and lower case letter forms

---

To make typed heads truly camera-ready, follow the rules for good typewritten copy on page 27. In addition, back up your typing paper with carbon paper rolled in the "wrong way". The result you want is carbon letters on the reverse side of your white typing paper so your typed letters appear extra dark. For even greater contrast, go over your typing twice. Assuming your machine stays in good register, you'll get the bold effect available on many word processer printers.

Transfer lettering. Dry transfer lettering is inexpensive and makes fine heads. Start with a catalog from a company such a Letraset or Formatt to learn about styles and sizes. The catalogs are also good to have because they show other graphics available on transfer sheets and give details on how to use the medium.

You can get transfer graphics catalogs at most art supply stores and some larger stationery stores. While those stores carry the widest selections of brands and styles, they also charge the most, reflecting the high cost of extensive inventories and highly-trained sales people. In larger cities you can save money by shopping at the warehouse-type graphics stores such as Arvey Paper. Another cost-cutting trick is to buy through catalogs such as Dot Paste Up Supply. Ask a local printer for the name of a regional graphics catalog or warehouse.

Transfer letters are often hard to set perfectly in line. A little sloppiness makes a big difference. Most makers help by printing tick marks or guidelines on the sheets. Place the lines over non-reproduction blue lines on graph paper or layout boards. To make the job easier and better, use a light table as described on page 100.

Done at desk:

Send in the Clowns

Done at light table:

Send in the Clowns

Misteaks in headlines are very obvious. If you make one using transfer materials, correct it with ordinary cellophane tape. Lightly cover only the wrong letters with tape, then peel it from the paper. The letters will come with it, leaving space for your correction.

Mist   s Mistakes

Headline making machines. There are two kinds of light-duty machines for making heads and display letters. One is a strip printer which works exactly like a hand-operated phototypesetter. The font is a strip of film inserted under a strong light. Each letter is exposed onto high contrast paper which is then developed in standard photographic chemicals.

The other type of machine works much like a label maker. The font is a large dial rotated to individual letters. When a button is pressd or lever pulled, the letter transfers to tape with a peel-off backing. The tape of finished headline is taken from the machine and placed above the story for camera-ready copy.

Headline making machines are common in small print shops and in-house graphics departments. Many sit idle for hours or days on end. If you're looking for services to be donated to your newsletter, access to one of these machines is a good candidate.

Typesetting. If you have body copy typeset, heads should be set at the same time. As an alternative, you might consider having only heads set, thereby getting top quality without the cost of typesetting text. In either case, typeset heads are top of the line in good looks—and cost.

Headline and display type sizes increase in six point units, not one point as with body copy. Strictly defined, anything 14 points or over is headline type. Most editors consider 18 point the smallest they would use. 24,30,and 36 points (half inch) are common in newsletter work.

"I'm always looking for fillers. You know, those little quotes from famous people, humor items.

"You have to watch it, though. The address for **Tumbling Topics** *is listed in a national guide to gymnastic organizations. We get newsletters from all over the country. Last summer I was desperate for material, so I lifted a whole article. Everybody loved it—everybody except the original author.*

"It turned out the newsletter I stole it from had stolen it from somewhere else without giving credit. It also turned out the author lives here in town. Of course, I hadn't checked on any of this.

"When the author saw the story in our newsletter with no credit line, he called and really gave me an earful.

Calendars

Readers often consider calendars the most useful news presented. Sometimes lists of forthcoming events are their only reason for looking at the newsletter.

Your calendar should be accurate, complete and visually interesting. It should be located ready to take out for placement on bulletin board or desk. Don't put it on the other side of the page with the membership form, map to annual picnic or list of key phone numbers. If you design the calendar well and have important information, you may even get the ultimate compliment: placement on the door of a refrigerator or vending machine.

The example below was made by reducing a standard 11 inch wide calendar to fit the 8 1/2 by 11 format. The editor then typed in events for the appropriate days and pasted up the results along with other material for the back page of her newsletter. Seven other editors took several different approaches, all trying to make calendars attractive and informative.

HOMEMAKER ACTIVITIES

February

4 - Heritage Quilting, 1:30 p.m., Trinity Lutheran Church (Multi-purpose Room), Waupaca

18 - Heritage Quilting, 7:30 p.m., Clintonville Urban Telephone Office (Meeting Room)

March

7 - Farm Institute, 10:30 - 3:30 p.m., Clintonville High School

10 - Candy Making Workshop

15 - The Hyperactive Child, Workshop at Waupaca High School, 9:00 a.m. - 3:15 p.m.

17 - Executive Board Meeting, 7:30 p.m. at the Manawa City Hall

18 - International Australia, 8:00 p.m. Manawa Little Wolf High School Commons.

April

1 - Leader Training "Eating at Low Cost" - Iola (afternoon and Weyauwega (evening) - tentative

4 - Leader Training "Eating at Low Cost" - Clintonville (afternoon) - tentative

8 - Spring Council, Iola

8 - Shara-Pac Spring Tonic, Waupaca

22 - Central District Homemakers' Spring Meeting (for county Education Chairmen), Waupaca.

For Sale: Cookbooks

The Oak Grove Homemakers of New London have put together a cookbook of recipes from their members. It has 47 pages of several different catagories. The club made extra typewritten copies and is selling the cookbooks at 50c a piece. If anyone would be interested in seeing or buying a copy, please contact Mrs. Del Otis, Club President, Route 4, New London.

JULY 1982

SUNDAY	MONDAY	TUESDAY	WEDNESDAY	THURSDAY	FRIDAY	SATURDAY
* JULY 1-2 - INDEPENDENCE TIME - Sing "Yankee Doodle" and get $1.00 OFF any order over $2.00. Show up in an Uncle Sam suit and get 100 FREE COPIES. * JULY 20th - MOON DAY - Bring us a "Moon Rock" to celebrate the 1st Moon landing and we'll give you 10 FREE COPIES. * JULY 26th - VISA DAY - 10% OFF if you charge on your VISA card.				*1	2	3
4 INDEPENDENCE DAY	5 Rabbit Show 12 Noon Expo Center	6	7	8 Holstein breeders sale 7:30 PM A-Barn	9	10
11	12	13 Dog License Committee meeting 7:00 PM	14	15	16 Domestic pet disease clinic 1:00 - 4:00PM Expo Center	17
18	19	*20 Dog License Committee meeting 7:00 PM--REPORTS ARE DUE	21	22	23	24
25	*26	27	28	29 Square dance lessons 7:00PM	30	31

CALENDAR

April

2 Sat.	9-4 p.m.	4-H Work Day, Upham Woods, Wisconsin Dells.
2 Sat.	9-4:30 p.m.	Distance Riding Seminar, UW-Madison, Room 212, Animal Science Building, Madison.
3 Sun.		Spring Recreation Laboratory, Upham Woods, Wisconsin Dells.
4 Mon.	8:00 p.m.	Green/Dane Counties Older 4-H Youth Volleyball Game, Monticello Schools.
5 Tue.	8:00 p.m.	4-H Photography Training, Ag Building, Monroe.
9 Sat.	1:30 p.m.	4-H House Plant Training, Ag Building, Monroe.
11 Mon.	8:00 p.m.	Adult 4-H Leaders Association, Ag Building, Monroe.
11 Mon.	7:30 p.m.	Dairy Goat Meeting, Courthouse, Room 208.
11 Mon.		Area Electricity Project Meeting #4, Electric Company Service Center, Watertown.
12 Tue.	7:30 p.m.	Countywide 4-H Foods and Nutrition Project Leaders Meeting, Courthouse, Room 208.
13 Wed.	8:00 p.m.	Dairy Project Judging Workout, Norvic Farms, Lake Mills.
13 Wed.	8:00 p.m.	Countywide Livestock Judging Meeting, Courthouse, Room 208.
13 Wed.	7:30 p.m.	Jefferson County 4-H Older Youth Board and Planning Meeting, Paul Schroedl Home, Jefferson.
14 Thur.	7:30 p.m.	4-H Dog Project Training, Pet Chalet, Monroe.
15 Fri.		DEADLINE: Dairy and Horse and Pony I.D. Forms.
15 Fri.		DEADLINE: 4-H Summer Camp Counselor Applications.
16 Sat.	9:00 a.m.	Southeastern Wisconsin 4-H Rabbit Show, County Exposition Grounds, Waukesha
17 Sun.		Naturalist Training Workshop, Upham Woods, Wisconsin Dells.
17 Sun.	2:00 p.m.	Northern Area 4-H Model Airplane and Rocketry Meeting, John Karstens Farm, Cambridge.
18 Mon.	8:00 p.m.	Home and Family Clothing Developmental Committee.
19 Tue.	7:30 p.m.	Southern Area 4-H Model Airplane Project Meeting, Koshkonong Community Center, Fort Atkinson.
20 Wed.	7:30 p.m.	Camp Counselor Planning Session, Orfordville.
21 Thur.	8:00 p.m.	Dairy Judging Training, Ag Building, Monroe.
23 Sat.	9-3:30 p.m.	Hoofers Riding Clinic, UW-Madison, Stock Pavilion.
25 Mon.	6:30 p.m.	Countywide 4-H Dog Obedience Training, Fairgrounds Activity Center.

1 Tri-Met. Public meeting on proposed route and
WED service changes. 7:30 p.m., St. Johns Community Center, 8427 N. Central.

2 Portland School Board. Proposed school closures. 7:30 p.m., Administration Building,
THU 501 N. Dixon.

2 Metro Council. 7:30 p.m., 527 S.W. Hall.
THU

Planning Commission. Comprehensive Plan map
TUE amendment, residential to industrial, for St. Johns Urban Renewal Area; Comprehensive Plan amendment initiation process, and amendment at S.E. 37th and Francis; Banfield Station Influence Area Boundaries; zoning code fee schedule. Noon, 621 S.W. Alder.

Metro Regional Development Committee. Hearing
WED on Urban Growth Boundary. 5:30 p.m., 527 S.W. Hall.

8 MCD Advisory Committee. 7:30 p.m., Southeast
WED Uplift, 5224 S.E. Foster.

Metro Regional Development Committee. Hearing
on Urban Growth Boundary. 5:30 p.m., 527 S.W. Hall.

9 Department of Environmental Quality. Hearing
THU on water quality control rules. 10 a.m., 522 S.W. Fifth.

Northeast Neighborhood Leadership Conference.
SAT 10 a.m., King Neighborhood Facility, 4815 N.E. Seventh. $3 fee includes lunch.

Tri-Met Board. 10 a.m., Water Services Building, 510 S.W. Montgomery.

13 Portland School Board. 7:30 p.m., Administration Building, 501 N. Dixon.

City Council. Morrison Street Development
THU Project. 2 p.m., Council Chambers, City Hall.

22 City Council. Proposed water towers in Ash
WED Creek area. 2 p.m., Council Chambers, City Hall.

Tri-Met. Public meeting on proposed route and
THU service changes. 7:30 p.m., Temple Beth Israel, 1931 N.W. Flanders.

Metro Council. 7:30 p.m., 527 S.W. Hall.

---

wood Cliffs, NJ 07632. Single issue, $.75. 6 issues. $2.95.

• Stone Soup may interest children who like to write as well as read. Published by the Children's Art Foundation of Santa Cruz, Calif., it is written entirely by kids. Readers are invited to submit their stories and poems for publication. To an adult, the stories in Stone Soup are both charming and revealing, but whether they interest other children is questionable. The possibility of being published in this magazine could, nevertheless, provide important encouragement for a young writer. Box 83, Santa Cruz, CA 95063. Single issue, $2.50; 5 issues, $12.00.

• Ebony Jr! is an interesting and well-written magazine primarily for black children. It contains a mature of fiction, nonfiction, news, puzzles and games. Many of the articles and stories are about Africa, past and present. A feature called Ink Links encourages children to write about actual events in their lives or to use their imaginations and create poems and stories about fictional people and happenings. In addition, winners of each month's story and poetry contests get to see their work in print. For an extra $2.00 a year, parents can subscribe to "A Guide for the Use of Ebony Jr.!," which stresses reading comprehension and further exploration of topics discussed in the magazine. 820 S. Michigan Ave., Chicago, IL 60605. Single issue, $.75; 10 issues, $7.00.

• Games is an adult magazine that has great appeal for bright children. It is made up entirely of puzzles, games and articles about games and how to play them. Recent issues have included hidden picture puzzles, mazes, logic and crossword puzzles and anagrams, plus articles about backgammon, chess, bridge and wari — the oldest game in the world. Games performs the dual function of keeping children happily occupied while sharpening their thinking skills. P.O. Box 10145, Des Moines, IA 50340. Single issue, $1.25; 6 issues, $7.00.

The Right Magazine
Is Out There, Somewhere

With the exception of Games, all of the magazines discussed in this article are designed primarily for children 8 to 12 years old. Clearly, you need not limit your search for reading material for your gifted child to publications directed at children in this age range. Many gifted children are bored by World but very interested in its "parent" magazine, The National Geographic. And a gifted child interested in model railroads is as likely to be a fan of these interest magazines for model railroading hobbyists as any adult. As in all matters, your child's interests and your understanding of them must be your guide.

By Susan Meyers, a book reviewer and author of the recently published children's book The Truth About Gorillas and the forthcoming book Pearson, a Harbor Seal Pup (both by Dutton)

---

dates to remember:

Dec. 9 Local School Committee Meeting – 7:30 p.m.
Dec. 11 Holiday Band and Vocal Concert at Whitford – 7:30 p.m.
Dec. 15 School Board Meeting at Errol Hassell – 7:30 p.m.
Dec. 18 Canned Food Drive
Dec. 22–Jan. 2 Winter Vacation
Jan. 5 Classes resume

Calendar

Dec. 16 Barnes Winter Program
7:30 p.m. Holiday Revue

Dec. 17 VIP luncheon with principal in the Art Room

Dec. 17 Barnes Carnival Committee
7:30 p.m. meeting, Staff Room

Dec. 19 All School Sing in the gym
9:15 – Canned food donations will
9:45 be presented to Fire District

Dec. 19 Last day of school 1980

Jan. 5 First day of school 1981

Jan. 6 Local School Committee
11:30-1 Luncheon meeting

Jan. 8 PTC Board meeting
7:30 13625 SW FarVista

Principal's Corner

Barnes School is dedicated to providing a positive learning environment for all students. Various instructional activities, resources and teaching skills are being used to achieve this goal.

The instructional program at Barnes is designed to meet the Beaverton School District and State of Oregon standards for elementary schools.

Barnes teaching staff have developed long-range plans for the next couple of years to best meet the needs of boys & girls.

Among Barnes' objectives for 1980-81 are the following:

An emphasis in meeting individual math skill needs using a system recently developed by the Beaverton School District called Managing Arithmetic by Objectives (MABO).

A continuing emphasis in energy education which features conservation, and appropriate uses of energy and natural resources.

An emphasis on career education, human relations and guidance goals as related to district and state standards through the use of the Learning Activity Guide, developed by Barnes teachers.

An active awareness of teaching strategies best suited to meet the needs of students.

An emphasis in providing effective communication with parents.

For more information regarding Barnes' plans and objectives for 1980-81, please contact your child's teacher or the principal. We welcome the opportunity to talk with you.

Our best wishes for a joyous holiday season.

Kathy Holstein

2

Mastheads

Although not required by postal regulations (unless you mail second class), your newsletter should have a masthead in every issue. The "mast" is simply the familiar box with information such as addresses, names and publication schedules. As a minimum, your mast should include:

- name and address of your organization,
- your name as editor,
- frequency of publication, and
- subscription costs, if any.

You might also include names of key officers and information about advertising. Potential contributors will look in your masthead to learn if you solicit articles and photographs and what you pay for them.

If you copyright your newsletter, the notice belongs in your masthead. Ordinarily your organization, business or agency would be the copyright owner. See pages 24 and 25 for details. You can also put an International Standard Serial Number in the masthead if not run as part of your nameplate. An eight-digit ISSN is assigned at no fee by the National Serials Data Program of the Library of Congress, Washington DC 20540. You should have a number if you want your newsletter filed in libraries, and you must have a number to mail second class.

Because your mast will usually not change from one issue to the next, it can be prepared well ahead of time to pasteup in the same location each issue.

REPORTLAND

Published Bi-Monthly By

Greater Portland Convention and Visitors Association, Inc.
26 SW Salmon
Portland, Oregon 97204
(503) 222-2223

OFFICERS

Paul T. Himmelman, President
Benson Hotel

Warne Nunn, Vice President
Pacific Power & Light Co.

John A. Kemp, Secretary
U.S. National Bank

B. Clyde Billman, Treasurer
Nendel's Management Company

EXECUTIVE COMMITTEE

Daniel A. Damon
Portland Hilton Hotel

Raymond A. Dodge
Imperial Tour & Travel

Gerald J. Fitzpatrick
Jerry Fitzpatrick Real Estate

Patrick G. Goss
Sheraton-Airport

Elmer E. Henry
TraveLodge - Portland

Murphy T. Landels
Portland Rose Motel

Ms. Pat Colwell Lewis
Professional Printing Services

John H. Maloney, II
Gray Line Sightseeing & Convention Services

Ronald W. Miller
Decorators West, Inc.

Keith A. Phildius
United Airlines

Robert J. Snider
Thunderbird / Red Lion Motor Inns Corporation

James W. Suiter
Portland Marriott Hotel

Ex-Officio Members

James A. Larpenteur, Jr.
Schwabe, Williamson, Wyatt, Moore & Roberts

Edward M. Perkins
PERSCHCO

A.F. Tony Ralter, Editor

PHOTO CREDITS:
Ankrom Capitol Photographers, Page 1
Jim Knight Photography, Pages 4, 6
David Mann Photography, Pages 1, 6
Oregon Historical Society, Page 5
Uptown Studios, Pages 4, 6
Western Forestry Center, Page 3

---

4) You should maintain an active blacklist with names of contract violators. No adoption should be approved without checking the blacklist.

5) The adoption contract must be legally binding (a cooperative attorney can help you work out the terms) with the following provisos:

- The animal must not be sold or given away to any other person or agency.
- The animal is never to be used for experimental purposes, for breeding or as a draft animal.
- The animal must be returned to the shelter if the adopter can no longer care for it.
- The animal remains the property of the shelter, and the shelter retains the right to confiscate it if the contract is violated.

6) You should set a standard adoption fee for each species. The adoption fees for purebred animals and mixed breeds should be the same, because these animals are to be adopted solely as pets, and mixed breeds offer as much pet potential as animals with pedigrees.

All pedigree papers that come in with animals should be voided and sent to the American Kennel Club, 51 Madison Ave., New York, NY 10010. This prevents anyone from using those papers for another animal and notifies AKC that the particular animal will be sterilized and cannot be claimed as the parent of a future litter.

7) If you have a spay/neuter clinic, the pet should be sterilized before it leaves the shelter. For infant animals, a deposit must be collected to be returned on proof of surgery.

8) You should check each applicant's home to verify the address and ensure the conditions are appropriate for the animal selected.

9) A regular and systematic follow-up system should be maintained to verify that the animal has been sterilized according to the contract.

Follow-up can be by telephone, postal card or form letter, and can be performed by a volunteer. It should include several questions about the animal's adaptation to its new home to verify that the adoption is successful. (This is also an opportunity for you to request an additional donation or to offer to add the adopter to your mailing list.)

SHELTER SENSE is published by The National Humane Education Center, a division of The Humane Society of the United States, 2100 L St., N.W., Washington, D.C. 20037, (202) 452-1100.

Subscription rate:
six issues — $5.00
additional subscriptions to the same address — $4.00 each

Photos:
John Dommers, cover;
Sumner Fowler, pg. 3;
Marc Asher, pg. 12.

HSUS Director of Animal Sheltering and Control . . . . Phyllis Wright
Editor, SHELTER SENSE . . . . Susan Bury Stauffer

---

SEPTEMBER 1981
Vol. 1 Number 1

THE LITTLE RED SCHOOLHOUSE
ISSN 0277-304X

Marjorie F. Brown
PRESIDENT
Char Dahl
SECRETARY

William C. Brown
MANAGING EDITOR
Suzy Peraino
SCHOOL EDITOR
Joella Connors
COPY EDITOR, COMPOSITION
Mikel Meyers
RESEARCH DIRECTOR
Roz Bryant
PROMOTION
Clement David Hellyer
SENIOR ADVISOR
Mary Workman
FUND ADMINISTRATOR
Rebecca B. Lacy
LEGAL COUNSEL

The Little Red Schoolhouse is published monthly by Midwest Meridian Limited to foster national exchange of information on schools, learning, and education in general. The description "reprinted" denotes material substantially intact from the original; "adapted," moderately abridged; "excerpted," substantially abridged. TLRS actively solicits letters from readers. Letters must be signed and address given, although only initials will be printed if writer so requests. All letters become the property of TLRS on publication and may be edited. Photo selection, headlines and captions are by the editors. Manuscripts and other material submitted must be accompanied by a self-addressed, stamped envelope.

Copyright ©1981 by Midwest Meridian Limited. All rights reserved. Although we carefully examine all submitted material, we cannot be responsible for damage or loss. Please submit all manuscripts to Article Editor, TLRS, N.E. 8595 Court, Bothell, Washington 98011. Subscriptions: U.S. & Canada $14 a year, $20 two years. Elsewhere add $1. POSTMASTER: Send form 3579 to The Little Red Schoolhouse, 8595 N.E. 8595 CT, Bothell, WA 98011. Telephone 206-481-7772.

"He says he wants to be a sexologist!"

Current
Official publication of Columbia River Girl Scout Council. Serving 13 counties in Oregon and Southwest Washington.
President: Mary Anne Wolfe
Executive Director: Grace Raymore
Editor: Gail Workman
Deadline: 10th of each month preceding publication. Submit news c/o Council Headquarters.

Telephone: (503) 224-6560.

Current

COLUMBIA RIVER GIRL SCOUT COUNCIL

Non-Profit Org.
U.S. Postage
PAID
Portland, Oregon
Permit No. 545

Mastheads can be built into address blocks.

Contents

If your newsletter has more than four pages, readers will appreciate a short table of contents. Label the box "contents," "inside" or "this month," or make it so graphically attractive that it commands attention. The three-dimensional effect below was made by using 50 percent screen to add deep shadows along two edges. See pages 60 and 61 for how to use screens.

The contents list should appear either on page one or as part of the address panel. What's the point of putting it anywhere else? List only material on inside pages, letting front page headlines speak for themselves. Somewhere on the inside pages consider a graphically similar list of future articles. Keep your readers looking forward to getting each issue.

Gifted Children Newsletter

JUNE 1980   VOL. 1 NO. 4   SPECIAL REPORT

Disciplining Your Child

Search for Young Scientists

An Interview With Joseph Renzulli

How To Explore a Museum

Update on Terman's Study Of the Gifted

Gifted Children Swap Lifestyles

Better Chance for Gifted Minorities

Plus: Book, Toy and Game Reviews; a Calendar of Events; And Spin-off, a Four-Page Pullout Section for Your Child

ADVISORY BOARD

A Critique of Kids' Magazines

Most parents of gifted children know the value of frequent trips to libraries and bookstores. They know that inquiring young minds need stimulation and that books are the food and drink of a growing intellect. Many of these parents, however, overlook another satisfying and readily available source of mental nourishment: children's magazines.

A good magazine can provide a child with a variety of experiences and pleasures — even its arrival in the mail is an exciting event. A smorgasbord of information and entertainment in the form of nonfiction articles, stories, poems, puzzles and games introduces children to facts and ideas they can read about in a single sitting or pursue for days. And, with the high prices of children's books, a year's subscription can cost as little as one juvenile title.

Among the fine children's magazines available, some are general interest, others are specialized. When making your selection, it is important to keep your child's interests and preferences in mind, for the most familiar and popular publications are not necessarily the best. Get single copies of the magazines you are considering — either at the library or by writing to the publishers — before sending in any subscription forms. As your child reads them, pay attention to his reactions. Does your child comment on the information? Does he ask questions or express a desire to find out more about newly discovered subjects? The following capsule reviews and your child's candid remarks and behavior will help you find a worthwhile new resource.

General Interest Magazines

• Cricket routinely publishes the very best children's authors and illustrators. Each issue contains at least one nonfiction article as well as a craft or game feature, but fiction — with considerable emphasis on

The Newsletter Forum

May 1981/Columbus, Ohio

November/December
931 West Third A...
PO Box 949
Columbus, Ohio 43...

Spin-Off of Business Wire

—Helvetica Heavy, 24 pt

Saucy Newsletter Serves PR, Media People

BY JOHN WOOD

A three-dot, accurate, terse, gutsy cross between Theodore Bernstein's *Winners & Sinners* and Jack O'Dwyers PR newsletter? That's Lorry Lokey's *Business Wire Newsletter*, published monthly from San Francisco.

"I don't try to be artsy," says Lokey about the newsletter, "but it's chock-full of news about PR and media people that Bizwire clients need . . . and otherwise might not get so fast, or not at all."

He talks choppy but to the point.

The communications network, which is the mainstay of the Bizwire operation, started in 1961. As a spin-off, the newsletter began as an infrequent periodical shortly after.

The communications network Lokey had put together in the San Francisco Bay Area was a 16-location, 70-mile network of teleprinters direct to newspapers and radio and television stations. The news releases that zipped over the teleprinters to the news media were supplied by corporate and agency public relations operations, who were charged a fee for the service by Lokey.

Front page of Business Wire uses abbreviated, staccato-style of writing to cram a lot of news into four quickly- produced typewritten pages. Emphasis is on information, not graphics.

something like the style of the newsletter.

Busine..s Wire Newsletter, valued for its brash public relations advice but not its graphics, is read by business communicators across the country

Every month 1,700 copies go directly to communications offices and pass from desk to desk in the *Fortune* 500 corporations and the top public relations agencies in America, all clients of the national *Business Wire* hook-up with the country's top press and broadcast outlets.

"At first, the newsletter reported who changed jobs . . . . pointers I thought everybody knew, like 'Don't call P.M. papers in the morning . . . call in the afternoon, or better yet, write!' It still does that. Reports on changes in the news game. Updates old hands and is something of a primer for journeymen and novices," Lokey says.

He reads a couple dozen business, trade and general news publications a day, along with countless news releases and gets constant telephone calls. The hardest part of the reporting, he says, is when a caller requests "I don't want to read this in your newsletter, but . . ." And he adds, "if they say that, I don't put it in unless I have the same item from a third party."

From these various sources, Lokey stuffs items in pigeon holes until near deadline time. Then on a week end, he spreads them out on his kitchen table and organizes them into topics.

The most recent issue: a lead on United Airlines closing all ten regional PR offices and pulling its nationwide PR operation to the Chicago headquarters; a few items on the changing technology of news reporting and dissemination; available news and public relations jobs; a candid item about lost dollars in 1980 from a nonpublic

page format. Typewritten on a proportionally-spaced typewriter with ragged right margins, the pithy items spit out on the page one after another, highlighted with underlined, left-hand slugs.

SEE SAUCY, page 6

4-5 What really determines what makes a newsletter a newsletter?

7 Search for Mr Goodboss continues with a look at the Creative One

8 What does "communications" really mean? A novel approach.

Plain talk, sometimes a little comfort, a bit salty, to make it real. Watch for hip-shooting and foot-in-the-mouth syndrome. The power of the printed word remains undiminished, so think through carefully what you want your company to say, then lay it out truthfully. Consumers and employees have an eternal ability to sense double-talk.

words verbatim: "How far is it to Augusta? Two six-packs,' I used to tell people. Your whole life revolves around that *bleep* bottle."

In another part of the story, the only one of the six recovering alcoholics who hadn't been divorced is offered an admiring comment about his wife: "She must be quite a

Con't on page 7

KEEPING UP WITH AMERICAN English Today™

Volume 2 No. 3
July 1981

The monthly newsletter for people who want to stay current with the modern language of the U.S.A.

Trademarks get lost in name of success

For every businessman dreaming of making a product such a success that it becomes "a household word," there must be ten lawyers with nightmares about fighting a hopeless battle against such a fate.

In the USA, the manufacturer of a product that is the first of its kind on the market is especially concerned about this dilemma. Ask the makers of **Formica**, **Styrofoam**, and **Scotch Tape** how hard it is to keep a balance between promoting public interest in their goods and protecting their proprietary rights to the brand name.

When you think of an **Instamatic** camera, are you aware that this is the brand made by Eastman-Kodak, or do you generalize the term to include all lightweight, fixed-focus cameras?

Do you use **Xerox** to describe all dry photocopying machines? Is the **Coke** you drink made by Coca-Cola, or do you refer to all cola drinks in this way?

Are all blue jeans **Levi's**? All petroleum jellies **Vaseline**? All decaffeinated coffees **Sanka**? All household

cleansers **Ajax**? All facial tissues **Kleenex**?

Despite vigorous efforts on the part of the companies to retain these brand identities, many Americans today do not make the connection between the manufacturers and their products, even though all of the above brand names are registered trademarks protected by the U.S. Patent Office.

Under US law, you may register as a trademark (TM) the symbol, name, title, or phrase that is associated with the identification of a product (or service).

A trademark is owned and used exclusively by a single company, to differentiate its product from those of competitors. Generally, a successful trademark is catchy, apt and easily recalled in connection with a given product.

There is no set pattern for coining words to be used as trademarks. You may combine words associated with the product, e.g., **AstroTurf** (from Astrodome + turf), **Instamatic** (instant + automatic), **Exercycle** (exercise + cycle), and **Ultramatic** (ultra-, meaning beyond, + suede). Sometimes the coinage is part of a fad (fee-O-Matic) or it may be a proper name (**Jacuzzi**, whirlpool baths).

In most cases, the trademark goes on forever. (Compare a "copyright" – for literary, artistic, and musical works – which eventually expires.)

Ironically, sometimes the more popular a trademark becomes, the more in jeopardy the company may be of losing exclusive rights to it because the word passes into the language as a common noun. That's what

In this issue   Page

New meanings of natural parenting

After all the thousands of years of parents begetting children, you'd think that this natural process would be unchanging. Not so.

Who are the **natural parents** of a child, anyway? Once there would have been no doubt. Only the **pair** whose genes combined to form the offspring would have qualified as "natural parents."

Today, however, you may hear adoptive parents referred to as the natural parents, particularly when they have adopted and reared their child from infancy.

Childbirth itself is thought of in new terms, too. In modern **natural childbirth**, the mother is awake and has been trained to assist in the birth through special breathing and pushing techniques, such as those taught by the Lamaze method. Much more sophisticated and studied than primitive (more natural?) births, the **natural childbirth** is contrasted to giving birth while partially or completely unconscious, i.e., anesthetized.

Fortunately, regardless of method, the outcome is almost always a natural child.

Massage parlor messages
Would a massage parlor offer the "adult" activity you're looking for? Find out about adult DWs on page 3.

Graphics

Graphics are pieces of art used to express ideas. Both parts of the definition are essential: art and ideas. The essence of graphics is a clear message pleasing to the eye — ideas through art.

Considering graphics as art applied to a purpose, your use of graphics should begin with a review of the goals of your newsletter. What are you trying to accomplish and how can graphics help?

- Graphics can convey a mood or image. Design, color and drawings suggest what kind of organization you are or want to become. Graphics can also convey ideas such as being rich or poor, passive or aggressive, slick or homey.
- Graphics can transmit information. A good sketch, chart, map or graph can replace several hundred words of copy.
- Graphics can establish an attitude, especially with art showing people. Gender, age and race make a difference. So does what they are doing. Visuals of people carry your opinions and reinforce or change readers' feelings.
- Graphics can make copy more attractive and readable. Borders, rules, screens and other devices help readers keep order and let editors focus attention on important material. Pictures and designs break up blocks of print which otherwise might seem too heavy.

The next twenty pages of this book deal with graphics. I have described where to get graphics and how to use them. In most cases, I have tried to practice what I'm preaching by using plenty of art. Enjoy!

"The whole idea of graphics always seemed so hard to understand. Even the word sounded complicated: graphics sounds like mathmatics. So I edited our newsletter for five years and never gave a second thought to visual effects.

"When we got a new editor, he showed how easy it could be. A week after he began, he went to the art supply store during his lunch break. He just told them he was doing a newsletter and wanted to make it look nice. He also showed them two or three other newsletters he liked and asked how their art was done.

"Well, our new man got a lesson that noon and for two more noons the same week. For twenty five dollars worth of clip art, transfer lettering, border tapes and other supplies, he also got a crash course in graphics. His issues don't look professional, but at least they are interesting. That's more than I could say when I was editor."

Use timely art.

Five simple sources

1. You can use transfer film material (ruboffs) available from most stationery and art supply stores. Letraset, Formatt, Cellopak, Microtape, Zipatone and Chartpak are some of the common brand names.

There are several tricks to transfer film materials. Never apply them to erasable bond or other high gloss paper. They may slip. Be sure letters and images are well-burnished before copy goes to a printer. Most packages include instructions and materials for proper burnishing. Soft plastic tools do OK for burnishing, but not as well as a rubber roller. The roller, available at any art or graphics store, is also the only good burnisher for larger pieces of copy stuck down with wax.

If you have a logo or other stock items you want on a transfer sheet, consider having a supply custom-made. The sheets are made from camera-ready copy like any other print job. Look in the catalogs of most major companies for complete information.

The cityscape on these two pages was created entirely from ruboff materials. Only the blimp and its banner were clip art.

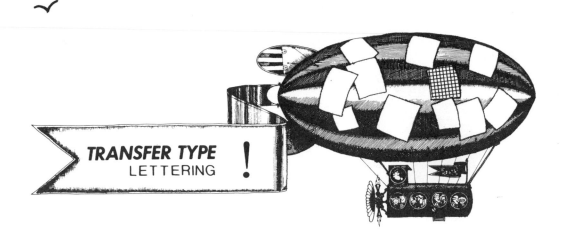

TRANSFER TYPE
LETTERING !

FILMS

2. For making copy more pleasing and readable, you have graphics at your fingertips. Your typewriting has accurate spacing and symbols to make designs and borders. Try using half spacing, half lining and whatever other features your machine offers.

```
><><><><><><><><><><><><><><><><><><><><
><                                    ><
><   Make borders with a typewriter.  ><
><                                    ><
><><><><><><><><><><><><><><><><><><><><
```

```
"""""""""""""""""""""""""""""""""""""""""
=========================================
^^^^^^^^^^^^^^^^^^^^^^^^^^^^^^^^^^^^^^^^^^
++++ Make lines with a typewriter.++++
```

```
][][][][][][][][][][][][][][][][][][][][
```

```
##########################################
##########################################
##########################################
###                                    ##
### Make screens with a typewriter. ##
###                                    ##
##########################################
##########################################
##########################################
```

3. You can take letters, symbols and drawings from newspapers, magazines and any other printed material. Simply cut out what you want and arrange it to suit your purposes.

There are hundreds of design and graphic books published for the printing trade. Books such as these may be found in most public libraries, book and art stores, and print shops. In libraries the books may be listed under art or advertising rather than graphics. The books are full of clip art: art designed to be cut out and pasted down to camera ready copy. Subjects and styles are virtually limitless.

If you plan to cut out clip art, be sure you own the book or have permission to take from it. Clip art should never be taken from library materials.

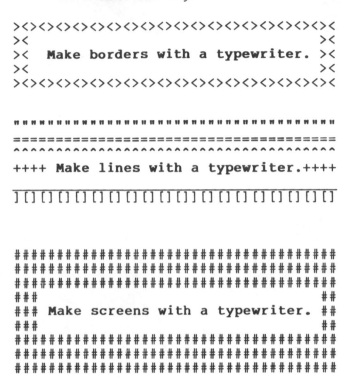

In addition to these books, typesetters, printers and graphic artists often have encyclopedias of design published for commercial users. Parts of these books may be reproduced without paying royalties or securing copyright permissions.

There are hundreds of other books with graphics you can use. Look in used bookstores, garage sales and summer cabins. Keep in mind the art in children's coloring books, posters and school books. Watch the discount tables in bookstores and catalogues from places such as Publishers Central Bureau and Marlborough Books. Finally, keep your eyes open for books and magazines published in the nineteenth century. Before the invention of halftones, pictures were published using steel engravings. Those engravings make fine graphic copy.

Books for graphics

Here are just a few titles:

William Rowe.	**Flora and Fauna Design Fantasies.**
Dan Solo.	**Special Effect and Topical Alphabets.**
Spyros Horemis.	**Optical and Geometrical Patterns and Designs.**
James Harter.	**Women: A Pictorial Archive from 19th Century Sources.**
Carol Grafton.	**Children: A Pictorial Archive from 19th Century Sources.**
Gregory Mirow.	**A Treasury of Designs for Artists and Craftsmen.**
Clarence Hornung.	**An Old-fashioned Christmas in Illustration.**
Flinders Petrie.	**Decorative Patterns of the Ancient World.**
Leroy Appleton.	**American Indian Design and Decoration.**
Edmond Gillon.	**Victorian Stencils for Design and Decoration.**
Suzanne Chapman.	**Early American Design Motifs.**
Martin Isaacson.	**A Treasury of Stencil Designs for Artists.**
Rudolpf Motel.	**Handbook of Pictorial Symbols.**
Melvin Pruitt.	**Computer Graphics: 118 Computer-generated Designs.**
Jorge Encisco.	**Design Motifs of Ancient Mexico.**
Ernst Haeckel.	**Art Forms in Nature.**
Matsuya Co.	**Japanese Design Motifs.**
William Hawley.	**Chinese Folk Designs.**
William Rowe.	**Original Art Deco Designs.**
Theodore Menton.	**Japanese Border Designs.**
Theodore Menton.	**Ready to use Headlines.**
Theodore Menton.	**Ready to use Borders.**
Dave Phillips.	**Graphic and Op-art Mazes.**

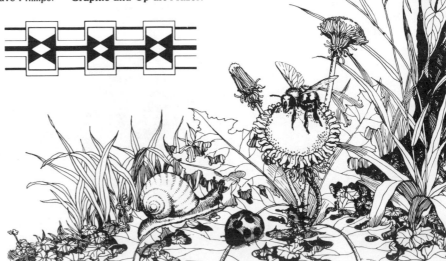

4. You can have graphics drawn for you. Your organization may have a member with talent in art. Perhaps a neighbor, friend or relative who does calligraphy would help. And don't overlook the skill and imagination of children. They might surprise you. Art departments at local schools and colleges are also good sources. Finally, of course, you can pay a graphic artist.

5. You can get special effects from other artistic media. Photography is one of the best because it can produce high contrast and sharp borders. Ask an amateur photographer with a darkroom to make some photograms. They are made simply by placing an object directly on a piece of photo paper, exposing the paper to light, then developing using standard procedures.

"I wanted to do something special for our holiday issue, but couldn't find any clip art I liked. Everything looked too commercial. Then my daughter showed me how to make photograms. We took some holly leaves and arranged them in a pattern we liked. Then we got some resin-coated printing paper, some developer and some fixer, a couple of big baking pans to hold the chemicals, a piece of clear glass, and a short string of red Christmas tree lights.

"We took the whole pile into the bathroom, plugged in the red lights as a safelight, and turned off the white light. Then we put the holly leaves on the paper and the glass on top of the leaves to hold them flat. We turned on the white light for a count of ten, took the glass and leaves off the paper, and developed our picture. The basin was our water wash tank.

"Here is an example of what we got. Of course, we didn't get it exactly right on the first two or three exposures, but pretty soon we were turning out our own original graphics."

Tips for graphics

▸ Be careful not to overdo it. Keep designs simple and images clear. Flowery graphics, like flowery words, may confuse your readers.

▸ Use graphics to draw attention down the page and to the right. Clip art especially should be placed to emphasize the least read area of the page.

Here are two diagrams showing the percentages of time people spend looking at different areas of a page.

41%	20%
25%	14%

61%
39%

"I always wanted some color, but thought I couldn't get it. Too much money. Then one rainy Saturday Alice and I cleaned up the mimeo machine and ran a thousand copies of our name-plate in red ink. Now we take page one of every issue from that stock. The copy is the same old black ink, but the bright heading makes the package jump right through the mailbox.

Next winter we'll run out of the thousand and it'll be time to clean the machine again. We're going to change ink twice and go for a two color head—red for words and blue for art. We'll have to run all the sheets through twice, but the result will make everyone know our business is top drawer."

▸ Be sure blacks are dense and uniform, edges sharp and clear. With copy lacking dense blacks and sharp edges, try outlining with pen and shading with lines or dots. This is especially important if you must use a photocopy instead of an original in your final paste-up.

▸ Make several photocopies of all materials so you will have trial copies during layout. Save the originals for final pasteup. When you make photocopies, use a machine which prints on plain bond paper (rough and dull) and not photostatic paper (smooth and glossy). Remember light colors will not reproduce well with photocopy or offset. Steer clear of warm colors and stick with colors as close to black as possible.

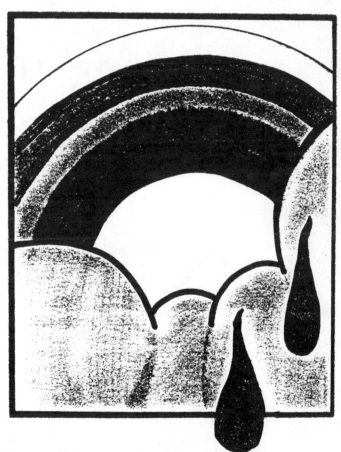

Rainbow and clouds above were drawn in colors, then photocopied. The example was printed from the photocopy. Top band of the rainbow was bright yellow. Then came green, red and dark blue. Bottom band was black. Clouds were light blue and the drops brown.

Different brands and settings of photocopy machines would give slightly different results, but the relationships among the shades would remain much the same.

Transportation Planning

Criminal Justice Planning

Combine graphics with standing headlines.

Question

ABS NT

MARRIAGE

ANGRRRY

PERI.D

TNNNEL

L°NELY

STROLL

Let your imagination turn letters and words into graphics.

Buy a template for the signs and symbols you draw most often.

Don't get carried away. Keep graphics in their place.

"We thought it was going to be easy! We both spent almost ten years as journalists, so thought we knew exactly how to make a living off a newsletter. All we had to do was write interesting articles about environmental issues and the money would start flowing in.

"What a laugh! We're making a living now, but it took us five years to get here. Five years of begging printers for credit and even moonlighting from our own business. When we started, we had absolutely no idea how to test a mailing list or develop spin-off products or even write decent advertising copy. Yet those kinds of things are the guts of the business.

"Meanwhile, whatever happened to journalism and high ideals? I'm lucky if I spend five hours a week actually writing. The rest of the time I'm a business manager, not an editor, and I'm not so sure it's what I want."

Lines and borders

Lines are probably the most effective graphic aid. They highlight text and give design a sense of order. Lines are also the easiest graphic to make. They are as close as a typewriter or pen. For better quality, a dozen companies make hundreds of products for rules, borders and boxes.

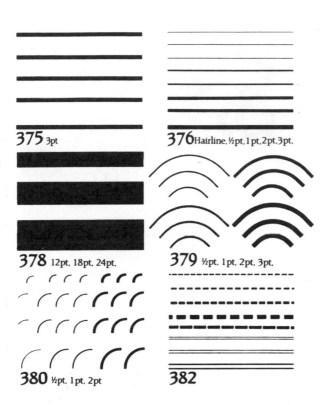

375 3pt.

376 Hairline, ½pt., 1pt., 2pt., 3pt.

378 12pt., 18pt., 24pt.

379 ½pt., 1pt., 2pt., 3pt.

380 ½pt., 1pt., 2pt

382

The same companies that make transfer letters use the process for sheets carrying lines and corners. Look in their catalogs for selections such as this.

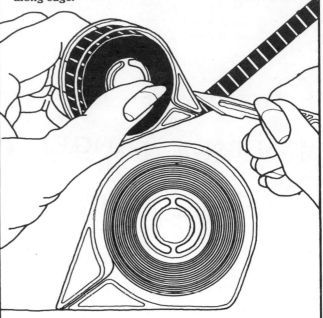

Lines from tapes. Draw the dispenser across the artwork surface and press into contact. Two methods to insure a straight line: 1. Draw a non-reproduction blue line along a ruler, then lay the tape next to that line. 2. Lay a straight edge (ruler, triangle, T-square) directly on pasteup surface and run tape dispenser along edge.

For cornering, overlap two tapes. Cut through both from outside to inside using a very sharp blade. Remove excess, then reposition tape to create a perfect mitered corner.

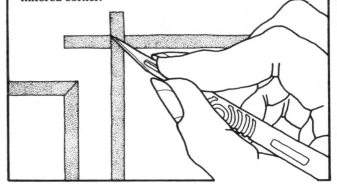

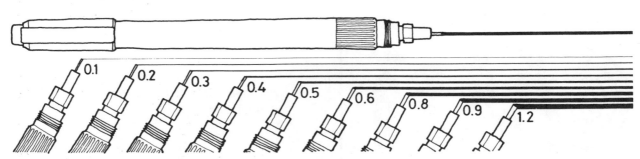

0.1 0.2 0.3 0.4 0.5 0.6 0.8 0.9 1.2

Use pens to make lines, never pencils. Common ball points or felt tips make lines that may be fuzzy or uneven. For best results, use pens made for graphics.

Ruling pens are drafting instruments with line width controlled by adjusting the screw. Dotted line pens are also technical drawing tools useful for newsletter work. Their wheels may be changed for line variety. Technical pens with interchangeable nibs produce precision lines. Line sizes above are in millimeters.

Sentences or phrases used to catch the reader's eye can be run as blurbs. The trick is especially good when used for quotations from the surrounding story.

Don't use a blurb at the optical center of a page or near the end of a story. Instead, place it as you would any other graphic to make the page look dynamic.

Make blurbs bold. They should seem deliberate parts of your design.

" Blurbs are great to fill leftover space. You can adjust the size of the box so copy runs to the end of the column. "

BORDER BOARD | **GRAPHIC PRODUCTS CORPORATION**

JOB DESCRIPTION
Copyright 1981 by Graphic Pr...

PASTE-UP BOARDS™
© Copyright 1982 by Graph Pak, Inc.   Portland, Oregon

JOB NAME

DATE   PAGE   OF   PAGES

Several companies make pasteup boards printed in non-reproducing blue. A good board should be sturdy enough to carry your materials, have a useful grid and be free from spots which might print. Some boards come with preprinted borders, saving time and assuring perfect alignment.

Identical design and copy looks quite different using lines in various ways. The rule between columns is called a floating rule and helps keep readers oriented vertically. The example at the right uses a box with strong bottom line to balance the large, bold nameplate.

Screens

Most printing is done with inks going on the sheet in a solid wash. Screens are ways to prevent some ink from reaching the paper. When ink is withheld, art or letters become lighter. Using screens to manipulate how much ink goes on, you can enhance both graphic elements and copy.

Lay an ordinary piece of window screen over a piece of paper, then spray the paper with paint. If you pick up the screen, the paper will be covered with small squares. Wire in the screen held some paint, making lines on the paper. Graphic screens produce the same effect.

Screens are described according to two traits: 1) how fine they are, and 2) what percentage they are. Fine screens have lots of dots per inch, coarse screens not so many. The top row at the right is very coarse at 30 lines; the bottom row rather fine at 85 lines. A screen that holds back most ink has a low percentage and looks very light. As percentages increase, more ink gets through and the image is darker.

Most printers will screen materials to your specifications. You can do it yourself, however, with press-on screens. Buy them from the same suppliers that handle transfer letters and border tapes.

While learning to use press-on screens, start with shapes having straight lines. Use scissors to cut both screen and backing slightly larger than your finished shape. Peel the screen from the backing then lightly place it down from its center outward to be sure it doesn't crease. To get the final shape, place

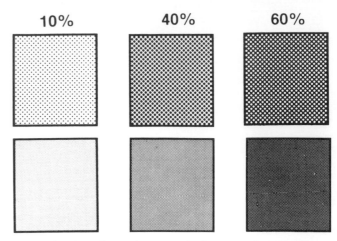

10%   40%   60%

a metal ruler along the straight lines and strip off excess screen with a sharp blade. Be careful only to cut through the thin screen, not the paper or pasteup board underneath.

There's an alternative way of doing screens using thin, clear acetate and a red film called rubylith. Both materials are common graphics supplies. Cut the acetate to the size of your pasteup board, then tape it to the top of the board like a flap. You can see your pasteup through the acetate. Next cut a piece of rubylith roughly to size and stick it to the acetate. Do a final trim as explained above so the rubylith precisely covers the area you want screened.

Using rubylith and acetate is called making windows. The red area held precisely in place by the acetate tells the printer's camera exactly where you want the screen. You specify screen size and the printer does the rest.

Examples of graduated and textured screens.

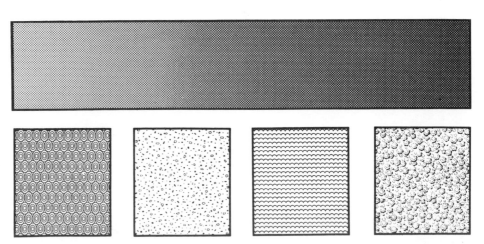

OPPORTUNITY

Summer 1981   Distribution Division   Editor: Chris Arnold

Mastering the rubylith technique opens several doors to more sophisticated design. For example, you can screen drawings like the one below. You can introduce additional colors—one acetate overlay for each color. That's how the blocks were made just below. And, as with these blocks, you can overlap colors. Orange and black screens, for example, would produce dark brown when overlapped at the right percentages. You can work with a graphics shop to produce designs mixing letters and art such as the nameplate above. Finally, ruby windows are a common way to tell a printer where photographs should be placed.

When one screen is printed over another at an angle it creates a moire pattern. The pattern looks like ripples on water or may only look cloudy, depending upon screen density and angle of overlap. Sometimes the effect is interesting, other times disastrous.

These five blocks show the range of effects possible using screens and two ink colors.

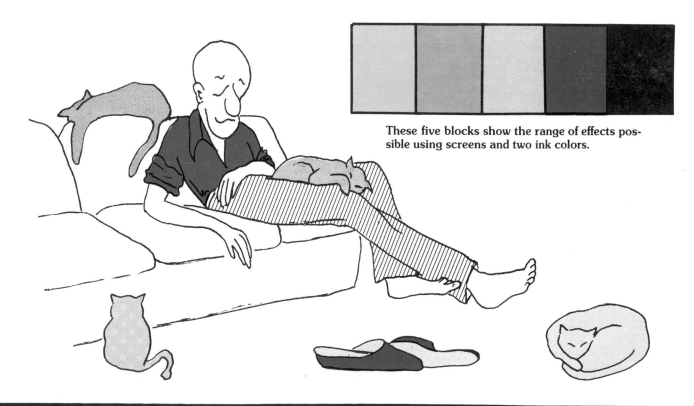

Graphs and charts

The ways of making graphics described in the last few pages easily combine for graphs and charts. These examples are all from a fine book called *Manual of Graphic Techniques*, by Tom Porter and Bob Greenstreet. I must confess, however, that I took the easy way to add colors. Instead of carefully cutting rubylith overlays, I merely made overlays of artists tissue. Using crayons, I colored the bars and backgrounds on the tissue. My printer followed these instructions to cut windows for the four negatives required for this page and the three negatives for page 63. Each negative is dark except for a clear space (window) where the color goes.

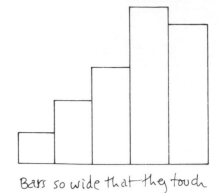
Wide bars on bold baseline

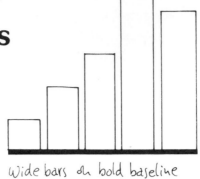
Bars so wide that they touch

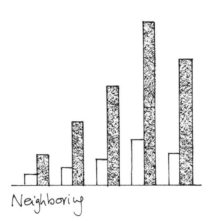
Neighboring

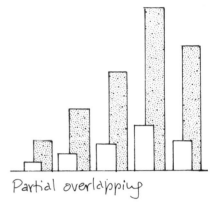
Partial overlapping

The bars shown in 3D:

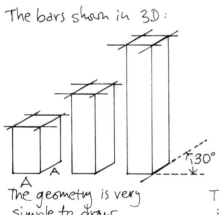
The geometry is very simple to draw

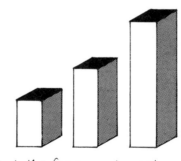
Tinting of the faces produces the illusion of lighting from different directions

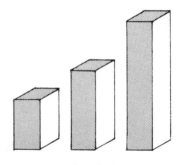
Lit from "behind"

An aggressive version

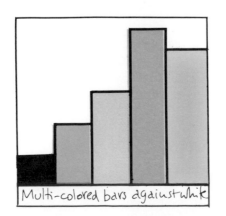
Multi-colored bars against white

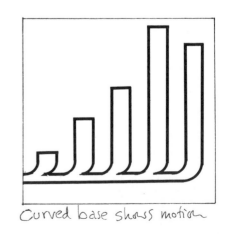
Curved base shows motion

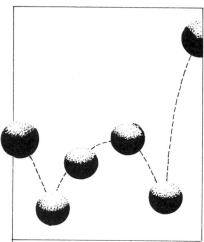

Dry statistics turned into symbolic graphics

Plain statistics embellished or humanized with pictures

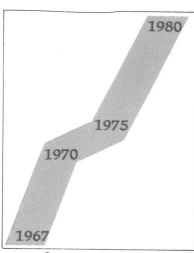

Significant information (e.g. dates) instead of dots

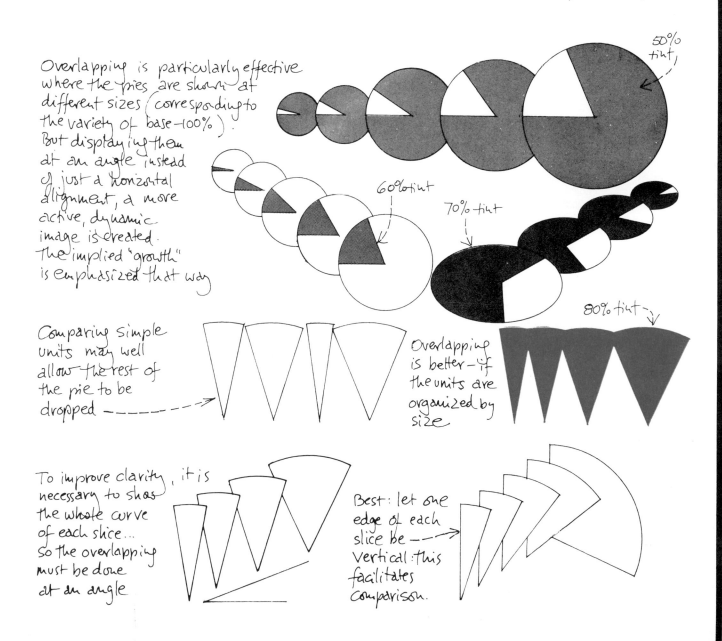

Overlapping is particularly effective where the pies are shown at different sizes (corresponding to the variety of base—100%). But displaying them at an angle instead of just a horizontal alignment, a more active, dynamic image is created. The implied "growth" is emphasized that way

50% tint

60% tint

70% tint

80% tint

Comparing simple units may well allow the rest of the pie to be dropped — — — →

Overlapping is better — if the units are organized by size

To improve clarity, it is necessary to show the whole curve of each slice... so the overlapping must be done at an angle

Best: let one edge of each slice be — — vertical: this facilitates comparison.

Nameplates

The nameplate is the first thing readers see when they open your newsletter. Its design and production are strong signals of how you want to be regarded. It is well worth your time to sketch several possibilities and ask for reactions from officers, staff, members and anyone else who will read your newsletter.

In addition to the name of the newsletter itself, the nameplate should include two other elements: the name of your organization and the date. If your organziation name does not clearly suggest your purposes or activities, those should be added. That is especially true if your organization name is an acronym. The words producing the acronym should be given and, if necessary, a few extra words of definition.

PAC Tales—If it is by the **Pacific Angling Club,** the club name is enough. If it is by the **Positive Action Center,** you might want to add something like "a focus for human potential development."

The white on black *Applegram* is a reverse made by putting white transfer lettering on black paper. To make the red letters and apple in the middle example, I used the tissue overlay technique

The cornucopia at the top was drawn by hand, carefully trimmed with an X-acto knife, then laid down over transfer lettering.

COUNCIL CIRCLE
News from the Urban Indian Council, Inc.

October, 1979   Vol. 2, No. 2

Even the most simple nameplate can look elegant. The *Garden Home Gazette* for a school PTA has a vague idea and poor execution. In the revised version, the editor used transfer letters for the top two words and border tape for the fence posts. The perfect arches came from tracing oval templates using a technical pen. The editor's sixth grader contributed the house and trees. Below, the *Portsmouth Biweekly* shows professional hand lettering at its award-winning best. The design is clean and contemporary — just the right note for this newsletter reaching 800 public employees.

OREGON STATE PARKS QUARTERLY

PARKS AND RECREATION DIVISION, DEPARTMENT OF TRANSPORTATION   **NUMBER 1, 1980**

NewsLetter
for Grantmakers

The Council

For Grantmakers

Council Takes Position on Payout Legislation

Legislation to modify the current private foundation payout requirement is likely to be introduced early this year in the 97th Congress. Current law requires private foundations to distribute annually 5% of their assets or their total annual income (less long-term capital gains) —whichever is greater.

A position paper prepared at the request of the Council's Committee on Legislation and Regulation outlines reasons for supporting a revised rule that would eliminate the total income payout requirement but retain the requirement that 5% of assets be paid out.

"In a time of high inflation," the paper states, "and correspondingly high interest rates, the requirement that all current income be distributed annually makes it virtually impossible for foundations to offset the effects of inflation. Thus, the current income payout rule is the practical equivalent of a requirement that foundations distribute a portion of their corpus each year, and thus progressively spend themselves out of existence." To continue on this course, the paper explains, will leave foundations with constantly deteriorating capacity to respond to grant applicants.

In tracing the history of payout requirements since the Tax Reform Act of 1969, the Council points out that "neither Treasury nor Congress devoted significant attention to the effect which the required distribution of current income would have in an inflationary environment." The paper notes that Congressional debate in 1969 and again in 1976, when Congress lowered the minimum distribution rate from an escalating 6% to a fixed 5%, "makes it absolutely clear that the payout rule was intended to require only that foundations distribute their real, as opposed to nominal, income, and that it was not intended to require distributions that would erode the real value of foundation assets."

see **Payout**, page 6

Results of Council Opinion Poll

In setting priorities for legislative actions, the Council's Committee on Legislation and Regulation has been guided by member responses to the opinion poll circulated last May. Of the 290 members providing an opinion on the payout requirement issue, 75% urge repeal of the provision that foundations be required to pay out income in excess of 5% of their assets. The Council has adopted the position that the 5% limit be retained but that income in excess of that should not be required to be paid out. Each foundation will, of course, be free to pay out more than 5% if it wishes.

Completed questionnaires provide evidence of significant erosion of foundation assets in the face of double-digit inflation and the requirement that foundations pay out all income. In the period from 1977 to 1979, foundation assets increased by only 5.7% (excluding gifts). During that same period, inflation was 19.8%, so that the assets of 96 foundations sampled actually declined by 11.6% in constant 1977 dollars. In addition to inflation, the level of gifts declined 64% from 1977 to 1979. In 1977, gifts were 1.5% of assets. In 1979, gifts were only .52% of assets.

A study just completed by the Charles Stewart Mott Foundation of Flint, Michigan, warns that if foundations continue on this course, they will, over time, spend themselves out of existence. In an article to appear in the March-April issue of Foundation News, business administration Professor J. Peter Williamson also points to the erosion of the future grant capability of foundations caused by market complications, inflation, and the requirement that all income be paid out.

— Data Provided by the Council's Research Department

Council on Foundations, Inc.   Volume 2 • Number 4 • February-March 1981

Nameplates at top and bottom each use strong lines, but in quite different ways. To set an outdoor mood, the *State Parks* editor used dark green borders. In *Kanata News* a 30% screen leads the eye into the title. *Council Newsletter* to the left uses fine lines to strengthen a strong design. At the far right, the editor broke the border line at the bottom to make words there actually part of the nameplate.

The Little Red Schoolhouse calligraphy title had to be on an overlay to prepare for color printing. The editor drew the borders and school building in black. Taking his creation to a typesetting shop that also did camera work, he asked for an overlay of his title letters. The result was a piece of acetate with letters fitting perfectly over his border and schoolhouse design. His printer lifted the acetate overlay to photograph the portion to run in black. Then the printer placed a white sheet on the pasteup, lowered the overlay, and photographed the letters to run in red.

Kanata news

CPAir

Volume 4 Number 5 October 1981

The Little Red Schoolhouse

September, 1981

"I never paid much attention to how newsletters looked until I got the <u>Cedar Millrace</u> job dumped on me. I guess I didn't even know what design was. I'm still no artist, but I thought it would be nice to have some color for the December issue. But how are we going to add color on our nickel-dime budget, especially when we only run 200 copies in the high school print shop?

"Simple! I paid five bucks for a rubber stamp and green ink pad, then put Happy Holidays in the white space. Instant color!"

Inside 24J

September 16, 1981

Salem Schools Staff Newsletter

School Begins!

On September 8, the Salem Public Schools welcomed 22,210 students back to school. Much excitement, and some confusion were apparent.

At Keizer elementary school, 4th grader Brian Azule can't seem to find his name on the class list.

Registration for these two McKay High School students came a little easier. As sophomores, they've been through the first day of school many times. Shelly Way and Ted Jones take a look at their new schedule of classes.

Walker Middle School student, Tracy Bremer, 8th grade, asks vice-principal, "Mr. Warren, what am I going to do? The computer cut me out of my biology class!"

SALEM SCHOOL DISTRICT 24J, SALEM, OREGON 97302

CEDAR MILLRACE

CEDAR MILL PTA
1980

HAPPY HOLIDAYS

Many THANKS to everyone who helped make the 1980 Holiday Bazaar a success!! We could not have done it without you! Much preparation and physical labor is involved in putting on an event like ours and we had many wonderful helpers.

Insiders' Report

enRoute Club

Vol. 2, No. 16, September, 1981
Published by **AIR CANADA** ✈

EXCHANGE NETWORKS

THE NEWSLETTER FOR NEIGHBORHOOD RESOURCE EXCHANGE NETWORKS

As this issue of *Exchange Networks* goes to press—the New Year still fresh in our minds and 1981 ushering in a new President, Administration, and Republican majority in the Senate—feelings ranging from enthusiasm and hope to cautious anxiety and a sense of impending doom hang in the wintry air over Washington. My personal feelings are a mixture of all four, though I'm confident that this will be an active and exciting year for those working to improve our communities. Barter, skills exchange, and self-help, I am told, are likely to be well received by the "new Washingtonians," and I have yet to find any evidence to refute that.

This issue marks the beginning of what I hope will be an informative and expanded year of *Exchange Networks*. More than any preceding it, this issue includes a great deal of nuts-and-bolts materials to assist existing and future skills exchange/barter networks. Many thanks go to Jessie Bond, a former intern at VOLUNTEER, for her informative article on establishing a model barter system, and to Laurie Bernhardt, for her review of *Exchange Networks and Community Politics*. Also contributed is an article by Steve Van Hook of the Jo-Co Skills Exchange on their very successful apprenticeship and tutoring programs, and another by Diane Simonson of SWAP on their innovative fundraising activities. Along with these articles are the descriptions of skills exchange/barter programs and listings of helpful organizations and publications which you're accustomed to seeing in EN. As always, I strongly encourage readers to send me suggestions for improvement and articles for inclusion in upcoming issues. I look forward to hearing from you and wish you a happy and successful New Year!—The Editor.

A Model System To Facilitate Bartering

Every local bartering program uses its own approach to recruiting members; cataloging their members' skills, interests, and needs; making matches; and recording the value of services rendered and received. Some systems are very simple, bypassing the credit hour accounting system altogether for example, while others are considerably more complex. In each case, an effort is made to keep the system as simple as possible while recording the information necessary to facilitate bartering and evaluate the effectiveness of the program in an ongoing fashion. The following model system is based on techniques used by a variety of existing barter programs, and incorporates other approaches not yet tested. An effort has been made to combine the successful approaches of each, and eliminate those techniques which are overly time-consuming, hard to manage, or have otherwise proven ineffective.

Since a record keeping system reflects the processes it monitors, it is best to start by outlining the major steps of the barter process. First is the presentation of the promotional brochure and the accompanying application process whereby individuals become members of the program. Next is the service request, when a member requests names of providers of the service

he or she seeks, and once the service has been provided, the reporting of the exchange to the barter program. Finally, the exchange is recorded in the appropriate files and ledgers.

There are five possible files or records that should be created and updated as the exchange process described above occurs:

- member file
- skills file
- tool file
- credit hour ledger
- daily hour log (optional)

The process by which this system functions can best be explained by following two members of a barter organization through each step of an exchange.

The Application

Dana has just moved into a new apartment—she wants to become involved in and contribute to the community. She has heard of a neighborhood barter group where skills can be exchanged. A photographer by profession, Dana has numerous skills and hobbies that she can share in her spare time.

Dana calls the barter group after hearing about it on the radio and they send her a brochure. The brochure and radio ads are part of a public relations

campaign to promote the barter program. At the minimum, this involves airing public service ads on radio, speaking to groups, posting flyers around the community, and distributing brochures. The brochure serves both as an explanation of the program and as an application form. The explanatory section includes a brief introduction to the barter program, guidelines for involvement, and a skills listing. Since members must use the skills listing when identifying and requesting skills, it is complete, yet simple. It consists of major categories (such as "Arts, Crafts and Theater", "Business and Law", "Communications", "Construction and Home Repair", "Education", "Gardening and Forestry", "Health", "Odd Jobs", "Music", "Repair", "Sports and Games" "Transportation") under which skills are grouped. Categories are constructed so that no skill appears in more than one category. The listing is usually the product of a brain-storming session during the center's planning phase by the organizers, since all the skills the community offers are not clear before the members sign up.

After reading the brochure, Dana decides to join. The application form is the first step in this process—it is the place where Dana gives information about herself. On the top half of the

♥ **VOLUNTEER:** The National Center for Citizen Involvement

Winter 1980.

The *en Route* editor used the PMTacetate overlay procedure described on page 66. *Exchange Networks* title is reversed out of black printed on light blue paper. (For this example, the light blue paper is simulated by using a 10% screen over the entire newsletter.) The colors work well, but I think the nameplate could benefit from a small graphic in the right portion of the banner to make the overall effect less heavy.

In *The DMSO Report* everything is pretty basic except those lines around the molecule and the three-line description in the upper right. Without the outlines, the art would fade into the screen and have equal weight with the letters. Yet the outlines must be perfectly aligned to look right. There is no room for error. Looking at this complicated design, the editor decided to let a printer do the work because it requires very tight registration. Quick printers usually do not do preparation work this complicated or have presses to register this close. The DMSO editor had to pay more to use a high grade commercial printer.

Accurate and timely information about dimethyl sulfoxide for general and professional readers.

The DMSO Report

Volume 7, Number 6

November-December, 1981

The business-like reverses above and below use the same techniques as *The DMSO Report*, but don't have its registration problems. Title letters for *JEMIMA* came already shadowed directly from transfer sheets. *Shelter Sense* simply uses a pre-printed vertical bar to set off its large lettered nameplate. The photograph in *Shelter Sense* was made with a 100-line screen in a home darkroom.

*"Fowler's book **Modern English Usage** expresses my feelings about government jargon better than I ever could. It says jargon 'may be ascribed to a combination of causes: a feeling that plain words sort ill with the dignity of office, a politeness that shrinks from blunt statement, and, above all, the knowledge that for those engaged in the perilous game of politics, and their servants, vagueness is safer than precision.'"*

Volume 4, Number 1
February 1981

SHELTER SENSE

A Publication for Animal Sheltering and Control Personnel

Your adoption program

by R. Dale Hylton

Hylton is an accreditation associate for The HSUS Accreditation Program (see page 4).

Your shelter's adoption policies should be formulated to assure the best level of care possible for the animals in your custody.

This responsibility does not end in the selection of an adopter who promises to provide a good home. It must include getting adequate evidence that the adopter has fulfilled the provisions of the adoption contract and the animal has adjusted to its new environment.

Here are some basic safeguards that you should use to achieve that goal:

1) Clear, concise adoption rules must be available on paper.

2) Your shelter must have interviewers who are capable of evaluating potential adopters and assisting them in selecting the right pet.

3) A personal reference should be required for all applications.

JEMIMA newsletter

Japan Electric Measuring Instruments Manufacturers' Association   August 1981, Vol. 5, No. 17

69

Photographs

Oralee Stiles

Often editors want to print photographs but are afraid of high costs, poor quality, or both. Neither fear is justified. If your newsletter is printed offset, you can include pleasing and inexpensive pictures. Even if your publication is done by mimeograph or photocopy, you should consider an occasional photographic image.

Why use photographs?

Adding photographs to your newsletter changes its image. The pictures make your publication seem more timely, professional and expensive. They may also bring out negative feelings from your readers. Pictures may make your publication seem too slick.

Whether or not you include photographs in your newsletter is a policy decision which should be discussed with the officers, board or advisory committee.

When you consider using any particular photograph, keep in mind the goals for your newsletter. If the picture doesn't help achieve some goal, don't use it. Photographs should meet the same standards as prose and graphics: they should convey ideas or information consistent with the purposes of the newsletter as a whole.

Here are some reasons you might use a photographic image. The picture might

- illustrate an article.
- give information by itself.
- please the photographer or subject when it appears in print.
- create a mood such as sympathy, anger, relief or pleasure.

Where to get photographs

Most organizations have lots of members who take pictures and usually one or two members who are good photographers. Ask these people to submit some prints or to work on assignment. In either case, tell the photographer exactly what you want. Give as much detail as you can about the sort of shots you would like and how they will be used in the newsletter. For examples:

Vague: Could you get some shots during the awards banquet?

Specific: Could you get some close-ups of the mayor talking with individual members and handing the trophy to the president?

Vague: Do you have any railroad pictures?

Specific: I'm doing a story on going to the state convention by train. Do you have any pictures about train travel?

You can also get free photographs from many other sources. Public libraries and museums often have collections organized by topic. Newspapers will usually give you prints of staff photos relating to your business or organization. Schools may have a photo class or club willing to work for you as an assignment.

One note of caution: sometimes amateur photographers will give you prints from pocket cameras using 110 film. The inexpensive lenses and small films usually turn out pictures not good enough for reproduction in print. The problems lie mainly with the focus which typically is not sharp.

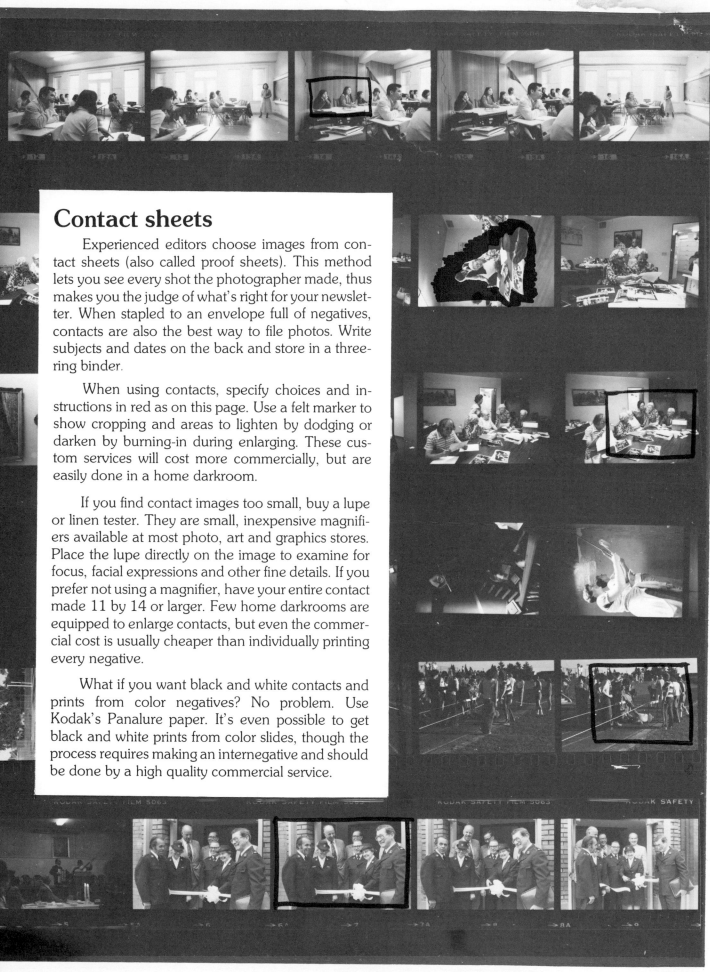

Contact sheets

Experienced editors choose images from contact sheets (also called proof sheets). This method lets you see every shot the photographer made, thus makes you the judge of what's right for your newsletter. When stapled to an envelope full of negatives, contacts are also the best way to file photos. Write subjects and dates on the back and store in a three-ring binder.

When using contacts, specify choices and instructions in red as on this page. Use a felt marker to show cropping and areas to lighten by dodging or darken by burning-in during enlarging. These custom services will cost more commercially, but are easily done in a home darkroom.

If you find contact images too small, buy a lupe or linen tester. They are small, inexpensive magnifiers available at most photo, art and graphics stores. Place the lupe directly on the image to examine for focus, facial expressions and other fine details. If you prefer not using a magnifier, have your entire contact made 11 by 14 or larger. Few home darkrooms are equipped to enlarge contacts, but even the commercial cost is usually cheaper than individually printing every negative.

What if you want black and white contacts and prints from color negatives? No problem. Use Kodak's Panalure paper. It's even possible to get black and white prints from color slides, though the process requires making an internegative and should be done by a high quality commercial service.

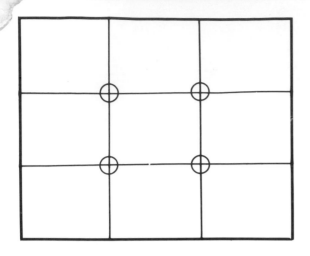

Pictures with impact

Most editors use photos as part of a story: to illustrate the news. Some go the next step of letting strong images stand only with small caption. All photos, however, must be interesting enough to attract attention to the newsletter as a whole.

Few people see a picture all at once. Most tend to read images much as they read words, going from left to right. Images, however, invite the eye to enter at the lower left and to follow curved rather than straight lines. In addition, an image whose focal points are off-center seems more alive than one with subjects in the middle. Thus the design rule of thirds, illustrated at the upper left, helps make interesting pictures.

Most newsletter pictures have people as subjects. Whether portrait or group shot, these images can easily include flowing curves and dynamic focal points. With individuals, avoid straight-on shots. It's hard to make them look much better than the average driver's license. Instead, go for a three-quarter angle of shoulders and face. Put a little more space in front of the subject than behind and plan layout so the subject is looking into the page, not away from it. Look at the senior pictures in your high school or college yearbook to see a variety of approaches and compare results. If your image shows the person's full torso, be sure to include the hands.

Kathleen Ryan

What about group shots? Too often photos of more than one person are either grip-and-grin or stand-em-in-a-line. Both are dull! To avoid the grip-and-grin, look for images showing emotion of the moment, not convenience for the photographer. Get the retiree smiling at some fond memory; snap the person to be honored talking with the mayor or president before receiving the plaque; photograph the dignitary after the formal greeting, but during those first few moments when business talk starts.

Solving stand-em-in-a-line photos is even easier. Use two or three images, thereby having fewer people in each. Use an odd number of people: three or five work best. Ask people to talk with each other, not look at the camera. Choose only

Kathleen Ryan

Kathleen Ryan

An action photo has more life than a posed, static image. Look for photos which make readers ask, "What's going on here?" This caption is set ragged right. For a justified caption also set eight picas wide, see page 74.

Kathleen Ryan

two or three people who symbolize the whole group instead of picturing everybody. Move in or crop close, cutting out feet and legs and distractions.

Here are other ways to add interest to pictures.

1. Watch for bright white distractions. Plastic coffee cups especially are the bane of photo editors.

2. Get clutter out of the background. Get dishes off the tables and ask people to stand away from signs (unless the sign needs to be in the picture).

3. Let people be doing something. Put action in the picture. Use props if you must, so long as subjects are not simply staring vacantly at the lens.

4. Look for verticals. Most photos are taken horizontally. Most newsletters, however, have vertical formats. You can't avoid using horizontal images, but running some verticals will add interest. Verticals also let you be more flexible with page design.

5. Find an editorial point of view. Look for the angle or detail that captures the story. Don't worry about showing the whole subject. Crop very close if you must to add drama.

6. Use background and foreground as props. Deliberately put buildings or foliage into the picture to establish a tone or context.

Kathleen Ryan

Changing the perspective of the camera can sometimes make a straightforward record shot more interesting. Here a 24 mm. lens used at a low angle captured these volunteer painters rehabilitating an old hotel.

Getting pictures ready

To get an original photograph off your desk and actually into print, you need a working knowledge of ten key words: contrast, glossy, crop, caption, credit, halftone, screen, halftone positive, velox and PMT.

Contrast

When a photo seems muddy or washed out, it has low contrast. When there is sharp distinction between blacks and whites, or between dark and light colors, it has high contrast.

A high contrast picture is vivid and bright.

If you want pleasing photographs in your newsletter, you must start with high contrast original pictures. Black and white originals will reproduce much better than color.

Glossy

The original print you plan to reproduce in your newspaper should be on glossy paper, not on mat or silk finish. The glossy surface reflects light perfectly uniformly for the offset master, photocopy machine or stencil scanner, thereby yielding clear reproductions.

Crop

Often an original print has too much information, especially if it will be made smaller to fit your format. You want attention only on the important parts of the image, so must eliminate portions which do not suit your purposes. You need to crop the picture.

There are three principles to keep in mind when cropping a picture.

- A good photograph has one subject or object of attention—only one area to which the eye is drawn to get the message.

- Pleasing pictures tend to be composed in thirds, not halves. It's especially important not to run a strong line such as the horizon or a light pole straight through the middle.

- Cropping should not eliminate something needed to tell the story. Don't make viewers suspect something is missing.

To test how a picture would look cropped different ways, cut two L-shaped masks about ten by four inches. By laying them over opposite corners of the image, you can adjust height and width for greatest

The original print for the picture above had too little contrast. A better print was made in the darkroom yielding the image at right.

Mark Beach

The nightclub image above is too cluttered. After cropping, the image below tells the story without the extra information.

Kathleen Ryan

What information or feeling do you want from pictures? The editor wanted mood rather than facts.

Oralee Stiles

impact. These cropping Ls also let you see how a part of a horizontal image might appear when presented vertically.

Once you've decided what portion of an image to print in your newsletter, you get best quality by having that portion made into a glossy in a darkroom. If that is too slow or costly, crop by trimming a velox or PMT halftone of the entire image. (These terms defined on page 77). As with all final copy, the trim should be made with a paper cutter, X-acto knife or razor blade to assure clean, straight edges. Cropping a picture for content also involves scaling it to dimensions to fit your format. See pages 98 and 99 for how to scale.

If you choose to have your printer make halftones, that service can also include cropping and scaling according to your instrucitons. Ask your printer to show you how crop lines and changes in size should be indicated so your instructions will be clearly understood.

Caption

Every photograph when published needs a few words of explanation. The caption says just enough to let readers understand the image. When people are the subject, the caption should always give their names.

When an entire photo is wrong for your story, try cropping to make an image that is right. And beware of backgrounds. The student below seems to have a flag sticking out of his neck.

Captions should be placed under pictures or, occasionally, to the side. Because captions should be read after the picture itself is seen, they should never be placed above.

Credit

Giving credit to a photographer is just as important as giving a by-line to a writer. Photographic credit can be given by listing a name under the picture, as part of the caption, or as part of a box elsewhere which mentions all contributors.

Kathleen Ryan

Halftone

An orginal photographic print has continuous tones. The greys, blacks, whites or colors blend into each other usually without sharp boundaries between them. Publishing processes, however, can only reproduce discrete tones—lines or dots or blocks of pure black or dense color against a light background.

To be published, original prints must be converted into a pattern of very small dots which, when viewed as a whole, make a picture. The pattern consists only of black or colored dots all of the same density. There are no grey dots. Greys and other shades are represented by the size of the black dots. As the dots become smaller they also become farther apart, giving the impression of grey tones.

The image which results from converting an original print into the pattern of dots is called a halftone. All published photographs are halftones.

Screen

To make a halftone, a printer uses a screen. It is a grid of lines just like an ordinary window screen, but the mesh is much finer and the lines are embedded in a thick plastic film. The screen is placed on top of the original print and a new photograph made of the whole package. That is, the new photo is made of the original print taken <u>through</u> the screen.

The size of screens is measured in lines per inch. A 65 line screen is coarse; a 150 line screen is very fine. The typical newspaper photo is done with an 85 or 100 line screen. Pictures in news magazines are usually with 120 or 133 line screens.

Results usually become more pleasing—more like the original—as screens become finer.

Your publication process largely determines the size of screen you may use. On coarse, highly absorbent papers such as mimeograph, an 85 line is typical. You might get away with 100 line using better paper and running the machine slowly. On papers usually used for offset printing, 120 line would be average. If you want a finer screen, your printer may have to use special paper or ink and also slow the presses.

Mark Beach

85 line screen.   **100 line screen.**   **120 line screen.**

Ball and the eye are each screened very coarsely to show the pattern and size of dots which make a printed photograph. Moving the page away from you has the effect of reducing the screen size, thus making the images more clear.

Halftone positive

Printing plates for published halftones are usually made directly from a halftone negative. Newsletter editors, however, usually want to do their own pasteup, so prefer working with halftone positive: an actual paper print of the halftone which can be used as part of the copy to be printed.

Halftone positives can be photocopied and the copies used to experiment for cropping, scaling and placement during layout. Thus halftone positives are another step toward quality control and should be used whether your newsletter is done by mimeograph, photocopy or offset.

There are three ways to make a halftone positive.

1. Take your original to a reproduction service such as a blueprint company or commercial photographer. This method will give you best results,

but is also the most expensive in time and money. Having you originals done all at once (called gang shot) is one way to cut costs.

Halftone positives made this way are usually done on a photographic paper called Velox, made by the Eastman Kodak Company.

2. Anyone with good darkroom skills can make a Velox print. It helps to watch a reproduction service do it first and will still require some trial and error, but it can be done. Here is how.

    Set up the negative paper as you would for any standard print. Put a screen of the proper size directly over the paper and make the exposure. You will get good results only when
    *   you use the right paper,
    *   the screen fits very tightly against the paper,
    *   focusing is on the paper, not the screen, and
    *   the whole package is properly flashed.

3. The Kodak Company also has a process for making halftone positives called photomechanical transfer—PMT. Most printers and many commercial typesetters can make a PMT for you. The PMT process yields a halftone positive a little faster and less expensively than the Velox process, but with a slight loss in quality. PMTs can also be gang shot, but only if the originals are all of roughly the same contrast.

Regardless of which method you use to get halftones, you must decide about screen size. Your halftones will make poor camera-ready copy if screens are not matched with paper and printing process. Even if you have your printer make halftone negatives, you should specify screen size.

Newsletter papers are discussed in detail on pages 110 and 111. Here, however, it is important to notice the paper change between pages 74 and 75. Page 74 and the fifteen pages before it are stock coated during manufacturing; page 75 and all the rest of the book are uncoated paper. When ink is applied to uncoated paper, it soaks in something like a blotter effect. Coated papers are less porous, so inks dry on the surface. Photographs consist of thousands of tiny dots. If each dot is fuzzy because it soaks in a bit, the photo doesn't look as sharp as it could. Thus, photos on coated paper look better than those on uncoated.

Photolayout

When editors use photos, most tend to stick with one per page. Text dominates. It is important to place the photo so it doesn't compete with your nameplate, headlines or other art. The editor of *Flyer* solved the problem nicely by running a photo similar to art in the nameplate. The *Metroforum* example shows how two photos work well when run at quite different size. If you have a strong image, don't hesitate to let it occupy a whole page—even page one. Magazines do this all the time to command attention to inside copy.

Picture stories are easy to lay out and very popular with readers. The trick is to let the pictures do the talking. Written copy should give only the minimum connecting narrative. Use five or six photos, then run them in story-telling sequence left to right. Let one dominate all others, even making it four or five times larger than the rest. Keep uniform spacing between images, allowing misalignments to happen at margins. These few guidelines lead to fine layouts like the one about scuba diving.

78

ON LOCATION

Anne was beside me now. We scooped up the filthy, frozen lambs in our arms, hurried back to the house, and laid them beside the wood stove, just six inches from the hot metal.

As soon as I opened the lambing-yard gate, I spotted her. The frantic mother, a big Suffolk, was trying to rouse her lambs—she'd had triplets—but they were all flat on the ground, motionless as boards. I ran back to the house and shouted, "Anne! Come quick!"

The ewe had done her best; she had cleaned each lamb as it came, and had tried to nudge them to their feet, but they were down now—muddy, bloody, and stiff. I wiped the birth mucus off their faces and forced my finger into their mouths. Cold. Ice cold. One lamb's

WITH RO

It's always chancy pulling brand-new lambs off their mothers. The bonding process, in which the mother recognizes the lamb as her own, is fairly delicate, and sometimes, when the process is dis-

---

Bout in a nice little restaurant ne and candlelight. We want to novie on a screen bigger than am about concerts, ballet, gallery openings, dancing. We long for what Anne calls "life in the fast lane."

Harrisonburg, our shopping town, is only forty miles away, but bad roads and mountains make for a slow trip: an hour and a half one way. When lambs are coming, we rarely go there together, but this particular morning we decided to chance it. The two ewes we'd been expecting to lamb did so, considerately, at 6:30 A.M. A good single, and twins. Most of our ewes twin, some single, and occasionally a ewe will drop triplets.

The ewe due to lamb next was Bouncer, a big young Rambouillet, who had proved her mothering ability the past year. She wasn't showing any signs of hurrying into labor. She wasn't pawing herself a nest, or walking aimlessly about, or licking her lips, or separating herself from the flock. A neighbor promised to check Bouncer at noon, so we took off.

The trip in was pleasant; we made good time and stopped for chili dogs at

Certain kinds of products have mysteriously escaped the chrome nameplate and the Technicolor decal. Furniture, for instance, still functions purely as furniture, ungarnished by promotion. But I don't think it will be long before we'll see convertible sofas with "Castro" stitched into the upholstery or rugs with "Karastan" worked into the weave. Clothes were once off limits in this regard, but now people seem to get a warm, participatory glow from wearing Adidas T-shirts, Yves St. Laurent ties, or designer jeans with "Gloria Vanderbilt" emblazoned across their backsides.

Even the Post Office has started to put its dowdy wares to promotional use. This winter my godfather, a Dante scholar, rushed through a purchase of fifteen-cent stamps only to discover later that they were of a new variety, no doubt devised to counter the Time Lady's attacks on written correspondence. Each of them was decorated with a floral generality and a motto: "Letters preserve memories," "Letters lift spirits," or "P.S. Write soon." The purchase thus transformed my godfather, of all people, into an involuntary press

that mar my appliances: "F/GM/Mark of Excellence/Frigidaire/Product of General Motors U.S.A./Imperial 170" on my refrigerator, "Sears Kenmore Magicord Powermate" on my vacuum cleaner. It sometimes seems to me, as I look around at the honky-tonk of my kitchen, that I've spent my money only to populate my shelves and countertops with ambassadors singing their companies' praises. Even now, as my typewriter taps out these words for me, it is advertising SCM's Smith-Corona Coro-

gy-saving tip from the Phone Center Store—form car pools and combine trips" is her message at this moment (10:12), but I have heard her take swipes at letter-writing, hawk push-button phones, and remind me of faraway loved ones whom I haven't called in weeks (although she has shown a curious lack of concern for loved ones within my toll-free area whom I haven't called in weeks).

She is a fund of advice and information, but she has a somewhat scolding, Dr. Joyce Brothers little voice and I always hang up with a mortified feeling. In fact, sometimes I get so snagged on her pitches and tips, so eager to close my fireplace dampers or call my Aunt Mary Alice, that I forget to hear what time it is and have to start the process all over again.

I hate to sound ungrateful, but since the Time Lady is paid for out of the profits the phone company makes by overcharging for its other services, I tend to regard her as part of Ma Bell's product line, and as such she demonstrates to me once again the increasingly preachy and grudging manner in which business has taken to dispensing its goods and services. Promotion, which was once an antecedent to actual commerce, now survives each product like flypaper. Indeed, I've lately gotten the feeling when I buy something that I've

turbed, the ewe will refuse a lamb and let it starve or even butt it to death in the lambing pen. You can raise lambs on bottles, but they never do as well as lambs raised by a good mother.

Ewes recognize their lambs by scent, but we had washed all the scent off the triplets. Ange eyed the clumsy, healthy lambs. "Fine," she said. "Now we have four lambs and two mothers that both want the big white one."

We would have to try and graft one of the triplets onto Big White's mother. The Suffolk could raise two lambs on one teat. Perhaps the ewes were so confused by now that they wouldn't know one lamb from another.

G1:30, the lambs were strong to go outside. The wind had died Ve each carried two lambs. As the ewes heard them, they went alling for the lambs, rushing back and forth. They were like woolly gunboats circling us, trying to get to the lambs, and when we stepped into the barn, all the other ewes, suddenly awakened and alarmed, started calling for their lambs. We laid the lambs in the straw of the lambing pens. The lambs found it hard to walk in the deep straw and weren't too certain of their direction, but they were in fine voice. The ewes fell silent. Reserving judgment, they extended their noses to sniff the lambs. With a soft nicker, and a swipe of her rough tongue, the Suffolk

Almost sure . . ." Then Lazarus let out a particularly lusty cry, and the ewe accepted the stranger and nudged her back toward her milk.

When Anne checked at one A.M., the lambs on the Suffolk had learned to take turns on her one functional teat.

When I went out at three, all four lambs were asleep, banked up against their mothers. There's nothing so smug as a lamb with a full belly. When I put my finger in Lazarus's mouth, she bleated in outrage.

ful and considerate reading of books, with such rereadings and ritings as individual taste may scribe, will give any man the ess of a liberal education even if devote but fifteen minut

Eliot's selections the advance mail had not been completed, but a nary list had been prepared salesmen. This list was on office that Collier had ope bridge.

On the night of June 15, 1909, someone from the *Harvard Crimson* filched the secret list from a locked desk, and the next day it was published in the student paper—the literary scoop of the year. The New York *Times* and many other newspapers picked up the hot news and published it *June 17* on page one, thereby setting off a nationwide controversy over the wisdom of the selections.

Newspapers did their best to heat up the controversy and make a contest out of the selection, seeking dissenting opinions throughout the country. In Houston, Texas, the president of Baylor University declared that the shelf should include a grammar, a dictionary, the Bible, and a collection of Mark Twain's writings. He commented: "I am decidedly of the opinion that a liberal education cannot be found in sixty inches of plank." A Vermont clergyman

free publicity the Harvard Classics received during 1909 and 1910 was beyond anything ever known before in publishing circles. At one time my clerks reported to me that we had pasted up in scrapbooks a total of over 1700 columns of newspaper free publicity."

Abbott Lawrence Lowell had assumed the presidency of Harvard in May of 1909. Commencement on June 30 was the occasion for ceremonial farewells to Eliot, who received honorary degrees of LL.D. and M.D. That night,

chusetts Institute of Technology, where his plan of reform was welcomed and set the pattern for chemistry teaching throughout the country.

Being a scientist, Eliot chose for the Five-Foot Shelf writings of such great just like to bring up this stuff and not art on any of it or expect anyone else to act on it either. Well, you've got me all wrong. During the course of writing this piece I think I've finally found a cure for our sickly pride of ownership.

As out that many of these logos complaining about are removplastic SCM/Smith Corona Super 12 logo plate, for instame off without a hitch, and after a little light scrubbing with cleanser and a sponge you'd hardly know anything had been there. And all it took was a few quick turns of a screwdriver and the Sears Craftsman logo plate came right off my push mower. I haven't had quite as much luck with the GE/General Electric Toast-R-Oven decal on the door of my toaster-oven, but I'm working on it. The only real problem I've had is with the logo plate on the refrigerator door. I pried it off easily, but it left a long scab of glue which gives the refrigerator a sullen look.

Removing the logo plates has given most of my possessions a pleasing, abstract quality, but I think what I'll have to do in cases like that of my refrigerator door is devise my own logo plates to paste over the scars the old ones leave. I figure I could find somebody who'd fashion a few for me out of brass or chrome, and I've been giving their composition a lot of thought. To set a good example for industry, I think I'll leave my name out of it and have it read in simple little letters: "A poor thing, but

One Hundred Army Years

Once in a while try cutting a photo as a silhouette and feature it coming out of body copy. Use scissors to cut carefully around a halftone positive, then stick it down as you would any camera-ready art. If you're having a printer make halftone negatives, rub down a piece of rubylith on an overlay and slip your full photo in the correct position underneath. Secure the photo with tape, then trim the rubylith to the shape of the silhouette. Put register marks on the edge of the photo and also on the overlay, remove the photo and pull away the trim from your photo mask. The printer places the halftone negative in the clear space made by your window and makes a printing plate from that union.

If you make silhouettes, remember that you must also plan copy to run around the image. Getting the copy to fit is sometimes more work than making the silhouette.

Making the Whole

Layout

To design your newsletter, you arrange copy and art in patterns that make attractive, practical pages. From an aesthetic standpoint, good design yields pleasing pages which invite your reader's attention. From a practical standpoint, good design yields an efficient format: pages produced at a minimum cost of time and money.

Page design is like graphics because its ultimate purpose is to be useful—to be art with a message. The ultimate test of design is whether people actually read the newsletter. Prizes and compliments are nice and efficiency is important, but readability is the key.

Design is also like graphics in that it conveys an image for your business, organization or cause. Just as with decisions about typesetting vs. typing or color vs. black nameplate, choices determining design also determine how others think of you. Your goals shape all these choices. If your goals are clear, your design will be appropriate and consistent. Without clear goals, you risk design choices putting you visually into a category you may think wrong.

Format

Good design begins with a good format—a useful page size and number of columns. Most editors work with 8½ by 11-inch pages because they are standard: paper is readily available and the printed product fits a file folder, three-ring binder, and #10 envelope. At the subconscious level, 8½ by 11 pages are at the same four-to-three ratio as index cards, TV screens and other familiar items.

The 8½ by 11 size is so convenient that almost eighty percent of all editors use it. The standard size is by far the most popular, regardless of number of readers, type of organization or cost of production.

Another ten percent of editors use closely-related sizes such as 8 by 11 and 8½ by 14. An additional five percent use the standard multiple 11 by 17, called a tabloid and usually printed on newsprint. (Note that page sizes here refer to folded or trimmed size and not to dimensions of paper for printing. For a discussion of printing sizes, see pages 108-112.)

Unless you have a tabloid page, use one of the three basic column counts: one, two or three columns per page. Pick the right one for you, then stick with it for every page and every issue.

One column, called full measure, is best suited to pica typewriter production. Subscription newsletters commonly run full measure to look most like up-to-the-minute business letters. One column formats are rather rigid, making it hard to work in illustrations and photos. The examples on pages 82 through 85 tend to be short on art.

A two-column format such as this book looks clean and is relatively easy to paste up. It gives a somewhat formal tone, especially because it's usually typeset and justified. Two columns yield more flexibility for art than one, as you can see from the examples on pages 86 through 89.

Editors who like lots of art and brisk design often use three columns. Pages divided into thirds have nice balance, copy can be ragged right without wasting too much space and art works in very easily. The three-column format requires more careful design work than one or two columns, especially because there isn't as much space to run one-line heads and the tight margins may make copy seem crowded. Pages 90-93 show three-column newsletters.

Regardless of page size or number of columns, your format should be clearly expressed on paper. That means writing down column widths, alleys, margins, and any other standard elements such as borders, running heads and numbers. And it means making a page map such as those shown here. The discipline required to make these decisions and commit them to paper pays huge dividends in efficiency and freedom. Now you know the basic pattern for each issue, so can concentrate on copy and art. Your support people, typesetters and printers, should also know your format so they can do their jobs accurately with minimum supervision.

Design

Designing newsletter pages is an artistic activity whose primary requirement is common sense. A piece of paper is your canvas; photographs, graphics, headlines and blocks of copy your materials. Your job is to assemble the materials on the page so people will read its content.

Start by looking at the page itself. It is white (empty) space about to become the frame for your creation. The biggest temptation you face—and the biggest mistake you can make—is to use up the whole page, leaving no frame. Readers need a context in which to view words and art. Take away that white space entirely and you ruin readability. Leading designer Polly Pattison summed it up when she wrote, "White space is NOT what is left over—it is an active participant in design."

1. **Simplicity.** Help your reader be efficient by keeping pages uncomplicated. Put short items in groups; use graphics and photos only with a specific purpose in mind; keep headline sizes and styles consistent. Simplicity yields a clean design.

2. **Unity.** Try to make everything on the page—or on a two page spread—visually related to everything else. A harmonious style of art and type helps. So does balance: putting large elements near the middle and smaller ones near the edge. Try to make the eye flow easily from top to bottom and page to page.

3. **Contrast.** On a simple, unified page, contrast means life. Instead of headlines or photos all of equal size, make one big and others small. Make boxes and screens call readers' attention to what you consider important. Use design elements for emphasis as you use gestures and voice tones in conversation.

4. **Proportion.** As with photographs, newsletter pages look most interesting when unequally divided. Rectangles seem more dynamic than squares and odd numbers of photos more lively than even.

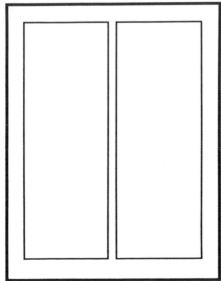

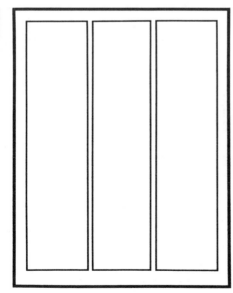

One column format should have margins at least 1⅛ inch (7 picas) at sides and top and 1¼ inch (7½ picas) at bottom.

Two column format should have margins at least ¾ inch (4½ picas) at side and top and ⅞ inch (5¼ picas) at bottom. Alley should be ¼ inch (1½ picas).

Three column format should have margins at least ½ inch (3 picas) at sides and top and ⅝ inch (3½ picas) at bottom. Alleys should be ³⁄₁₆ inch (1 pica).

The Kerr Report
The Monthly Report Devoted to Success in Manufactured Housing Developments

Mid-April 1981 ... #11

. . . ANOTHER BILL ON "SEVENTEEN YEAR RULE" . . .

A third bill is before the Legislature to change existing law which allows mobilehome park management to require, at the time of resale, the removal of a singlewide more than 17 years old or of a double-wide more than 20 years old. Assembly Bill 1546 has been introduced by Assemblyman Dave Elder, a Long Beach Democrat.

The bill would eliminate existing removal-upon-age stand-ards and, instead, allow management to require removal only if the owner of the mobilehome cannot present a "certificate of compliance" with the standards of Health and Safety Code Sections 18550 and 18605.

The certificate of compliance would be issued by the State Depart-ment of Housing and Community Development only after an inspection and payment of fees.

This bill, we're told, was introduced by Elder at the request of three mobilehome parks in his district.

As a quick update on the other two "seventeen year rule" bills, instead of dropping his bill as was rumored, Senator Paul Carpenter (D-Orange County) has amended his SB231 to provide that the party requesting a health and safety inspection of a mobilehome for the purpose of requiring its removal from the park would be required to pay for the inspection by the enforcement agency. Carpenter's bill would restrict removal on sale to mobilehomes in rundown condition and in violation of health and safety standards. SB231 is set for hearing on May 5 in the Senate Judiciary Committee. No hearing date is set for SB401 (Craven), the third bill to eliminate the "seventeen year bill."

For additional information on this issue and on SB231 and SB401, see the mid-March 1981 edition of THE KERR REPORT.

. . . TENANTS PROMOTE CHANGES IN LAW . . .

State Senator Jim Ellis (R-San Diego County) and Assemblyman Chet Wray (D-Orange County) have large mobilehome park constituencies in their districts. They have, accordingly, introduced tenant-promoted changes in the Mobilehome Residency Law.

Both AB1977 (Wray) and SB1077 (Ellis) would change existing law to prohibit charging to a tenant for a guest who does not stay "for more than 30 consecutive days in any calen-dar month." (Why, you ask, don't they just simply prohibit guest charges instead of this nonsense?)

Continued...

THE KERR REPORT (ISSN 0973-9796) is Copyright 1981 by Thomas P. Kerr ● 601 University Avenue, Suite 150 ● Sacramento, California 95825. Reproduction in whole or in part by any means, including photocopying, is prohibited. Annual subscription (12 issues) $75.00

Single column formats are popular with editors of commercial newsletters having subscribers who pay for up-to-the-minute news. Typewritten copy looks like a a business letter and can be written just moments before printing. The wide margins also leave plenty of space for punched holes so copies can be stored in ring binders.

Often graphics and photos don't mix well with copy in full measure formats. Art seems to intrude. White space and bullets, however, prove effective reading aids with the otherwise long lines of type. It may also help to mix typesetting with typewriting as in *Government Marketing News*.

Shipyard Weekly is justified via text editor. The front and back illustration of *Real Estate Intelligence Report* shows how editor John Gornall writes news like a personal letter to subscribers. The two-line, typeset masthead for *Kerr Report* adds a balancing touch at the bottom of the page, an effect missing from the *APHA Letter*.

The APHA Letter
THE AMERICAN PRINTING HISTORY ASSOCIATION

No. 41   1981, No. Three

This newsletter, a publication of the American Printing History Association, is sent without charge to all members. See back page for mailing address information. Edited by Prof. Catherine Tyler Brody. Assistant Editor: Barbara Jones.

ANNUAL REPORT FOR THE YEAR 1980. Annual Meeting. At the sixth annual general meeting, January 26, 1980, held in Columbia University's Butler Library, the following officers were elected for two-year terms: Catherine T. Brody, President; Philip Grushkin, Vice President for Programs; Jack Golden, Vice President for Publications; Pat Taylor, Vice President for Membership; Jean Peters, Secretary; Philip Sperling, Treasurer. In addition, the following were elected as three-year trustees: Edna Beilenson, Stephen O. Saxe, and Lili Kronker; and as a one-year trustee, Greer Allen. The 1980 APHA Award was presented to APHA's founder, J. Ben Lieberman for his contributions to print-ing history. Dr. Lieberman's acceptance speech, "The Transcendent Purpose of the American Printing History Association", will be issued as an APHA monograph. Publications. Five numbers of the APHA LETTER, under the editorship of Catherine Brody, appeared in 1980, and a sixth will appear early in 1981. Numbers Two and Three of the APHA journal, PRINTING HISTORY, were issued during the year. Susan Thompson continues as editor and Jack Golden as art director. The fifth annual APHA conference was held on September 27, 1980, in Wood Auditorium, Avery Hall, Columbia University. The topic was "The Permanence of Ephemera." Conference co-chairmen were Alice Schreyer and Daniel Traister, and speakers were: Katharine F. Pantzer, Houghton Library, Harvard University; George B. Bumgardner, American Antiquarian Society; Michael Twyman, University of Reading (England); Stephen O. Saxe, Harcourt Brace Jovanovich; and Peter C. Marzio, Corcoran Gallery (Washington). Membership. At the end of 1980, APHA member-ship stood at approximately 1,400. (Jean Peters, Secretary)

TREASURER'S REPORT FOR 1980. Treasurer's Report for Annual Meeting: January 24, 1981 covering January 1, 1980 through December 31, 1980. (All figures rounded to nearest dollar)

CASH BALANCE: Chemical Bank as of January 1 $ 6659.00

INCOME:
Membership Dues $16360.00
5th Annual APHA Conference   3475.00
Advertising in Journal: Printing
    History Issue Nos. 2 & 3   2537.00
Misc. Lists Sold, Publications, etc.   2217.00   24589.00
                                                              31248.00
EXPENSES:
Paid to New York Chapter   1290.00
Membership Maintenance, Mailings
    APHA Newsletters, Etc.   5520.00
Journal: Printing History Issue No.2   7578.00
    "   "   "   " No.3   8534.00
5th Annual APHA Conference   4042.00
Postage   389.00
Newsletter (typing)   110.00

SHIPYARD WEEKLY
SHIPBUILDERS COUNCIL OF AMERICA
800 NEW HAMPSHIRE AVE. N.W. | WASHINGTON, D. C. 20037

Thursday, August 21, 1980 - No. 34

GOVERNOR REAGAN OUTLINES HIS SHIPBUILDING POSITION

In shipyard setting on Tuesday (Aug. 19), Republican Presidential Candidate Ronald Reagan called for "New Begin-ning" to arrest decline in U.S. shipbuilding employment and "to put America back in the captain's chair of world maritime powers."

Speaking at Sun Ship, Inc., Chester, PA, Governor Reagan projected decline of shipyard employment at 75,000 workers by 1983 with "a serious 'spill-over' effect on related indus-tries." He said:

"Should our shipbuilding capability continue to de-cline, America's mobilization potential will be se-riously undermined because a large reduction in a skilled shipbuilding workforce today makes any in-crease tomorrow very difficult. This is a dangerous threat to our national security, jobs and a key U.S. industry. The truth is, the Carter Administration has no coherent, long-range shipbuilding or maritime policy.

"America is a maritime nation. Yet our maritime industry is at a critical stage. Ninety-five percent of our trade moves in foreign vessels - a serious situation. Our active U.S.-flag fleet has declined to 533 ships - about 1/3 the total lost - 1,787 - by our country during World War II.

"As the world's leading trading nation, as an island of have-nots in the area of strategic commodities, and as the chief guarantor of freedom of the Western World, the U.S. is in dire need of a rational, reasonable and effective maritime policy. Let's begin to move today!"

To "revitalize and reinvigorate our nation's shipbuilding and maritime industry," Candidate Reagan put forward these proposed "steps":

• "First, early next year I would convene a conference of top maritime and shipbuilding leaders with the appro-

"Sure we're out for profit, but we're also out to serve our readers. And the two go hand-in-hand. The more honest we are with our readers, the more they trust us and recommend us. That's why we don't shrink from controversy. In fact, we welcome it so we can show readers we are objective and not afraid to print the truth.

"I used to publish a newspaper. Almost three-fourths of our income came from advertising. Sometimes one hand was writing editorials criticizing advertisers while the other hand was scratching their backs. It's quite a trick! I like the freedom I have publishing a newsletter with no ads."

Vol. 6 — No. 5
May 1981

GOVERNMENT MARKETING NEWS
Reporting on Strategies, Techniques and Opportunities

Holtz's Capital Hill Feature

MARKETING OR SALES?

To a large degree, success in selling to the government lies more in marketing--finding out where and what the needs are--than in salesmanship. As one Washington veteran often puts it, "It's easy to sell to the government when you find the right doors; it's finding those doors that's tough."

Reading the Commerce Business Daily is, of course, one obvious way to find out about some of the needs--perhaps 10% of them, at most. Filing copies of Standard Form 129 will get you on bidders lists, and that will bring some more requirements to your attention. Calling on procurement offices and visiting bid rooms helps some, too, in learning who needs what. But all of these methods are the same as those followed by others: in a sense, they serve only to help you "get in the hat," along with a lot of competitors. Of course, you'll do better if you can find some opportunities others have missed and don't know about. And it is precisely by doing this that some contractors survive and prosper. Some even refuse flatly to bid anything that's competitive because bidding is an expensive process for most companies, and the chances for success are not mathematically too great.

(Please turn to page 2)

May's Highlights

OFFICE SPACE FROM OLDER SHOPPING CENTERS

Makings of Next Commercial Real Estate Boom. Two current real estate trends could be coupled to produce big profits for investors willing to act now and cash-in in 4-5 years: (1) Suburban malls are dying; and (2) Office space (in general) is the most sought-after property right now. According to Michael Hirshfield, chairman of Garrick-Aug Associates Store Leasing, Inc. (the nation's largest retail space broker):

- Suburban centers will be largely out of business within the next 2 decades--replaced by urban malls, huge multi-level covered pedestrian spaces built under office towers.
- Retail stores will be smaller as a reaction to escalating rents and utility costs.

Office Space Pressure Great. While the recent inflation, recession and oil shortage years cut into retail sales in the suburbs, the office space demands continued due to the establishment of more regional offices by major insurance companies, high technology industries, computer-oriented operations and small service firms. So-called "secondary" office space is ideal for many businesses today and suburban retail centers with problems have profit potential as office centers. The attractions are lower rents, less commuting for owners and employees, convenient free parking for customers and better access to airports for business travel.

Downtown Rebirth "Polarized" City and Suburbs. The emphasis the last 5 years of rehabilitation and revitalization of inner city real estate has put much city property beyond the rents many medium-sized businesses can pay. The movement "back to the city" is developing a growing non-commuting population that, in the years to come, will live, work, play and shop in the city. Likewise the suburbs and satellite towns near big cities will develop their own work, shop, play near home pattern.

Evaluating Potential Sites. Commercial property is a specialized field and the help of an experienced broker can give you is usually worth the commission or fee. Here are some tips on locating retail property for potential reuse:

- Never deal long distance. Visit the site, stand in front of it. Get a feel for the traffic pattern.
- Get demographic studies of the area and traffic counts from a broker or from municipal offices.
- Before making an offer call in a contractor or architect and obtain estimates on rehab costs and new-use alteration expense.
- Have your lawyer review the deal. You may want to structure a contract which provides for retail tenants to renew leases for another lease period allowing you time to fine-tune your plans for conversion to offices later on.
- If you are investing in the property as a member of syndication or partnership, have your financial advisor review the sales agreement.

Trends Encourage Investment. With the costs of land and of construction twice what they were 5 years ago, with new shopping center construction off, and with office users willing to pay $30 per square foot, this investment looks promising.

John Gornall

John Gornall, Editor

P.S. Congratulations to the 2 winners of our Second Annual Real Estate Sweepstakes. They are Charles W. Walter of Tallahassee, Florida, and R. Hergonson of Bellflower, California. They won respectively $150 and The Arnold Encyclopedia of Real Estate.

ISSN 0194-6900

Phillips Publishing, Inc.
Actionable Information for the 80's

Real Estate
Intelligence Report

July, 1981
Washington, D.C.
Vol. 4, No. 9

Dear Subscriber:

The situation today is similar to that of a year ago: mortgage rates between 16-17%; the prime hovering around 20%, changing almost day to day. Interest rates, as I predicted here 6 months ago, are not down. High interest rates are here to stay--at least until late this year, and probably beyond. By High I mean mortgage rates that are adjustable and flexible, bracketed to a prime rate no lower than 16% and often up in the 20% neighborhood for the next 6 months. And maybe longer.

Short-term interest rates are in the midst of a downward trend but economists are not unanimous on what will happen by the end of 1981. Some say the rates will drop considerably lower while others say the rates will soar again to the 20% level or higher. Meanwhile, the Federal Reserve Board, taking the big brother role, is watching and won't hesitate to apply the brakes if it feels the trend is getting out of hand. A further drop in short-term rates would help the thrift industry, now caught in a squeeze because of unprecedented money costs brought on by inflation and the federal deregulation of interest rate ceilings. But for the savings and loan associations and savings banks things may get worse before they get better. The National Savings and Loan League sees losses for S&Ls of $1.25 billion to $1.5 billion for the first half of 1981. Some bank executives see savings banks losing as much as $250 million.

With the large number of new mortgage plans, I've provided a glossary to help you through the alphabet jungle recently created. But whatever happens in this field, you'll need money-making possibilities. One is group tenants (see page 4); another is suburban commercial space (see page 8). Planning ahead is the topic of our legal adviser, Larry Shulman, who outlines ways to keep your real estate "estate" in order. And now to this month's issue.

KEY DUE-ON-SALE RULING GOES AGAINST REAL ESTATE INVESTORS

Lenders Position Upheld In Virginia. A federal appeals court in Richmond, Virginia, has upheld a practice lending institutions have been using to rid their portfolios of old, low-interest mortgage loans. Sellers of mortgaged property in Virginia now must pay off outstanding mortgages immediately. The loans cannot be passed along to buyers. New buyers are forced to get a new mortgage from a lender at today's higher rates rather than assuming the lower rate from the seller.

The ruling in Virginia could affect cases pending in other states. Meanwhile, the Minnesota Supreme Court ruled recently just the opposite--that the state could stop lenders from exercising due-on-sale powers against borrowers.

Supreme Court Appeal Certain. Virginia attorney Paul D. Scanlon, who has represented Jeff-

John Gornall has more than 22 years of "hands on" realty experience. While an executive with U.S. Steel, he helped guide that corporate giant into real estate investment for the first time. He also helped create the first profitable "new town": Montgomery Village, Maryland.

John is a licensed Realtor, a popular real estate speaker and consultant, and a successful real estate investor. He's written a syndicated real estate newspaper column and is co-author of a book on new town development. He also has produced an award-winning film about real estate. John's inside real estate knowledge will help you prosper with your real estate investments.

MORTGAGE FINANCING WITH BONDS

With interest rates holding at or near all time highs there is continuing interest in the prospect for financing of residential properties with tax exempt revenue bonds, such as the Houston Home Finance Corporation did through its $200,000,000 issue in 1980.

There have been deterrents to further use of this program - the overhanging presence of the Ullman bill, which passed the House but not the Senate - the disarray in the bond markets which negated any chances of Texas participation because of our 10% usury provision - the subsequent passage by Congress of legislation supplanting the Ullman bill, but imposing new limitations on bond financing for mortgage financing purposes.

The new legislation contains no income limits, but purchase price cannot exceed 90% of the average purchase price in the community. In economically distressed target areas the ceiling is 110% of the area average.

Prohibited is bond financing for families who have owned a home in the past three years, except in targeted areas.

Each state's annual allocation is to be split 50-50 between state agencies and localities unless the state government changes the split.

In rental project financing with tax exempt bonds at least 20% of the units to be financed must be held for families whose income is below 80% of the area median income, thus eligible for Section 8, although there need not be an allocation of Section 8. In targeted areas the requirement is lowered to 15% of the units.

The allowable spread between bond cost and interest rate to the public has been cut from 1.5% to 1%. This creates administrative difficulties for housing finance corporations.

This act allows financing until December 31, 1983. All of you who favor this type of financing vehicle, although not necessarily the restrictive elements, would be well advised to start now convincing your representatives in the Congress of the benefits of tax exempt revenue bond financing.

Single column formats especially benefit from lines and borders. For example, headlines often seem lost, even with off-center designs which place heads next to rather than above stories. The editor of *Executive Report* used fine lines run over both head and story to make a visual link and pleasing page pattern. With the line tying head and story, the head itself can be set downstyle instead of all caps as in *Falcon Flyer*.

Communication News shows boxed body copy offset to the left, creating a bold right margin taking readers' eyes directly to the news. The *Kovels Letter* groups photographs with copy to illustrate text about the highly-specialized market for antiques.

Cartoon art helps make an elementary school newsletter such as *Barnes Bulletin* attractive to children as well as adults. Clip art services often have cartoon illustrations which leave space within for you to put your own message.

"We have lots of ways to measure success for <u>Medical Rounds</u>. When the legislature is in session, we see copies among working papers on desks at the capitol. Newspapers around the state use our stories as editorials. House organs in hospitals run our statistics or entire articles. Public media people call us for up-to-date information on medical topics.

"We'll publish as long as we continue doing our job well. When we stop meeting our goals we should, and will— in the jargon of hospitals—expire."

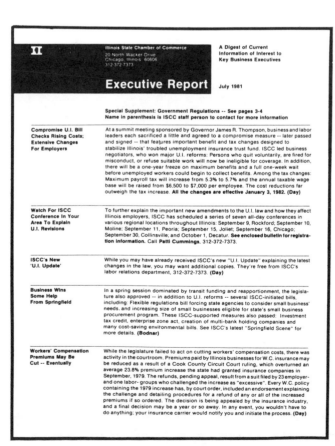

THE FALCON FLIER

FIVE OAKS INTERMEDIATE SCHOOL   Beaverton, OR.

November 1980

CAFETERIA SUBSTITUTES NEEDED
- Schools, like other instututions, are in constant need of good help on days when regular employees are ill or absent. The Beaverton School District is especially in need of additional substitutes for cafeteria work during the winter months. The substitutes generally work four hours a day and are paid at a rate of $3.35 per hour. If you are interested, please call Ethel Parr at 649-0425 for more information.

PUMPKIN CARVING CONTEST
- During the week of Oct. 27th, the Instructional Materials Center sponsored its first annual Pumpkin Carving Contest. The results were very creative. Judges were Julie Harris, Michaele Becker and the Media class. The winners were <u>Biggest</u> - Kevin Turley, <u>Smallest</u> - Pat McNeill, <u>Weirdest</u> - Shaun Hughes, Most Original - Michele Steinke, <u>Most Professional</u> - Brian Goff, <u>Cutest</u> - Laura Lewis, <u>Best Character</u> - Jill Heuring. <u>Honorable Mentions</u> went to Kelly Kaiser, Marvin Nichols, Dana Kent, Dunn Rice and David Porter.

We offer our appreciation to all those who participated and helped make our Halloween Week special.

INCLEMENT WEATHER INFORMATION
We are entering the season when inclement weather may delay or prevent the opening of school on a given day or days. When those conditions exist, opening of schools and schedules of buses may be delayed for one hour. Five Oaks would then begin at 10:00 a.m. This schedule is known as Snow Day Schedule.

In severe weather, Five Oaks would not be open for school. Radio stations which have agreed to carry announcements of snow day schedules between 6:00 a.m. and 7:30 a.m. include KGW, KISN, KPOJ, KYXI, KUIK and KWJJ. We have received word from station KXL-AM that the announcements will be made twenty-five minutes after the hour and five minutes before the hour. On KXL-FM announcements will be made on the hour and on the half hour.

II   Illinois State Chamber of Commerce
20 North Wacker Drive
Chicago, Illinois 60606
312-372-7373

A Digest of Current Information of Interest to Key Business Executives

Executive Report   July 1981

Special Supplement: Government Regulations -- See pages 3-4
Name in parenthesis is ISCC staff person to contact for more information

Compromise U.I. Bill Checks Rising Costs; Extensive Changes For Employers
At a summit meeting sponsored by Governor James R. Thompson, business and labor leaders each sacrificed a little and agreed to a compromise measure -- later passed and signed -- that features important benefit and tax changes designed to stabilize Illinois' troubled unemployment insurance trust fund. ISCC led business negotiators, who won major U.I. reforms: Persons who quit voluntarily, are fired for misconduct, or refuse suitable work will now be ineligible for coverage. In addition, there will be a one-year freeze on maximum benefits and a full one-week wait before unemployed workers could begin to collect benefits. Among the tax changes: Maximum payroll tax will increase from 5.3% to 5.7% and the annual taxable wage base will be raised from $6,500 to $7,000 per employee. The cost reductions far outweigh the tax increase. **All the changes are effective January 3, 1982. (Day)**

Watch For ISCC Conference In Your Area To Explain U.I. Revisions
To further explain the important new amendments to the U.I. law and how they affect Illinois employers, ISCC has scheduled a series of seven all-day conferences in various regional locations throughout Illinois: September 9, Rockford; September 10, Moline; September 11, Peoria; September 15, Joliet; September 16, Chicago; September 30, Collinsville; and October 1, Decatur. **See enclosed bulletin for registration information.** Call Patti Cummings, 312-372-7373.

ISCC's New 'U.I. Update'
While you may have already received ISCC's new "U.I. Update" explaining the latest changes in the law, you may want additional copies. They're free from ISCC's labor relations department, 312-372-7373. **(Day)**

Business Wins Some Help From Springfield
In a spring session dominated by transit funding and reapportionment, the legislature also approved -- in addition to U.I. reforms -- several ISCC-initiated bills, including: Flexible regulations bill forcing state agencies to consider small business' needs, and increasing size of small businesses eligible for state's small business procurement program. These ISCC-supported measures also passed: Investment tax credit, enterprise zone act, creation of multi-bank holding companies and many cost-saving environmental bills. See ISCC's latest "Springfield Scene" for more details. **(Bodnar)**

Workers' Compensation Premiums May Be Cut -- Eventually
While the legislature failed to act on cutting workers' compensation costs, there was activity in the courtroom. Premiums paid by Illinois businesses for W.C. insurance may be reduced as a result of a Cook County Circuit Court ruling, which overturned an average 23.8% premium increase the state had granted insurance companies in September, 1979. The refunds, pending appeal, result from a suit filed by 23 employer- and one labor- groups who challenged the increase as "excessive". Every W.C. policy containing the 1979 increase has, by court order, included an endorsement explaining the challenge and detailing procedures for a refund of any or all of the increased premiums if so ordered. The decision is being appealed by the insurance industry, and a final decision may be a year or so away. In any event, you wouldn't have to do anything; your insurance carrier would notify you and initiate the process. **(Day)**

COMMUNICATIONEWS

Written especially for the professional association communicator

MARCH 1981

SECOND-CLASS POSTAGE RATES: GOOD NEWS AND BAD NEWS

New postage rates for all classes of mail go into effect March 22. Even though it had wanted stiffer rate increases than those recommended by the Postal Rate Commission, the Postal Service Board of Governors accepted the new rates under protest and asked the PRC to reconsider its recommendation.

Under the new rates, you may pay a lot more or a little less for mailing periodicals, depending on your percentage of advertising, now far your subscribers are from your mailing location, whether you have been mailing at controlled circulation rates, and other variables. The new rate package includes discounts for mailers who presort their publications by Zip Code destination.

The board of governors did not approve a surcharge for expedited Red Tag delivery of second-class publications. For the time being, at least, Red Tag service will continue to cost the same as regular delivery.

Here are highlights of the new second-class rates:

	Old Rate	New Rate
Regular second-class publications		
Nonadvertising portion, per pound	13.1¢	10.6¢
Advertising portion, per pound (based on subscriber's distance from mailing location)	17.5¢-31.8¢	14.2¢-34.8¢
Per piece (based on level of presorting)	4.4¢-7¢	5.4¢-8¢
Nonprofit second-class publications		
Nonadvertising portion, per pound	6.4¢	6.3¢
Advertising portion, per pound (based on distance)	9.6¢-18¢	9.3¢-18¢
Per piece (now based on level of presorting)	2.6¢	1.9¢-2.8¢

In addition to the new postage rates, the Postal Service will do away with the controlled circulation category that sharply decreased postage for some publications. Publications that were mailed at controlled circulation rates will now go as second class—meaning that they must pay per-pound zoned rates on their advertising portions. By July 1982, these publications must comply with another requirement: At least 50 percent of the subscribers must have requested the publication or paid a nominal subscription fee to receive it.

AD REVENUE TO HELP PUBLICATION EXPAND ITS COVERAGE

Many association publications are beginning to take advertising to help stretch their budgets. For instance, <u>IABC News</u>, the monthly publication of the International Association of Business Communicators in San Francisco, now accepts

Published monthly by the Communication Section of the American Society of Association Executives. 1575 Eye St. N.W. Washington, DC 20005. Telephone (202) 626-ASAE. Brandi Sullivan, Section Manager. Merry Falconer, Editor.

Cedar Hills Happenings

DECEMBER 1980 PTC NEWSLETTER FOR PARENTS, TEACHERS, STAFF AND STUDENTS

THE PTC THANKS YOU ALL!!

On behalf of the P.T.C. Board, I would like to publicly thank Eileen Rodeen and Rodgie Larsen for chairing the Gingerbread House Breakfast and Bazaar. I would also like to thank all the the committee chairmen; Joan Lundin, Nancy Mittelstadt, Jan Johnston, Linda Hammack, Sue Weakley, Jan Kalberer, and Betty Holloway. ......To the cooks, the servers, the 6th grade chorus, Santa, Cinnamon Bear, Talking Tree, Clowns, and our surprise Gingerbread Man, a large THANK YOU!! A very special thanks to Mr. Zabel, our librarian's husband, who designed and made our delightful Talking Tree. WE APPRECIATE YOU ALL.

Thank you also to all the parents that stood in line for an hour waiting to eat. We really appreciate your support!

Through your help we netted about $850 to go toward play ground equipment, "Tears of Joy", and an all-school Art Fair.

Happy Holidays to you all!

Your PTC Board

FAMILY FUN NIGHT!!

KEX vs. C.H. ELEMENTARY
January 19, 1981 Monday
7 p.m.
Cedar Park Jr. High

This basketball game will be a fun evening of entertainment, matching the KEX D.J.'s against our Cedar Hills team made up of staff and parents. Plan to come!!

****

JANUARY CALENDAR

Jan. 5	School Resumes
Jan. 5	PTC Board Mtg. 7:30 Rodgie Larsen's
Jan. 6	Local School Comm. Mtg. 7:30 pm School
Jan. 30	Teacher Workday No school
Jan. 30	End of 2nd Quarter

SCHOOL CLOSURES AND LATE OPENINGS DUE TO WEATHER

School may be delayed one hour or closed for the day due to inclement weather. Announcements will be made between 6:00 and 7:30 a.m. on radio stations KGW, KEX, KPOK,KXXI,KOIN, and KWJJ. Certain bus routes may be changed or delayed because of certain roads.

Two column formats allow more flexible arrangement of words and art. Type sizes can be smaller with shorter lines, thus allowing more words per page. Headlines are more easily tied to stories, especially to short items. Don't, however, let a headline overpower your nameplate as in *Cooper Mountain News.*

Cedar Hills Happenings is printed from a paper master which picked up a shadow line under the word "happenings." Avoid this problem by brushing a bit of correction fluid around the edges. The handsome nameplate for *Neighbor to Neighbor* uses issue number and date as a major design element. The justified columns of typed copy look fine individually, but seem to float because the alley is too wide.

Three newsletters on these pages use reverses, all to quite different effects. The congressional seal in the *Ron Wyden Report* has very fine lines, so tends not to show well. The reversed logo in *Image Digest* looks distinguished, but reversed standing heads seem to compete for attention. By opening the reverse at the top, the designer for *Emphasis* made the straightforward announcement of purpose part of the dynamic nameplate.

Cooper Mountain Views

Published by the PTC for parents, students and staff   November 1980

SYMPHONY COMES TO SCHOOL

Children in all grades at Cooper Mtn. will be participating in the Symphony Suitcase program this year. This new program sponsored by the Oregon Symphony Association offers monthly workshops which school volunteers attend. At these workshops they are provided with material for instructing students at their schools on different aspects of music appreciation. The material is co-ordinated with the presentations of the Youth Symphony programs.

Joan Weil and Pat Reiter represent Cooper Mtn. in this program. Once a month they will share what they have learned with students during their regular music class. During October the 1st and 2nd grades were introduced to the instruments in the different parts of the orchestra. The older students will also have an opportunity to attend some of the symphony presentations later in the year. For more information about this program please contact Mrs. Beach, the music teacher at Cooper Mtn.

2 FOR 1 ON 10

On Friday, Oct. 17, the 2nd graders performed "10 in a Bed" for the 1st graders. Performing on xylophones and percussion instruments were Deanna Gardner, Lindsey Beal, Nicole Smith, Kimberly Yap, Alan Vestergaard, Mike Everhart and Jennifer Vickers. Teresa Roberts was "the little one" who finally managed to get the big bed all to herself.

dates to remember:

Nov. 4 ELECTION DAY   VOTE
Nov. 4 Local School Comm. 12:30
Nov. 4 PTC Meeting 7:30
Nov. 10 NO SCHOOL Veterans Day
Nov. 11 NO SCHOOL Teachers' Work Day
Nov. 17-21 Conferences
Nov. 17-21 Book Fair
Nov. 17 School Board Meeting
Nov. 20-21 NO SCHOOL Thanksgiving

P Promotional Image Contract Associates, Inc.
THE IMAGE DIGEST

CHARTER ISSUE
- Corporate I.D.
- Networks
- PR
- Commentary
- Letters
- FYI
- Mirror/Mirror

CORPORATE I.D.

Many large companies have recognized the importance of having well-dressed employees. This is particularly critical for those who are continually in the public eye. Your mode of dress is an important consideration for work performance as well as for promotion. It is not enough to be able to perform and produce effectively, you must also be aware of your personal appearance. The skirted suit, while scoffed at by many, has risen to become the mainstay of the necessary "corporate uniform", for most "company women". Like it or not, the skirted suit is a MUST! If you do not already own one, then make it your first priority apparel purchase above all else. If you want to be a part of the system, then you have to learn how to play the game.

Picture yourself in this situation: Got up late one morning, rushed to get dressed, wore an old standby outfit, got to work, boss was ill, boss was scheduled to make presentation to the board, and guess what happened! You had to stand in for boss in

that old standby outfit! Well, this scenario may never happen to you, but you should never leave yourself vulnerable, even if it means having a "spare" ensemble on hand. Remember the Boy Scout motto "Always be prepared".

NETWORKS

There are many organizations that have been formed to help women become more effective and to serve as a springboard for support. Of these, The National Association of Female Executives and the American Society of Professional and Executive Women, stand out as two organizations that excel in their offerings. The concept of "networking" has been around for a long time, but only recently have women begun to understand and utilize this resource. Networking is a mechanism by which individuals collaborate for collective personal or career opportunities. It can be very structured or it can be very informal. Information can be

page 1

"The thing that just gets me mad about our local paper is that they are always moving the funnies. One day they're in with sports, the next day just after editorials, and the day after that behind the used car ads.

"That got me thinking about how readers like to have various features always in the same place. The newspaper tries to be too clever. In our newsletter I always have the calendar on page four, feature photo on page one, and so on. Everything in its place every month. My readers get something they can depend on. It's easy for me, too. My layout is half done before I even start."

NEIGHBOR TO NEIGHBOR
YEAR 8
ISSUE 7
JULY-AUG. 1981

Highway Funding Sources Short

By Vickie Rocker

All the highway improvements planned for the Portland region are based on the availability of federal aid interstate or interstate transfer funding. Right now, both funding sources are coming up short.

The current program to complete the state-wide interstate system exceeds one-half billion dollars. Oregon is only receiving about $43 million each year for the interstate program; therefore, delays in completion must be expected. In Portland, the number one interstate priority is I-205. Completion of this freeway has recently been rescheduled for 1986 because of the constrained flow of interstate funding. This setback also means that funding needed for other projects will be delayed. R.N. Bothman, Metro Administrator for ODOT, says that it is now doubtful that the Portland region interstate projects can be completed until after the year 2000. That project list includes the Greeley ramp project connecting Swan Island to I-5 North, the I-405 extension in Northwest Portland, the Marquam Bridge ramps to the Central East Side Industrial area, the Jantzen Beach (Slough Bridge) section of I-5, and the North Tigard/South Tigard Haines interchange project on I-5 south.

Withdrawal of the Mt. Hood and the I-505 freeways entitled the Portland region to $482 million in transfer funds for substitute projects. We requested $84 million to meet the region's needs in 1987 and received only $39 million---$21 million for highways and $18 million for transit. The insufficient flow of federal funds is seriously impacting the ability of the region to build the projects.

Topping the list of major interstate projects in the Portland area is the Banfield Transitway with a $306.1 million price tag. ODOT officials are committed to completing this project on schedule.

However, the lack of transfer funds may have an impact on the 50 plus projects identified in the city including the I-505 alternative project ($26 million) and plans to improve McLoughlin Blvd. ($23 million). Portland will be faced with prioritizing projects to receive the available funding.

ODOT and City transportation planners are now working on a revised schedule for completion of highway and transfer fund projects, and this should be completed by the fall.

━━━━━━━━━━━━━━━━━━━━━━━

A LAND BANKING AND LAND REVITALIZATION WORKSHOP sponsored by ONA will be held Friday and Saturday, July 10th and 11th, at 8:30 a.m. at Southeast Uplift, 5224 SE Foster. Admission is free; lunch is available at cost. Call 248-4519 for more information.

━━━━━━━━━━━━━━━━━━━━━━━

Clearinghouse for
Sexuality and Population Education Program Materials

Emphasis

Highlighting people and programs in the field of sexuality and reproductive education.

Volume 1, Number 3   Spring 1981

Capitol Idea: The Men's Center

Gary Simpson, Director, Men's Center and client

In Washington, DC a successful community event celebrating all fathers evolved because of Gary Simpson's (Director of The Men's Center of Planned Parenthood of Metropolitan Washington, DC) feelings of respect for his own father. "When Mother's Day started rolling around I asked myself, 'What am I going to do for Father's Day?' My father had just been in the hospital and I wanted to do something special. I thought about all the fathers I saw at the clinic -- fathers in the military, teenage fathers and single fathers -- and I was frustrated because there weren't many places to refer them for help. So I decided to involve the community. It was my Father's Day present to my father," stated Gary.

"What does father mean to me?" was a city-wide high school essay contest sponsored by the Men's Center in Spring 1980. The winners read their essays at a one day conference, "The Changing Roles of Fathering in our Society," presented by social workers, lawyers, teenage parents and single parents.

The conference, presented on Friday, June 13, 1980, at the National Baptist Church, included workshops and dialogs addressing the problems men face in their contemporary role as fathers. Traditional roles of fathers and new alternatives were addressed in four sessions: "Fatherless Children: The Need for Role Models"; "Teenage Fathers: Children With Children"; "The Single Father: Equal Rights and Responsibilities"; and "Fathering: Personal Views and Unique Lifestyles."

More than 100 participants spent the day hearing about the economic, psychological, emotional and legal aspects of being a father in our society. Gary said, "We left excited and we're starting to see some follow-up. A direct result is a lot of community organiza-

Department of Education
Planned Parenthood Federation of America, Inc.

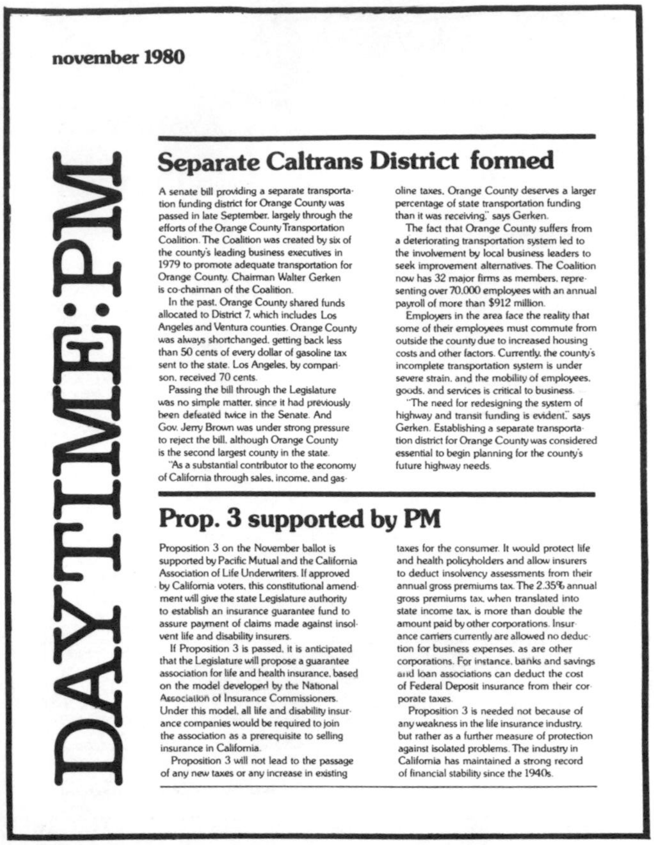

november 1980

DAYTIME:PM

Separate Caltrans District formed

A senate bill providing a separate transportation funding district for Orange County was passed in late September, largely through the efforts of the Orange County Transportation Coalition. The Coalition was created by six of the county's leading business executives in 1979 to promote adequate transportation for Orange County. Chairman Walter Gerken is co-chairman of the Coalition.

In the past, Orange County shared funds allocated to District 7, which includes Los Angeles and Ventura counties. Orange County was always shortchanged, getting back less than 50 cents of every dollar of gasoline tax sent to the state. Los Angeles, by comparison, received 70 cents.

Passing the bill through the Legislature was no simple matter, since it had previously been defeated twice in the Senate. And Gov. Jerry Brown was under strong pressure to reject the bill, although Orange County is the second largest county in the state.

"As a substantial contributor to the economy of California through sales, income, and gasoline taxes, Orange County deserves a larger percentage of state transportation funding than it was receiving," says Gerken.

The fact that Orange County suffers from a deteriorating transportation system led to the involvement by local business leaders to seek improvement alternatives. The Coalition now has 32 major firms as members, representing over 70,000 employees with an annual payroll of more than $912 million.

Employers in the area face the reality that some of their employees must commute from outside the county due to increased housing costs and other factors. Currently, the county's incomplete transportation system is under severe strain, and the mobility of employees, goods, and services is critical to business.

"The need for redesigning the system of highway and transit funding is evident," says Gerken. Establishing a separate transportation district for Orange County was considered essential to begin planning for the county's future highway needs.

Prop. 3 supported by PM

Proposition 3 on the November ballot is supported by Pacific Mutual and the California Association of Life Underwriters. If approved by California voters, this constitutional amendment will give the state Legislature authority to establish an insurance guarantee fund to assure payment of claims made against insolvent life and disability insurers.

If Proposition 3 is passed, it is anticipated that the Legislature will propose a guarantee association for life and health insurance, based on the model developed by the National Association of Insurance Commissioners. Under this model, all life and disability insurance companies would be required to join the association as a prerequisite to selling insurance in California.

Proposition 3 will not lead to the passage of any new taxes or any increase in existing taxes for the consumer. It would protect life and health policyholders and allow insurers to deduct insolvency assessments from their annual gross premiums tax. The 2.35% annual gross premiums tax, when translated into state income tax, is more than double the amount paid by other corporations. Insurance carriers currently are allowed no deduction for business expenses, as are other corporations. For instance, banks and savings and loan associations can deduct the cost of Federal Deposit Insurance from their corporate taxes.

Proposition 3 is needed not because of any weakness in the life insurance industry, but rather as a further measure of protection against isolated problems. The industry in California has maintained a strong record of financial stability since the 1940s.

Two column pages do not have to be centered. Both *Daytime: PM* and *Pathfinder* reduced column width to allow large left margins. Both use the margins for design elements. *Pathfinder* is a good example of building white space into design. The nameplate has gold letters running over the mountain outline. The total effect of gold reversed out of black set off by white mountains shows how color and design interact to make graphics art with a message.

Three pages from *Gifted Children Newsletter* show several design elements. Oversize capital letters begin each story. The letters break up blocks of text which otherwise would seem too heavy. The letters themselves, however, are screened at about 30 percent, thus do not overwhelm other elements such as headlines. And the initial letters are always the same height, making run arounds easy to plan.

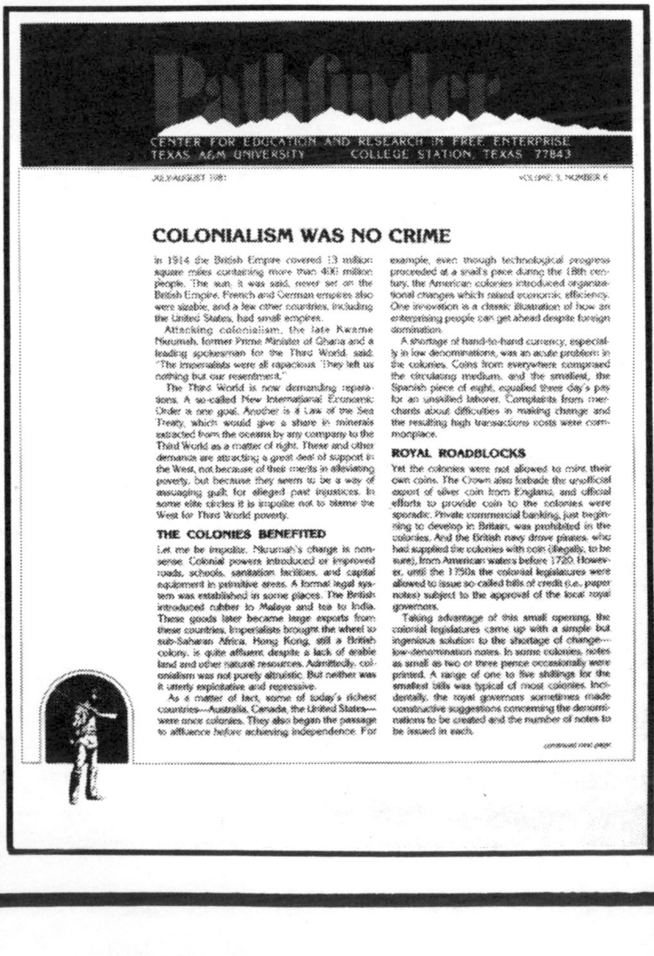

Pathfinder

CENTER FOR EDUCATION AND RESEARCH IN FREE ENTERPRISE
TEXAS A&M UNIVERSITY COLLEGE STATION, TEXAS 77843

JULY/AUGUST 1981 VOLUME 3, NUMBER 6

COLONIALISM WAS NO CRIME

In 1914 the British Empire covered 13 million square miles containing more than 400 million people. The sun, it was said, never set on the British Empire. French and German empires also were sizable, and a few other countries, including the United States, had small empires.

Attacking colonialism, the late Kwame Nkrumah, former Prime Minister of Ghana and a leading spokesman for the Third World, said: "The imperialists were all rapacious. They left us nothing but our resentment."

The Third World is now demanding reparations. A so-called New International Economic Order is one goal. Another is a Law of the Sea Treaty, which would give a share in minerals extracted from the oceans by any company to the Third World as a matter of right. These and other demands are attracting a great deal of support in the West, not because of their merits in alleviating poverty, but because they seem to be a way of assuaging guilt for alleged past injustices. In some elite circles it is impolite not to blame the West for Third World poverty.

THE COLONIES BENEFITED

Let me be impolite. Nkrumah's charge is nonsense. Colonial powers introduced or improved roads, schools, sanitation facilities, and capital equipment in primitive areas. A formal legal system was established in some places. The British introduced rubber to Malaya and tea to India. These goods later became large exports from these countries. Imperialists brought the wheel to sub-Saharan Africa. Hong Kong, still a British colony, is quite affluent despite a lack of arable land and other natural resources. Admittedly, colonialism was not purely altruistic. But neither was it utterly exploitative and repressive.

As a matter of fact, some of today's richest countries—Australia, Canada, the United States—were once colonies. They also began the passage to affluence before achieving independence. For example, even though technological progress proceeded at a snail's pace during the 18th century, the American colonies introduced organizational changes which raised economic efficiency. One innovation is a classic illustration of how an enterprising people can get ahead despite foreign domination.

A shortage of hand-to-hand currency, especially in low denominations, was an acute problem in the colonies. Coins from everywhere comprised the circulating medium, and the smallest, the Spanish piece of eight, equalled three day's pay for an unskilled laborer. Complaints from merchants about difficulties in making change and the resulting high transactions costs were commonplace.

ROYAL ROADBLOCKS

Yet the colonies were not allowed to mint their own coins. The Crown also forbade the unofficial export of silver coin from England, and official efforts to provide coin to the colonies were sporadic. Private commercial banking, just beginning to develop in Britain, was prohibited in the colonies. And the British navy drove pirates, who had supplied the colonies with coin (illegally, to be sure), from American waters before 1720. However, until the 1750s the colonial legislatures were allowed to issue so-called bills of credit (i.e., paper notes) subject to the approval of the local royal governors.

Taking advantage of this small opening, the colonial legislatures came up with a simple but ingenious solution to the shortage of change—low-denomination notes. In some colonies, notes as small as two or three pence occasionally were printed. A range of one to five shillings for the smallest bills was typical of most colonies. Incidentally, the royal governors sometimes made constructive suggestions concerning the denominations to be created and the number of notes to be issued in each.

continued next page

UPDATE

May/June 1981
Volume VI, No. 3

LATIN AMERICA

Congressional Committees Deny "Moral Reparation" to Argentine Military

Over Reagan Administration objections, the Senate Foreign Relations Committee and the House Foreign Affairs Committee voted to require that U.S. military assistance and arms sales to Argentina be contingent on a presidential certification of significant progress in human rights. The Committees acted in response to an Administration proposal to repeal a 1977 amendment (Section 620B) that prohibits all military assistance and arms sales to Argentina.

While agreeing to repeal the prohibition, a strong bipartisan majority in both committees specified that no assistance or sales could be made until the President certified that the Argentine government has made "significant progress" in human rights. The amendment specifies that "in defining significant progress, special attention shall be paid to whether 1) the government of Argentina has made every effort to account for those citizens listed as disappeared . . . and 2) the government of Argentina has either released or brought to justice those prisoners held at the disposition of the National Executive Power (*PEN*)." The amendment, offered by Senators Percy, Pell, and Zorinsky in the Senate and by Congressman Barnes in the House, passed in the Senate by a 11-1 margin and by a clear majority in a voice vote in the House, although a similar proposal had been defeated five days earlier.

If passed on the floor of the House and the Senate, the new amendment will fall short of the unconditional repeal of the prohibitions that the Administration promised General Roberto Viola during his visit to the U.S. just days before he assumed the Argentine presidency on March 30, 1981.

General Viola's visit, hailed as a success by the Argentine government, was marred by contradictory statements made to U.S. politicians and the Argentine press. When asked about the possibility of lifting the embargo on arms sales to Argentina, Viola quipped, "We don't need arms, but it would be a moral reparation." In its testimony before the House Subcommittees on Inter-American Affairs and Human Rights, the Washington Office on Latin America discouraged Congress from taking measures that would be interpreted as offering moral reparation to the Argentine armed forces for their actions over the last five years.

After Viola's meeting with members of the Senate, Senator Claiborne Pell reported that Viola had promised to provide a listing of people known to have disappeared. However, at a closed meeting with members of the Argentine press at the end of his visit, General Viola explained that his government was not going to publish a list of the "so-called disappeared," without being certain they were dead, and hastened to clarify that under no circumstances did he imply any investigation of the military. Viola said, "One cannot attempt to pass judgment on the victors, because this has not been the case historically. For example, if the Reich's troops had won the last World War, the (war crimes) tribunal would have been held not in Nuremburg, but in Virginia."

The *Buenos Aires Herald*, Argentina's outspoken English language newspaper, commented on Viola's statement. "This was an astonishing, and perhaps a revealing thing to say . . . Does he believe that in war everything is permissible to the victors, that nobody has any right to call them to account for their violations of the military code? . . . Viola, after all, is supposed to be

IN THIS ISSUE

- **Bolivia: Garcia Meza Attempts to Gain Legitimacy**
- **Central America: Washington Sets Sparks in a Conflictive Zone**
- **Brazil Negotiates Changes in Foreigners Laws**
- **Honduras: Last Chance for a Peaceful Change**
- **NEWSBRIEFS: Chile, Nicaragua, Peru, Colombia**

Washington Office on Latin America • 110 Maryland Ave., NE • Washington, D.C. 20002 • (202) 544-8045

"Cut costs? Believe me, there's only one way: keep up with technology. Learn about computer text management and perfecta presses and optical character readers.

"How do I do it? Well, I don't read much. It's all too complicated. No, I let the salesmen teach me. I go to trade shows—and not just in graphics, either. I go to shows for secretaries and photographers and artists and writers—anyone whose job title is one part of being a newsletter editor. And while I'm at shows, I let the reps invite me to seminars or exhibits they do for their customers. That way I get free instruction and free coffee in the bargain."

FOR THE PARENTS OF CHILDREN WITH GREAT PROMISE

Gifted Children Newsletter

JUNE 1980 VOL. 1 NO. 4

Disciplining Your Child

Search for Young Scientists

An Interview With Joseph Renzulli

How To Explore a Museum

Update on Terman's Study Of the Gifted

Gifted Children Swap Lifestyles

Better Chance for Gifted Minorities

Plus: Book, Toy and Game Reviews; a Calendar of Events; And Spin-off, a Four-Page Pullout Section for Your Child

ADVISORY BOARD

Alexinia Baldwin, assistant professor of curriculum and instruction, State University of New York at Albany, and former president of the Association for the Gifted. **Joseph S. Renzulli**, associate professor, Department of Educational Psychology, University of Connecticut. **Dorothy Sisk**, professor of exceptional child education, University of South Florida at Tampa, and former director of Office of Gifted and Talented (HEW). **E. Paul Torrance**, Alumni Foundation Distinguished Professor, Department of Educational Psychology, University of Georgia. **Steve Allen**, comedian, author, composer. **Fred Rogers**, creator of "Mister Rogers' Neighborhood."

Copyright © 1980 by Gifted and Talented Publications, Inc. *Gifted Children Newsletter* is published 12 times a year by Gifted and Talented Publications, Inc., 530 University Avenue, Palo Alto, California 94301. Second class permit pending at Palo Alto, California and additional offices.

SPECIAL REPORT

A Critique of Kids' Magazines

Most parents of gifted children know the value of frequent trips to libraries and bookstores. They know that inquiring young minds need stimulation and that books are the food and drink of a growing intellect. Many of these parents, however, overlook another satisfying and readily available source of mental nourishment: children's magazines.

A good magazine can provide a child with a variety of experiences and pleasures – even its arrival in the mail is an exciting event. A smorgasbord of information and entertainment in the form of nonfiction articles, stories, poems, puzzles and games introduces children to facts and ideas they can read about in a single sitting or pursue for days. And, with the high prices of children's books, a year's subscription can cost as little as one juvenile title.

Among the fine children's magazines available, some are general interest; others are specialized. When making your selection, it is important to keep your child's interests and preferences in mind, for the most familiar and popular publications are not necessarily the best. Get single copies of the magazines you are considering – either at the library or by writing to the publishers – before sending in any subscription forms. As your child reads them, pay attention to his reactions. Does your child comment on the information? Does he ask questions or express a desire to find out more about newly discovered subjects? The following capsule reviews and your child's candid remarks and behavior will help you find a worthwhile new resource.

General Interest Magazines

• *Cricket* routinely publishes the very best children's authors and illustrators. Each issue contains at least one nonfiction article as well as a craft or game feature, but fiction – with considerable emphasis on

(Continued on page 14)

HOME AND SCHOOL BRIEFS

Stay Involved And Keep Talking

A high level of parental involvement in a child's education and a lot of verbal stimulation at home and at school can boost a child's scholastic performance, according to Ronald Edmonds, a Harvard University professor and assistant to the chancellor of the New York City schools. During a panel discussion last fall, Edmonds argued against James Coleman's view that family background and luck have more to do with success than school does. Despite Coleman's stance, Edmonds won a major point in the debate when Coleman, a University of Chicago professor, conceded that children exposed to a lot of verbal stimulation at home and students with teachers having good verbal abilities did better than other students.

Researchers studying inner-city schools in Detroit found a high level of parental involvement among the characteristics present in schools with high levels of student achievement. Studies done by Edmonds, as well as the one in Detroit, revealed several other characteristics common to schools with good student achievement levels:

• a strong instructional leader as principal
• clear academic goals—established, understood and adhered to by the faculty
• a well-defined testing program used to diagnose student and program problems
• a clean, pleasant, secure environment
• high expectations for all students.

Gold-Medal Winners In Children's Literature

The glut of children's books on the market makes it difficult to sort out the winners from the also-rans. A good way to identify quality reading for your children is to use a book published by the Children's Book Council.

Children's Books: Awards and Prizes (Children's Book Council, 1979, $8.95), revised biennially, lists all the books that have won honors in the English-speaking world, plus some others. For example, *The Voyages of Doctor Dolittle* won honors in the prestigious Newbery Medal competition in 1923; James Thurber's *Many Moons* received the Randolph Caldecott Medal for its illustrations in 1944; and *Charlotte's Web* by E.B. White was voted best book by Canadian schoolchildren in 1972.

Kids Hold "Meeting of the Minds"

What would Eleanor Roosevelt say about the Equal Rights Amendment? How would Leif Ericson deal with the Iranian crisis? These are questions being posed by gifted students at Northeast Junior High School in Northglenn, Colo., a suburb of Denver. Following up on suggestions from their students, teachers of the gifted junior high youngsters contacted TV personality Steve Allen for permission to re-create his "Meeting of the Minds" program, which had inspired the kids to undertake a similar project. Allen gave his permission and volunteered some ideas for adapting the program. Students, however, must do their own research. By identifying with a character and determining what his or her "mind set" might be on contemporary problems, "our students are stretching their minds," said Principal Lynn Albi. As on the TV program, students in the classroom act out characters' opinions on current issues at round tables. Students' videotapes of their presentations (although not professional quality) may be of interest to other schools and are loaned out by Albi's staff.

Northeast's gifted program, started just over a year ago at the urging of the district's superintendent, combines special activities—such as the "Meeting of the Minds" project, designing a community park and developing a computer program for scoring a district wrestling tournament—with regular course offerings. The school has selected about 22 students, out of a student body of 900, to participate in the Horizons Program for the gifted. Students in the school's three grade levels (7-9) meet together for homeroom class every morning. They are also grouped together for regular classes, which are taught by the dozen teachers on the school's gifted team.

For more information, write: Lynn Albi, 11700 Irma Dr., Northglenn, CO 80233.

Disciplining Your Child

Like all youngsters, gifted children can be classroom behavior problems. But disciplinary methods that have an effect on other children may not be successful with gifted children, according to Joanne R. Whitmore, associate professor of psychology and education at George Peabody College for Teachers in Nashville. Behavior modification techniques, for example, may be successful for short periods with many young gifted children. "Significant numbers, however, are little influenced by such methods, and, even when these techniques are initially useful, they are insufficient for gifted children, who quickly perceive 'the game' and generally become increasingly unresponsive to it," she wrote in *Roeper Review*.

She recommends strategies that make use of gifted youngsters' ability to reason, apply knowledge and become self-directed. To help them identify and evaluate the consequences of specific behaviors, develop an understanding of their self-control problems, and design alternative ways of handling emotions and needs, she suggests one-to-one dialogues between adult and child, class meetings in which other youngsters support the child in solving a specific problem, and involving the child in establishing personal guidelines and goals.

Gifted Children Are Victims of Ignorance

A new study shows that regular classroom teachers, school administrators, community leaders and the general public have significantly less favorable attitudes toward gifted children and programs designed for them than do the parents and teachers of the gifted. The groups with the less favorable attitudes toward the gifted have little direct contact with them yet are the most influential in determining support and funding for their programs. The authors of the study, Barbara Nash Mills of the John Tracy Clinic in Los Angeles and Gordon L. Berry of the University of California at Los Angeles, say that the findings should alert parents and teachers of the gifted to the need "to educate their colleagues in the schools and those people in the broader community to the importance of providing specialized programs for the gifted."

Discovering Scientists

When David Gleba, 17, of La Jolla, Calif., was very young, he became fascinated with traffic lights. His parents agreed to buy him one and string it up in the living room. Then his interest turned to burglar alarms. He installed them everywhere. At one point his mother could not enter the laundry room, except on Mondays between one and three, without an alarm going on.

Recently Gleba was one of 40 young scientists who went to Washington, D.C., as finalists in the Science Talent Search sponsored by Westinghouse Electric Corporation. He brought along a computer that he had designed to replace one at the Salk Institute. His, he explained, was more flexible than the Salk model and one tenth as expensive: Salk's occupied an entire wall, while his was the size of a breadbox.

Brian R. Greene, another Science Search finalist, also told of his early development as a scientist. He first discovered his gift in science in the third grade, he said, when he came home from school and asked his father, a

musician and playwright, what a light year was. When his father explained that it was the distance traveled by light in a year, Greene proceeded to figure out just how far that was. Greene's project for the Talent Search—a mathematics paper on the theory of partitions—would earn him a Ph.D. at some universities.

Some Science Search finalists had less happy memories and told of traumatic childhoods during which they were ridiculed for daydreaming in class or for not doing their homework. As exceptionally capable high school seniors, however, all seemed pleased with their gifts. They were concerned, though, about classmates regarding them as "brains" or "Einsteins" and treating them differently from everyone else.

Of the 40 finalists in the national search, only 10 are chosen as winners. Judges evaluate the youngsters for motivation, mental flexibility, curiosity, initiative, resourcefulness and their commitment to the field. Logical thinking is important, but the special abilities being sought go beyond that. "We like jumps too," said judge Russell D. Johnson, a chemist. "Sometimes we ask a question and can actually see the kids look the answer up on the page. We take him along until we can't look it up any further. Some students then will stop. The others don't."

Since the Science Talent Search began in 1942, three of the competition's winners have gone on to earn Nobel Prizes.

How To Visit Museums

Enter museums with a sense of wonder, says psychologist Bruno Bettelheim, not with a determination to make children learn. A museum-goer since he was a child, Bettelheim remembers that his mother never explained "intrinsic meaning" to him or told him how to view works of art. "If somebody in authority had asked me to appreciate art as he thought I should, I would not have been made more secure in my appreciation of art—and the experience of looking at art would have lost most of its meaning for me," he says.

Today, parents, teachers and museum directors are trying to heed Bettelheim's charge to respect children's native enthusiasm and curiosity and to develop programs that give gifted children an active part in keeping their sense of wonderment alive. Children's museums already exist in many large cities, and established museums are adding personnel to work closely with kids. Program organizers with a variety of approaches are helping parents and teachers take advantage of museum resources:

• The Smithsonian Institution is at the forefront of helping teachers show children that visiting museums can be a lifelong enjoyment. It has shown teachers how the museum collection can be used to develop interdisciplinary studies. Write: Paul Perrot, 2467 Arts and Industries Bldg., Smithsonian Institution, Washington, DC 20560.

Three column formats allow for lots of creativity in design. Of course, this is a mixed blessing. More design options may just complicate your job.

Although three columns require smaller margins than two or one columns, you still need to frame the copy. The editor of *On the Level* let copy fall off the bottom of the page. Floating lines on *The Trader* contain copy even on outer margins. The bottom line on *Intercom* nicely repeats the broken nameplate line while giving the page a finished look. *Ways and Means* repeated its nameplate screen at the bottom of the page, actually finishing the nameplate with some curved lines to soften the otherwise angular effect.

Notice the difference between justified and ragged columns. *Ways and Means* is well aligned and orderly, but seems more formal than pages with ragged copy. *Oregon State Parks* shows how ragged copy can be informal almost to the point of seeming empty. Floating lines help contain the internal white space created by ragged right copy. *Animator* takes a creative middle ground, pushing white space to the outside by using narrow justified columns.

ON THE LEVEL
WITH NEIL KELLY PEOPLE

Summer Job Tours
highlight variety, teamwork, trends

The periodic job tour has become a fixture at Neil Kelly Company. An occasion for designers to "show off" their work, the tour reinforces a feeling of pride in the workmanship of Neil Kelly craftspeople. The job tours produce another important benefit, as well. They provide an excellent opportunity for the NKC team to learn from one another. The 17 jobs on this summer's job tours were no exception. Each was unique, interesting and well done. Taken as a whole, they also pointed up some interesting trends.

Represented on this summer's tours were a wide variety of projects. The jobs on view ranged from a complete condominium renovation to the creation of a fresh, new appearance -- without doing any major remodeling. Creative solutions were evidenced in the production of a commercial kitchen/business lunchroom, and the installation of a challenging new roof. Each individual job toured had numerous noteworthy features, so selecting those to highlight was a difficult task. The brief summaries that follow are choosen as indicative of the variety, teamwork and trends found throughout all the jobs toured.

The Phil and Gaynor Artz project done by Mary Paige, CKD, included a room addition, complete kitchen remodel and addition of a bay window to the living room. A nice effect was achieved by combining existing glass-doored cabinets, very traditional in style, with a contemporary custom built door, painted and trimmed with oak. Wood floors, laminate counters with custom tile highlighting the backsplash and a custom built open shelf unit complete the kitchen.

Ken Stanley, CKD, created more living space for the Asaphs while maintaining the colonial theme of their home by designing a curved brick retaining wall and archway leading to the

...continued on page 3

Artz

JULY · AUGUST · SEPTEMBER 1981
Vol.7 No.4 PORTLAND, OR

The Trader
A news update for the members of the Chicago Board of Trade

Volume 4, Number 12 — **July, 1980**

CBT submits 1,000-ounce silver contract to CFTC

The Chicago Board of Trade has submitted a 1,000-ounce silver futures contract to the Commodity Futures Trading Commission for approval, as of June 20.

The directors of the exchange voted to establish trading in a smaller silver contract at their regular board meeting on June 17.

The board acted on the recommendation of the exchange Metals Committee. According to Committee Chairman C.C. Odom, this new contract is designed to appeal to small commercial interests who presently are subject to great price volatility and who customarily trade in units of less than 5,000 ounces.

"A smaller contract would be more manageable, allow greater flexibility of positions, and add liquidity to the silver market," said Odom.

"This increase in liquidity should lead to increased use of the market, greater market efficiency and an improvement in the market's performance as a price discovery and hedging tool," said Odom.

The 1,000-ounce contract would trade simultaneously with the current contract of 5,000 ounces.

(Continued on page 9)

C.C. Odom, II

Survey shows members' attitudes on several issues

The major problems or challenges facing the Chicago Board of Trade in the future are government interference in the free market, increasing competition from other commodity exchanges and the need to improve the exchange's public image, according to the results of a recent survey of the attitudes of 715 CBT members.

The survey received a 37 percent response from CBT members and was conducted by the Public Relations Committee, using the marketing research firm of Elrick and Lavidge.

Survey results provided a comprehensive picture of members' attitudes and opinions on a number of issues affecting the CBT. Carl Zapfle, chairman of the marketing research subcommittee of the Public Relations Committee, said, "For the first time,

we have a statistical tabulation of how members feel on a wide variety of issues. It will be beneficial in making plans for the future of the exchange and will serve as a benchmark to measure future results of exchange programs."

Survey results also provided a commodity-by-commodity breakdown of trading activity by each respondent, and the respondents' reasons for trading in certain commodities and bypassing others. Conclusions reached from this portion of the survey will be used by exchange member committees and staff in planning new contracts and upgrading existing ones.

The survey asked members to assess non-members' perceptions of the exchange, and to compare the CBT with other exchanges. Members rated the

CBT's floor operations, clearing mechanism and contract specifications especially high in comparison to other exchanges.

Members said changes the CBT most needs to institute are increased trading space, more extensive promotional and advertising programs and improved relations with the CFTC.

A total of 14 questions with over 100 subcategories were asked in the three-page survey. Space also was provided for written comments on areas not covered in the survey.

Zapfle said, "These numbers are worth their weight in gold to the board of directors and other committee members, because now they know where the full membership stands on the issues."

OREGON STATE PARKS QUARTERLY

PARKS AND RECREATION DIVISION, DEPARTMENT OF TRANSPORTATION — **NUMBER 1, 1980**

BALLOT MEASURE NO. 1

MEASURE 1 on the May 20, 1980, primary election ballot is a Constitutional Amendment referred to the voters by joint resolution (SJR 7) of the 1979 session of the Oregon Legislature.

MEASURE 1 restricts revenue collected from state gas taxes and driver and vehicle registration fees to the construction, maintenance, and operation of public highways, roads, streets, and roadside rest areas in Oregon.

It permits the use of revenue collected from recreational vehicle fees for the acquisition, development and maintenance of parks and recreation areas.

It permits revenue from commercial vehicle weight/mile taxes to be used for the inspection and enforcement of truck weight, size and equipment regulations.

If approved by a majority of voters, the provisions of MEASURE 1 will take effect about one month after the May 20 election.

The provisions of a Constitutional Amendment apply to all levels of government within Oregon.

Oregon State Parks Quarterly is available at no charge. If you would like to be on the mailing list, or if your address is incorrect, please send your name, address, city and zip code to: State Parks Quarterly, 525 Trade St. SE, Salem, OR 97310; phone 378-2796.

Parks, police and travel information have had long and historic ties with highways in Oregon.

The state parks system began, for example, when the Highway Department was authorized to acquire roadside rest areas in 1921.

Highway department truck inspectors became the first deputized state law enforcement officers in 1924.

A travel information section was added to the Highway Department in 1935 to promote tourism, in order to boost gas tax revenues.

The ties were so close that when a dedicated Highway Fund was established by Constitutional Amendment in 1942, it permitted financing of parks, police and travel publicity as well as road construction and maintenance.

After World War II, booming auto and truck use nourished a Highway Fund capable of financing development of many parks, an expanding state police force, a growing variety of informational, recreational, and historical programs, as well as extensive road building.

But by the late 1960s, the cost of living index began catching up with Highway Fund purchasing power. The 1973-74 oil embargo. Road construction costs jumped 37 percent in 1974, while gas tax revenue actually dropped 5 percent.

Faced with a declining Highway Fund and a deteriorating state highway system, the Oregon Legislature began transferring financing for various non-highway functions to the state General Fund.

Items transferred out of the Highway Fund since 1975 include: State Parks, State Police, Columbia Gorge Commission, Travel Information, Natural Area Preserves, Capitol Guides, Board of Health, Marine Facilities Grants, Public Museum Grants, Law Enforcement Data Systems, Movie Promotion, Division of State Lands, Forestry Department.

The process was completed in 1979, with the total removal of State Police and State Parks from the Highway Fund.

All campgrounds opened April 18. See back page for more information.

"It took me a long time and some expensive mistakes to learn two really important things about the printing business. First, lots of printers don't know much. They can run the machines all right, but they're not creative. They're business people who print by formula.

"The other thing I learned is that buying good printing is like buying house painting or repair work on an old car. There aren't many rules—just a few guidelines. Customers have to be well-informed to get what they want."

intercom

CITIZENS BANCORPORATION

VOLUME 1.   NUMBER 1   JANUARY 9, 1981

Planning for the regular publication of INTERCOM are from left Elaine Gassmann, Associate Editor, Debra Coopman, Design-Layout and Julie Krier, Editor.

INTERCOM: Communication Opportunity

With the new year comes a new publication produced by and for Citizens Bancorporation employees at all locations. Titled INTERCOM, this newsletter is designed to promote regular communication among people at all levels within the corporation. As corporate growth continues, so does the need to widen our perspectives and broaden our basic knowledge of our company and its activities.

INTERCOM will be published every other Friday and distributed with the payroll. Unlike previous publications, it is not considered confidential and you are encouraged to share INTERCOM with your family.

As a corporate publication, INTERCOM will provide information and insight on a variety of timely topics relating to Citizens employees and their association with the corporation. The newsletter format can accommodate in-depth interpretative articles as well as very brief news items and updates. Several regular sections such as people will also be included.

It is said that the number one source of creditable information about any organization is the firm's employees. Thus, the editorial staff encourages each one of you to contribute ideas, articles or photographs to INTERCOM, either through your correspondent listed in the masthead on page 3, or one of the editors.

Gillett bank to join Citizens

The recently announced affiliation of Citizens Bancorporation and the Gillett State Bank (GSB) brings to the Citizens family a well-established institution located in Oconto County on the west shore of Green Bay.

Gillett State Bank is in the $40,000,000 class with branches in Oconto Falls, Abrams and Mountain. The four GSB offices encompass an oblong market area stretching from one end of Oconto County to the other.

Strong in recreational and vacation facilities, the Oconto County area is also known for its many industries. The affiliation with GSB solidifies Citizens northern position and expands our market area radius to the northwest by 30 miles. With offices in both Brown County (CAB) and Oconto County, our lakeshore position is strengthened and extended northward as well as our position in metropolitan, northnortheastern Wisconsin.

The affiliation has been approved in principle by the boards of both companies, but is subject to approvals by the shareholders of GSB and the Board of Governors of the Federal Reserve System. The affiliation is not expected to take place until mid-1981.

PUBLISHED FOR AND BY THE EMPLOYEES OF CITIZENS BANCORPORATION AND AFFILIATES

Animator

Fall 1981   Published Quarterly by the Northwest Film Study Center Number 26

Talking With Gene Youngblood

We are witnessing a genuine, scientific revolution of historic magnitude. By the 1990's, the big issue will be switched video or conversational video. The question is: at what point do we have sufficient technology to start proposing worlds to ourselves?

— Gene Youngblood

Gene Youngblood is the author of Expanded Cinema (1970), a classic work on experimental media theory and criticism, numerous articles on the media arts, and The Future of Desire, a soon to be published analysis of the electronic media revolution. He is a member of the Rockefeller Foundation Video Artists Fellowship Program, on the film selection committee of the L.A. International Film Festival, and on the faculty of the California Institute of the Arts.

Editor's note: the following comments were gathered from conversations with Gene Youngblood during three, exhausting, 17 hour days that he spent during the 56 films, 43 videotapes and 10 slideshows entered in the 9th Northwest Film and Video Festival.

Gene Youngblood: Oh goodness. You're not going to do this to me . . . If only (this cassette tape) fed out to a solid state display and printed out what it was hearing so that you could see what you're saying as literature, even as you spoke it.

Animator: What do you think of the work that you've seen over the last few days?

G.Y.: I was surprised at the relative infrequency of really inspired work. I would like to make a distinction between independent and personal work. Independent usually carries a strictly economic connotation. For instance, you don't get your money from the Pentagon or something, but that says nothing about art or what one does with one's own independent money. So I find a lot of stuff that's called independent, looks exactly the same as the stuff that comes from Exxon, and I wonder why it matters why it's independent. So the issue is really personal and autonomous and not independent. Most of the things that were submitted to the Festival were indistinguishable from commercial, industrial product. This kind of bothers me.

However, it's kind of unfair to impose these utopian ideals on mortal humans who have to make a living. Not everybody is willing to suffer and be poor for their art. There's got to be a way of talking about this without sounding critical of people who have joined the poor, the elderly and those living on fixed incomes in using food stamps and other federal programs to reduce their food bills.

ANI: Did you have any expectations?

G.Y.: I didn't know what to expect. I think that what I saw seems reasonable. What else would one see? This isn't New York where you have that intense art trip going on, and it isn't L.A. where you have that plastic world going on.

I think that somehow when work is really good, it's always for a reason that has nothing to do with regionalism. It's not good because it's regional, it's good because it's universal. The winners would stand up anywhere. They would be respectable in New York or anywhere, because they're good, period. So it's interesting that out of all this very regional, documentary oriented and not particularly ambitious or inspired work comes a program of 90 minutes that's first rate. And the highlights are not outstanding winners, but they are competent, creative works. The region seeps through . . . attitude . . . interest in the environment.

ANI: Was interest in the environment an outstanding characteristic (of the work that you've seen)?

Continued on page 7.

Ways&Means

Reporting on Innovative Approaches to State & Local Government

Vol. 4 No. 2   March-April, 1981

Federal cuts, inflation require solutions

DIRECT MARKETING: STATES FIGHT HIGH FOOD COSTS

by Maggie Kennedy

Soaring food costs are a serious economic problem for a growing number of Americans. In recent years, millions of working people have joined the poor, the elderly and those living on fixed incomes in using food stamps and other federal programs to reduce their food bills.

The combination of continued increases in retail prices of 10.5% per year and the proposed cuts in federal food programs could spell disaster for many of these people. Direct marketing of farm produce is one important option which should be considered by state and local officials and community organizations searching for ways to avert this potential disaster.

The purpose of direct marketing programs is to eliminate activities like packing, shipping, handling, brokering, processing, wholesaling, distributing, advertising, and retailing. Combined, these activities were responsible for 70% of food price increases between 1970 and 1977.

Direct marketing has something to offer both the grower and the buyer. By circumventing the marketing sector of the food system, the grower receives a greater share of the sales dollar. In addition to increased profits, direct marketing creates new outlets for farmers' produce where the grower sets the price, standard container costs are eliminated, low volume is not a handicap and cash payments from buyers are immediate.

For the consumer, the benefits are equally as rewarding. The produce is fresher because it has travelled through a shorter marketing channel with less handling. Retail prices are lower because many of the marketing activities have been eliminated and the consumer has the opportunity to interact directly with the producer helping to restore the missing link between farm and city.

Several state legislatures have taken an aggressive, action-oriented approach toward direct marketing by enacting legislation to establish state-run farmer's markets and encourage institutional purchases of locally grown produce. West Virginia has one of the best state-run market programs. Begun in 1948 with a combination of state and federal funds, the state Department of Agriculture sponsors seven markets which sell a variety of farm products such as eggs, fresh vegetables, fruit, honey and nuts. Farmers bring their produce to the market and place it on consignment, where trained market personnel sell it to wholesalers, retailers and consumers.

Weekly checks are mailed to producers for the total amount of all goods sold, less a 10% commission. By consigning their produce to a state market, farmers are relieved of the time-consuming task of making sales contacts to move it.

The state-run system also offers several other advantages. Each market makes buyer contacts and has established outlets for various products. The markets have grading equipment and storage facilities. Finally, they transport goods from one market to another, in state-owned and operated trucks, depending on need. Georgia, Louisiana, and Florida have similar state-run programs.

Another approach, with minimal administrative costs, is the institutional purchase program of locally grown produce. Two states, Maine and New York, have passed extensive institutional marketing legislation.

Enacted in 1979, the Maine law requires the state's 14 purchasers to buy as much of their food as possible from resident farmers and fishermen. The state's purchasing agents must accept bids for Maine products at five percent above similar bids for out-of-state food. This "preference option" declines to three percent in 1983, where it will remain fixed.

(continued on page 7)

In this issue . . .

A special 4 page policy report outlines a progressive agenda for state and local tax reform . . . . p. 3

Agricultural direct marketing comes of age . . . . p. 1

Union support grows for state plant closing legislation . . . . p. 2

Conference on Alternative State & Local Policies

The RCI Communicator

November 1980 ISSN 0193-5482

THE TRAINING AND DEVELOPMENT NEWSLETTER

Judging the Value of Work

"You never know how you're doing. He's a good supervisor, but I sure wish he'd honestly tell me what he wants."

The exact wording may vary but the message is often the same. Employee attitudes in all parts of the country are changing. In response to these changing attitudes, many companies are rethinking the process of employee evaluation. In the past, many companies assumed worker satisfaction. Or, if they didn't assume satisfaction, they were able to work out methods of feedback and job rewards through the union negotiation process or informal discussions. More and more individual workers and worker groups are asking for something new. One thing they are demanding is more specific knowledge of what is expected of them on the job

and specific feedback about their own competencies. Many companies are responding by initiating Performance Appraisal Systems. Some such systems can be purchased and the external agency will come into the company, install the system, and train workers and supervisors to use it. Other companies prefer to investigate their own needs, discuss possible solutions at various job levels, and eventually implement their own method and procedures. Awareness of goals and possible obstacles to effectiveness is essential, regardless of how performance appraisal is instituted.

A good performance appraisal system is not a once-a-year supervisor/subordinate job review. It is an ongoing process requiring continued commitment to individual and company growth. Good communication is the

key. In companies which recognize this, almost any system can work; however, in companies which assume good communication without giving specific training, almost no system will work. Since we've attempted to research the entire spectrum of performance appraisal, and because one of our goals at RCI is to help you stay informed on new methods of communication skills, we want to share what we've found.

Some basic communication skills good supervisors and managers use every day are useful for appraising employee performance. First and foremost, the ability to listen is crucial. Research says we generally listen at about a 25% competency level. What that can mean on the job is that we often choose not to hear when employees are expressing

Continued on next page

The RCI Communicator November 1980

Three column formats lead to narrow columns which, when justified, have lots of hyphenated words. Ragged columns eliminate hyphenation and put white pace at the end of lines rather than between words. Here are several examples of how full borders effect both ragged and justified columns. Notice the extra touch designer Polly Pattison used with *Que Pasa*: the bottom and top border lines stronger than the side lines, adding a slight sense of weight to the page and allowing her to use white space at the top of inside pages to repeat the feeling of the nameplate on page one.

Both *RCI Communicator* and *Que Pasa* show that strong photos and art can be run big. The large photo in *Que Pasa* is placed into the right two columns so its subject is looking into the page, not off it. The image also balances the off-center nameplate design.

NAIS Reporter

A quarterly newsletter

May 1981

NAIS News

Board supports tax credits

The NAIS Board of Directors voted 14-8 to support a tuition tax credit bill (TTC) during a meeting in Boston on February 25. The group has previously recorded its interest in government aid that helps families not now able to afford private education, provided that the aid does not limit the critical spectrum of schools.

In making its decision, the board noted that it speaks for itself and not for all independent schools, and that most of its debate about the issue focused on concern for public education. The board's specific action approves a bill that

• Disallows credit to families with children in schools that discriminate on the basis of race, color, or national or ethnic origin

• Limits the amount of credit per child in any taxable year

• Provides that tax relief is for parents, does not constitute federal assistance for schools, and does not subject schools to additional government regulation

• Emphasizes that tax credits are in no way intended to diminish support for public schools

• Ensures speedy judicial review to confirm the constitutionality of the bill.

The board also hoped that legislators would investigate the possibility of including a provision for differential eligibility based on family income.

"The board is concerned about the education of all American

children," NAIS president John Esty said after the meeting. "As private educators, board members have a basic belief that families should have options and choice in the matter of their children's education. Unfortunately, the financial aid funds of most independent schools aren't able to meet the needs of many low- and middle-income families."

"The board hopes that tax credits will help independent schools extend the diversity of both their student bodies and the educational opportunities they provide," he reported. "Moreover, members aren't certain that TTC, by itself, would undermine public education. Other undermining forces are much more serious." He noted that NAIS member schools currently educate less than 1 per cent of the nation's 50 million elementary and secondary students, and that most of these schools are fully enrolled.

During the debate many board members expressed reservations about TTC, and eight of the 22 finally voted against support for the bill. One dissenter feared "a backlash from teachers' unions, the

NEA, public school administrators, school boards, and state governments." A bill recently proposed in New Hampshire, for instance, would allow the state to levy taxes on independent schools.

Another felt that the board should offer to cooperate in solving the problems of public education. "If we vote to support TTC, we may create a barrier to cooperation," he said.

Proponents of the plan believed that TTC would broaden "family choice" in education, but some board members wondered if it would really bring improvements. "TTC would help schools where the tuition ranges from $400 to $800," one member pointed out. "But how many additional families will be able to choose independent schools if credit is limited to $250-$500 per child?" In 1980-81, the median tuition for NAIS day schools was $3,196, and $6,153 for boarding schools.

But 14 members—almost twice the number of those opposed—favored a resolution supporting TTC. "Arguments for supporting the bill outweigh the possible negative results of such support," one person commented. "The principle of family choice has always been important to the board, and support of this principle should influence action to provide assistance for both public and nonpublic schools."

"TTC has a lot of moral aspects," another supporter said. "Most important, it will help schools that have a hard time raising funds necessary to strengthen enrollment of minorities and lower-income families."

"TTC will be passed whether we want it or not," one member argued. "Should we be silent on

---

ISSN-0272-1392

KEEPING UP WITH

AMERICAN English Today™

Volume 2 No. 3
July 1981

The monthly newsletter for people who want to stay current with the modern language of the U.S.A.

Trademarks get lost in name of success

For every businessman dreaming of making a product such a success that it becomes "a household word," there must be ten lawyers with nightmares about fighting a hopeless battle against such a fate.

In the USA, the manufacturer of a product that is the first of its kind on the market is especially concerned about this dilemma. Ask the makers of Formica, Styrofoam, and Scotch Tape how hard it is to keep a balance between promoting public interest in their goods and protecting their proprietary rights to the brand names.

When you think of an Instamatic camera, are you aware that this is the brand made by Eastman-Kodak, or do you generalize the term to include all lightweight, fixed-focus cameras?

Do you use Xerox to describe all dry photocopying machines? Is the Coke you drink made by Coca-Cola, or do you refer to all cola drinks in this way?

Are all blue jeans Levi's? All petroleum jellies Vaseline? All decaffeinated coffees Sanka? All household

cleansers Ajax? All facial tissues Kleenex?

Despite vigorous efforts on the part of the companies to retain these brand identities, many Americans today do not make the connection between the manufacturers and their products, even though all of the above brand names are registered trademarks protected by the U.S. Patent Office.

Under US law, you may register as a trademark (TM) the symbol, name, title, or phrase that is associated with the identification of a product (or service).

A trademark is owned and used exclusively by a single company, to differentiate its product from those of competitors. Generally, a successful trademark is catchy, apt and easily recalled in connection with a given product.

There is no set pattern for coining words to be used as trademarks. You may combine words associated with the product, e.g., AstroTurf (from Astrodome + turf), Instamatic (instant + automatic), Exercycle (exercise + cycle), and Ultrasuede (ultra-, meaning beyond, + suede). Sometimes the coinage is part of a fad (Ice-O-Matic) or it may be a proper name (Jacuzzi, whirlpool baths).

In most cases, the trademark goes on forever. (Compare a "copyright" – for literary, artistic, and musical works – which eventually expires.)

Ironically, sometimes the more popular a trademark becomes, the more in jeopardy the company may be of losing exclusive rights to it because the word passes into the language as a common noun. That's what

Massage parlor messages
Would a massage parlor offer the "adult" activity you're looking for? Find out about adult DWs on page 3.

New meanings of natural parenting

After all the thousands of years of parents begetting children, you'd think that this natural process would be unchanging. Not so.

Who are the **natural parents** of a child, anyway? Once there would have been no doubt. Only the pair whose genes combined to form the offspring would have qualified as "natural parents."

Today, however, you may hear adoptive parents referred to as the natural parents, particularly when they have adopted and reared their child from infancy.

Childbirth itself is thought of in new terms, too. In modern natural childbirth, the mother is awake and has been trained to assist in the birth through special breathing and pushing techniques, such as those taught by the Lamaze method. Much more sophisticated and studied than primitive (more natural?) births, the new natural childbirth is contrasted to giving birth while partially or completely unconscious, i.e., anesthetized.

Fortunately, regardless of method, the outcome is almost always a natural child.

"Sharon didn't know about a couple of tricky practices in the printing trade. One is that printers own the negatives they make unless the customer specifies differently right at the beginning. The other is that printers only guarantee to come within ten percent of the number you order. Both practices are known as "customs in the trade" and don't even appear on most contracts. You just have to know about them.

"When I took over the editing job, I thought we had enough copies of page one stock to run three issues. When I got out the supply for that third issue, it was obvious we would have hardly enough to get started. Then I learned we didn't even own the negatives. We had to pay a rush fee to get that issue out in time. Then we had to pay to have the negatives made all over again when we changed printers."

Vol 11, No. 2   WHAT'S HAPPENING AROUND MISSION VIEJO COMPANY   FEBRUARY 1981

Planting at Casitas test site completed

Mission Viejo Company officials have announced the completion of initial planting of an innovative drought tolerant landscape material test site.

Located along Marguerite Parkway just south of Estanciero, the three-acre Casitas test site is designed to test a number of concepts associated with the company's drought tolerant planting program and seek feasible ways of reducing water usage in connection with landscape irrigation.

Randall Ismay, MVC's administrator of water resource management and supervisor of the program, said the Casitas test site was conceived to test new plant materials, irrigation and timing equipment plus erosion control methods. In addition, the site will hopefully refine other areas of existing drought tolerant program.

He explained the company has been successful with drought tolerant groundcovers, shrubs and trees planted in the community over the past two years, but is seeking to expand the number and variety of plant materials that would flourish in Mission Viejo's semi-arid climate.

"Part of the Casitas program is to test plants that have never been grown in California. Some have been imported from as far away as Australia. We want to see how these plants do in the community's environment," Ismay said.

Ismay hopes the Casitas test

PLANT PROGRESS — Randall Ismay, water management resource administrator, inspects growth of a drought tolerant plant at Casitas test site.

site will help determine which species grow best in various parts of Mission Viejo.

"Within the community are varying climatic and soil conditions. We want to establish a wider variety of plants that will be adaptable to most any condition within Mission Viejo."

(see Casitas, page 2)

Casitas...
(continued from page 1)

"For example, in the southern and western portions of the community, there is a stronger ocean influence. The areas tend to be cooler and more humid. This would affect the growth rate or even survival of some plants.

"Another variable is soil. Some plant materials will thrive in one type of soil, but if moved a short distance to a different soil they might not do as well. So, we're trying to develop a comprehensive program that will put the right tree, shrub or groundcover in the right micro-climate," said Ismay.

Along with Casitas' technical side, Ismay said the test site will show community residents what various drought tolerant plant materials look like.

The program's ultimate goal is to reduce the amount of water imported from far away places such as northern California and the Colorado River.

Gerry Ognibene, vice president of community service operations, said reducing the amount of water imported to southern California not only conserves water resources, but reduces the energy consumed in pumping the water great distances.

"We recognize that water, like soil, is a finite resource and our company has made a commitment to find ways of conserving both of these commodities," said Ognibene.

He said the company is convinced significant gains in resource conservation can be made through projects like the drought tolerant landscaping program.

"Another goal is to inform homeowners that drought tolerant plants aren't just for slopes

and other common areas in the community. Our preliminary studies indicate residents could cut their individual water bills by as much as 30 percent by installing and properly maintaining drought tolerant materials," Ognibene said.

Mehta finds Mission Viejo's "twin" in India

Vinnie Mehta literally has had the best of both worlds, east and west.

Most of the past year found Mehta working as manager of community facilities construction in Mission Viejo, California, the most successful planned community in the United States.

And for three weeks last month, Mehta and his wife, Nita, vacationed in Chandigarh, another highly acclaimed planned com-

Vinnie Mehta

munity in northern India, said to be far and away that nation's most beautiful city.

But it's not enough that Mehta works in one highly successful planned community and vacations in another, Chandigarh,

(see Mehta, page 3)

REPEAT WINNER — Steve Trammell (center), vice president of residential construction, accepts California Landscape Contractors Association award from Dennis Holder (left) and Roland Tittle of Habco Landscape and Irrigation of El Toro for work on newly installed medians on Marguerite Parkway south of Oso. The award was one of four major honors MVC received from the CLCA as a result of landscaping performed by Habco.

Mehta...
(continued from page 2)

160 miles north of New Delhi, and Mission Viejo have some striking similarities, ranging from cleanliness and beautiful landscaping (including gently rolling hills on the outskirts) to a pristine manmade lake designed for recreational use. Both are located on similar lines of latitude and have nearly indentical climates.

Mission Viejo and Chandigarh reclaim waste water for irrigation and utilize highly sophisticated sewage treatment systems. Both are primarily residential communities.

Another uncanny resemblance is signs around Chandigarh which proclaim it "City Beautiful," a slogan almost identical to "Beautiful Mission Viejo."

However, whereas Mission Viejo will ultimately have 90,000 residents occupying 30,000 dwelling units, Chandigarh's master plan calls for 350,000 residents upon buildout.

Chandigarh, which literally means home of the goddess of strength, is the brainchild of Le Corbusier, the French architectural master. The 15-square-mile city is divided into 47 self-supporting units known as sectors. Each sector is 800 by 1,200 meters and contains a small shopping center along with open space and residential housing.

Sectors are bordered by roads which run in a gridlike pattern connecting the entire city.

"Chandigarh is laid out like a human body," said Mehta. "The head is where governmental offices are located (Chandigarh is the joint capital of the states of Punjab and Haryana), the limbs contain the industrial and educational areas on opposite sides

and the torso has the central business district. The lungs are 'breathing' or open spaces."

Homes are individually designed and more spacious than those in the rest of India. A color scheme with rigid architectural requirements exists for all buildings.

Chandigarh has provided for all age brackets, with schools, health care facilities and shopping centers.

Unlike Mission Viejo and other American cities, Chandigarh places the greatest value on the pedestrain. "The whole city is geared toward him," Mehta said.

Due to considerably lower wages than Western workers, very few Indians can afford cars. Only about 10 percent of Chandigarh's residents drive, Mehta noted. The rest walk or ride bicycles and scooters. All of Chandigarh's populace works within the city limits.

"The design of the city is such

that someone can walk to the central business district in a relatively short period of time from any sector. Walkways bordered by plants and trees connect each sector," said Mehta.

Mehta, a native of India, has more than a passing interest in Chandigarh. He lived in the city for six years, five of those while attending the school of architecture, studying urban planning and architectural design.

The campus is considered to be one of the finest in Southeast Asia. The school's philosophy of instruction, by no coincidence, was established by Le Corbusier. Mehta designed some of Chandigarh's homes and did the conceptual plans for several private and municipal buildings.

Mehta says his sentiments toward Chandigarh are echoed throughout India. He exclaimed, "Once you've lived in Chandigarh, you don't feel like living any place

(see Chandigarh, page 4)

MAD HATTER — Gerry Ognibene, vice president of community services operations, looks in disbelief at oversized cowboy hat worn by Jack Haynes, general manager of CADA. The hat belongs to Tom Pekar, husband of Lynda Pekar, CADA, and is used as a prop in Tom's musical group.

Copyfitting

Throughout this book I have urged you to make some basic decisions, then stick with them. In particular, I've suggested you select type sizes for body copy and headlines and that you choose a regular format. Here's one place those decisions pay off. Fitting copy to available space calls for careful planning followed by simple arithmetic. The planning is most important, for without it the arithmetic is useless.

Copyfitting is based upon character count. Figure each letter, numeral, space and punctuation mark as one character. To fit a story, you need to know 1) how many characters it has, and 2) how many characters per line you get in your format with your type size.

There are two easy ways to count characters. First, you can start at the beginning of each story and count. This method is simple and accurate. It's also boring. As an alternative, you can type each story to an exact line length. Any length will do, so long as each line ends exactly right. Because all typed characters occupy equal space, you can now count lines and multiply by the number of units per line. Short lines at the ends of paragraphs still must be counted individually.

To make the line count approach most efficient, set your typewriter margins at the same character count as your typesetting. Each typewritten line will equal one typeset line. In this way you'll know almost to the last period how much space a story takes before it ever goes to the typesetter.

Once you have figured a character count per line and per column inch for your format, you'll find copyfitting happens as much by instinct as calculation. You will develop a sense of where in each issue a story will go and how much space it will take. From that point on.

1. Remember space for headlines. A major head might take out four lines of copy, a minor one two or three.

2. When working with word counts, figure six characters per word. That's five letters and one space. This average works for most subject matter. When counting words, be sure to include them all—even those of only one letter.

3. Most important, remember that fitting usually requires editing as well as counting. Your story may have to shrink or expand depending upon what else is going into the same issue.

```
     When typing material for this book, I figure fift

y five characters per line.  First lines of paragraphs

lose five characters for indentations.  I set my typew

riter margins at 55 and make all lines end there with

no hyphens.  Spaces between words and punctuation mark

s each count one character; spaces between sentences c

ount two characters, so are typed as in a normal manus

cript.

     When I'm done typing, I simply count lines - one

line of typing to equal one line of typesetting.  Beca

use I get six lines of typesetting per column inch, wi

th half a line lost for extra leading between paragrap

hs, I can look at my typing and know within a line how

many column inches it will occupy.
```

Headlines

Headlines are much easier to copyfit than text. With typewritten heads, all characters occupy equal space. One character count will tell you exact line length. Transfer letter and typeset heads are proportionally spaced, so require more careful figuring. The system is based upon counting letters and spaces according to whether they are wide, medium or narrow.

Wide: Lower case m and w; all caps except I; symbols such as $ and %; numerals.
Narrow: Lower case f, i, j, l, r, and t; captial I; all punctuation and spaces.
Medium: everything else.

To use this system, you must know your column width and headline point size. Using those facts, you can figure how many units you have for each line of bold type. Columns in this book, for example, are twenty picas wide. With 18 point heads, figure 51 units per line. Thus the title *Shaping and placing headlines* when expanded to 18 points should fit perfectly across one line.

Shaping and placing headlines

Writing good headlines to fit your format is the hard part. Placing them to do their job is easy. Simply follow these six basic rules.

1. Run heads flush left. Reading starts at the left and the eye comes back to the left. Be waiting there with your headline. Starting flush left also gives you a fixed beginning for copyfitting count.

2. Make headlines visually part of the story. Put them closer to copy below than copy above. Don't let headlines float alone.

3. For heads set above the column, try to have each line almost as wide as the column itself. White space after a short headline looks more like a hole you forgot to fill.

4. For two or three-line heads, ragged right is OK. Set them tight with no leading.

5. Don't run heads opposite each other. One large head across two or three columns is OK, but two heads must be visually separated.

6. Underlining is rarely necessary. When used, it runs under the descenders rather than breaking in mid-word.

---

7 December 1981

The Huenefeld Report

FOR MANAGERS AND PLANNERS IN MODEST SIZED BOOK PUBLISHING HOUSES

SELLING BOOKS TO CANADA THROUGH ITS MAJOR RETAIL CHAINS

A MAJOR PORTION OF CANADIAN BOOKSTORE SALES are acheived within the more-than-400 branch stores of the three major bookselling chains (suggesting no greater centralization, incidentally, than the U.S. with its two dominant super-chains). All three of these Canadian chains are headquartered in the Toronto area (two in the same suburb); you can direct-dial their area code 416 from the U.S. without going through an international exchange or operator. So we concluded that any small publisher from the U.S. or elsewhere hoping to make export sales of general interest books in Canada would do well to focus on these three chains as "the heart of the market." To help you do it right, we interviewed key executives in their three purchasing organizations, who were gracious about discussing how they think you can best go about selling them appropriate books from the U.S. or other countries. This issue summarizes their responses.

While we did not specifically concern ourselves with selling procedures of the numerous small Canadian publishers who are among our loyal readers, we point out to them that most of what is reported below is indeed equally applicable to them.

WE ARE INDEBTED to Ms. Helen Babiak, the mass market buyer for *Coles Book Stores Limited*, to D. W. Quick, vice president/ marketing for *W. H. Smith Canada, Ltd.*, and to Leonard Berger, vice president/purchasing for *Classic Bookshops, Ltd.*, for their time and the patience they extended in not only answering our direct questions about their own policies and procedures, but in bringing us up to date on recent trends in Canadian bookselling. While there were some modest differences in the policies, organization, and viewpoints of the three chains as these executives expressed them, by and large their assessment of your Canadian exporting opportunities (from other countries) and their recommendations as to effective sales approaches were remarkably consistent.

Just to get them in perspective, be aware that the 1981 *American Book Trade Directory* indicates that Coles operates 224 stores (including "the world's biggest bookstore," in Toronto), Classic operates 108, and W. H. Smith operates 72. The former two operate on both sides of the U.S./ Canadian border.

THE MOST OVERWHELMING IMPRESSION WE GOT from these interviews is that many small American publishers vastly overestimate the interest their books will attract on the other side of the border. Two out of our three respondents estimated that their chains' sales of books from all-but-the.giant U.S. publishers accounted for "less than 1%" of their annual sales volume. The third

THE HUENEFELD REPORT is prepared fortnightly by the specialized book-publishing management and planning consultants of The Huenefeld Company, Inc., P.O. Box U, Bedford, MA 01730, USA. One year (26 issues) $68.00, two years, $118.00; outside North America, add $22.00 per year if you wish Air Mail delivery.

© 1981 The Huenefeld Company, Inc.

Typed headlines set above white space clearly show beginning of each article.

Cars, Plane, Train

Travel Can Be Economical

Recent budget and energy constraints placed on agency travel reinforce the need for choosing efficient and economical means of getting state employes from place to place.

The state car is the most economical means of travel for single travelers going short to moderate distances. For longer distance trips, public transportation can be a better alternative. Special excursion rates offered by Air Oregon make it possible to make trips to Klamath Falls and Pendleton at a cost less than or equal to the cost of driving. AMTRAK, Greyhound, and other transit systems also make sense for the single traveler in terms of energy and out-of-pocket costs.

Often overlooked as means of employe travel are the aircraft owned by the Aeronautics Division and the Department of Forestry. These can be used as a tool to reduce travel time and cost in the following cases:

- Where groups of four or five persons from the same agency are traveling long distance. (Stops can be scheduled to meet passenger needs.)
- Where a single traveler can airpool with three or four persons from other agencies. By coordinating trips to a destination

with others, cost per person is minimized.

The following should be considered when choosing any means of travel.

1. Cost of the option; including travel, meals, and lodging.
2. Time involved with the mode of travel. A three-day car trip to Ontario can be made in one eight-hour day by air. Time spent in transit is often unproductive, and becomes an added "cost" of travel.
3. Travel conditions (driving fatigue, scheduling conflicts, commercial air stopovers, etc.).
4. Energy conservation. Public transportation offers an excellent way to reduce state fuel use. The agency plane is also fuel efficient if traveling at near capacity (per seat gas mileage on the Aeronautics aircraft is estimated at 48 to 49 miles per gallon).
5. State limits on mileage. Public transportation and agency aircraft use does not count in agency mileage totals.

For more information, contact Linda Getchell, Executive Department, 378-4366. For information on state aircraft availability and trip planning, contact the Aeronautics Division, 378-4800, or the Department of Forestry, 378-2373.

Resource Manual For Training Is Available

A comprehensive Training Resource Directory has been developed by the Executive Department Personnel Division. Intended for the use of training managers, trainers and line managers, the Directory is organized into two sections as follows:

Section I, Professional Development and Consultation Resources, contains two resource charts. The first chart includes Equipment, Space, Materials, and Programs organized by Name (contact person), Telephone, and Agency. The second chart includes 15 clusters of Personal and Professional Skills also organized by Name, Telephone, and Agency.

Section II, Management Development and Consultation Resources, includes the following lists of resources: (1) Film List organized by title, running time and summary of content; (2) Sound-Slide and Film Presentations by title; (3) Audio Tape List by title; (4) State Agency Meeting Room List organized by agency/facility, contact person, and room capacity; (5) Commercial Facilities Training Room List organized by name, location, room name, capacity, fee, and other explanatory information; and (6) Consultant Registry organized by name, address, telephone, and areas of expertise.

If you have questions or need additional information, call Jerry Jacobson, Executive Department, Personnel Division, 373-1848.

Merry Christmas

SMA Officers Are Elected

State Management Association officers elected at the annual conference in Eugene are: President, Sam Haley (Employment Division); Vice-President, Lydia Taylor (Intergovernmental Relations) and Secretary-Treasurer, Jim Tanner (Department of Human Resources).

These officers and the immediate past president, Chalmers Jones, together with the four members-at-large and the six regional

directors (to be appointed by the incoming president with the approval of the Board), will constitute the Board of Directors for the Association's 1980-81 year.

The resolution proposing amendments to the association's by-laws to regionalize the association and to allow for more representative and statewide membership involvement and participation was approved by the membership present at the meeting. For more information, phone Sandra Talbert at 362-1705.

One family of type faces yields heads and kicker in several sizes and styles.

Reducing and enlarging

As you do layout you will often discover some of your copy is too large or too small. Copyfitting problems usually involve photographs, but also may concern art, text and headlines. For example, you may have a calendar of events or membership form which you have typed but need to reduce.

Methods for changing size

With photographs, the darkroom is the best place to determine final size. Ideally, the original print will be made to fit your layout. Properly cropped and scaled, it will be ready for conversion to a halftone positive with no further work.

If your original print is not already the right size, it can be adjusted in the process of making its halftone positive. You must specify the new dimensions before the halftone is made. After it is made, your only remaining method of changing a photo size is to crop by cutting away portions of the halftone.

Note: Photoreduction methods used to change the size of a halftone positive will also change the size of its screening and therefore affect the quality of printing.

With line copy (text, graphics and headlines), you could change sizes photographically via either an ordinary negative, the PMT process, or through a photostat. While these procedures would each yield good camera-ready copy, all would require extra time and money. There is a faster and less expensive method.

Most quick printers and many institutions have photocopy machines with reducing capacity. Buttons on the machines change its lenses so allow you to reduce copy by predetermined amounts. For example, the button marked Reduce One might give you copy 75 percent of original size.

Choices about photocopy reduction sizes vary from one machine to another. Ask the machine operators to explain the capability of their equipment, then experiment with your copy. As you try this method, keep two points in mind.

► Each time you make a photocopy you lose some print quality. Even the best machines will not make blacks as dense and edges as clear as your original. The problem is especially acute with large black areas such as headline letters.

If you have solid blacks, look for a photocopy machine which shoots with strobe flash. Those machines usually give better copies than the continuous-light types. If that doesn't work, take your materials to a printer or blue-print shop for a PMT.

Lettering Lettering Lettering

▶ While any specific photocopy machine may offer only one or two reduction sizes, you may consider them as starting points rather than limitations. For example, you could think of your 75 percent reduction as a new original and make a reduction of the reduction.

If you use this method, the restoration becomes very important. Your second reduction has become a second generation photocopy, and even more quality is lost as compared to the original.

Here's a little block of ten pitch pica typing to show how typed copy looks when reduced. The first box on the right is shrunk 25%, the second 35%. The effect is to cram extra words onto the page, a job perhaps not necessary for one who properly edits in the first place.

Here's a little block of ten pitch pica typing to show how typed copy looks when reduced. The first box on the right is shrunk 25%, the second 35%. The effect is to cram extra words onto the page, a job perhaps not necessary for one who properly edits in the first place.

Here's a little block of ten pitch pica typing to show how typed copy looks when reduced. The first box on the right is shrunk 25%, the second 35%. The effect is to cram extra words onto the page, a job perhaps not necessary for one who properly edits in the first place.

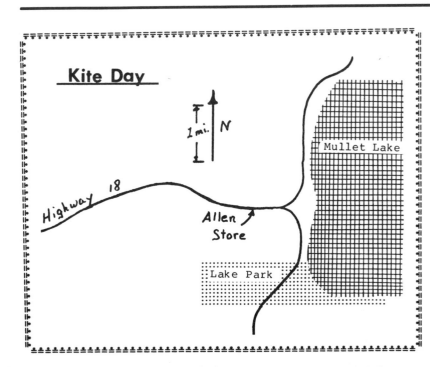

Kite Day

1 mi. N

Mullet Lake

Highway 18

Allen Store

Lake Park

"Learning how to make creative use of photocopy reductions helps me make maps like this one for our Kite Day. First I made the border and shading using equals and periods on the typewriter. The cross-hatching I did by hand. I reduced all three to 65% to make a basic stock. Then I did the title with transfer lettering and the other letters and lines by hand. Last I typed the lake names on peel-off labels and cut them down to size.

"With all my supplies done, I stuck everything in place with rubber cement. Then I reduced the whole thing to 75% to fit my layout.

"Here is the result."

How to scale copy

When you reduce or enlarge copy, you change all of its dimensions. Both height and width will become larger or smaller. Scaling copy is simply determining what the new height and width will be.

To scale copy, you must think of all items in your layout as rectangles. You know the height and width of the original. With that knowledge, you then have one of the two following questions:

1. My new size will be _____ inches high: how wide will it be?
   or
2. My new size will be _____ inches wide: how high will it be?

There are three easy methods to answer either question. All three are based on the fact that the vertical, horizontal and diagonal lines of rectangles change in proportion to each other as the size of the whole rectangle is changed.

> Newsletters are a highly individual form of communication. Most editors know many readers personally. Thus newsletter content and design can be planned with specific tastes in mind. In addition, editors can depend upon personal contacts for reactions to past issues and information for future ones.

Think of all items as rectangles.

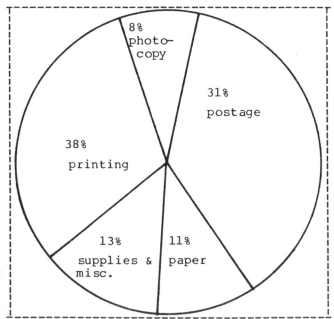

Diagonal line method

- If the piece of copy is not already in rectangular form, draw a rectangle which will enclose the item (as shown in the examples below).

- With a rectangle the size of your original copy, make a diagonal line from the bottom left corner through and beyond the right corner.

- Starting at the bottom left corner, measure off either the height or width of the new size you want.

- From the end point of your new vertical or base line, draw a line at right angles to your diagonal.

- Complete your new rectangle with another right angle line drawn either across or down from your diagonal. You now have the size of your reduced or enlarged copy.

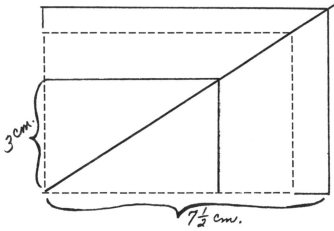

"I sweated over six issues of <u>Garden Leaves</u> before learning how to cut my layout to half an hour. My columns are all three inches, so I do a mock-up with nothing but a pencil and my 3 by 5 index card. I draw lines around three sides of the card, finish off the bottom line as far down as I know the print for a story will go, and there are blocks of copy to exact size."

Scaling wheel method

People in the print trade keep handy a device called a scaling wheel or proportional scale. They are inexpensive and easy to use. Most wheels come with instructions printed on the inner dial. You can buy a wheel at any store selling art supplies.

Solving ratio method

If you are handy with arithmetic, you can omit the task of actually drawing new rectangles. Simply set up a ratio equation with your three known dimensions and solve for the fourth. For example:

a. original size is eight by ten inches
b. new width wanted is four inches
c.

$$\frac{\text{original width}}{\text{original height}} = \frac{\text{new width}}{\text{new height}}$$

d.

$$\frac{8}{10} = \frac{4}{x} \qquad 8x = 40 \qquad x = 5$$

e. your new height is 5 inches

Let's do another example, this time with an enlargement and solving for width.

a. original size is two by five inches
b. new height wanted is five inches
c.

$$\frac{5}{2} = \frac{x}{5} \qquad 2x = 25 \qquad x = 12.5$$

d. your new width is 12.5 inches

Scaling with two unknowns

Here is a scaling technique for the mathematically minded.

What if you know neither height nor width of your new size? You can still scale from your original if you know the relationship between areas. Given your new area as a decimal of your original area, you can compute the new dimensions.

Recall that the vertical, horizontal and diagonal lines of a rectangle change proportionally as the shape is enlarged or reduced. Thus there must be a constant which expresses the proportion of change. That constant is the square root of the decimal comparing the new area to the old.

Consider a shape fifteen by ten inches. Its diagonal is eighteen inches. As your original, its area is 100 percent. Given a new area half (.5) of the original, what are the three linear measures? Simply multiply any original linear measure by the square root of .5 (.71) for the corresponding linear measures of your new rectangle.

As an added benefit, this process also works with a circle. Given new area as decimal of the original, its square root times the original diagonal will produce the new diagonal.

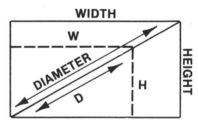

Area	=	100%
New Area$_1$	=	50% = .5
$\sqrt{.5}$	=	.71
New Width$_1$	=	.71 Width
New Height$_1$	=	.71 Height
New Diameter$_1$	=	.71 Diameter

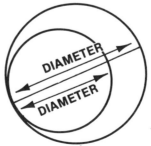

Area	=	100%
New Area$_1$	=	75% = .75
$\sqrt{.75}$	=	.87
New Diameter$_1$	=	.87 Diameter

How to build a light table

A light table is nothing but a box having one translucent surface and a source of light inside. The word "table" is actually a misnomer. The box is usually small enough to place on a desk or table while in use, then store easily until needed again.

A good light table can be made in a home shop within a few hours. The job is an ideal way for a handyman or woman in your organization to contribute to the newsletter.

The sketch below is only to illustrate the components and concept of a light table, not to specify dimensions and materials. Most materials will already be on hand in the average shop. Probably the only purchases necessary will be fluorescent tubes and sockets and a piece of acetate plastic.

Guidelines:

► The working surface should be roughly double the height and triple the width of your page size. For standard 8½ by 11 sheets, a table about 20 by 30 inches would do fine.

► Whether you want the surface level or slanted depends on your working style. If you stand to do pasteup, a level surface will do. If you sit, a surface slanted at about 30 degrees would be handy.

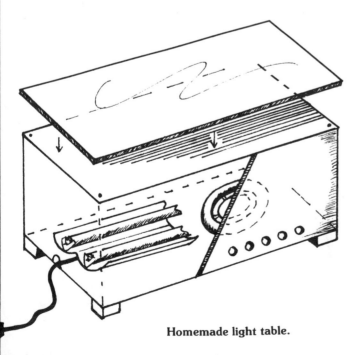

Homemade light table.

► You will need two fluorescent tubes—either straight ones in bayonet sockets or round ones which fit ordinary threaded sockets.

► The distance of the tubes from the plastic surface will depend on wattage of the tubes and thickness of the acetate. You will need to experiment. Ten inches is a good starting point to get a uniformly lit surface.

► The acetate should be covered by a piece of glass so the plastic is never scratched. Fasten the glass to the edge of the table using corner molding or aluminum angle strips. Whatever you use, be sure your edges are straight so your t-square will yield uniformly parallel lines.

Proofreading

It is said in courtroom circles that a lawyer who defend herself has a fool for clients. The saying applies equally well to writers and editors who do there own proofreading. Once you have created the material, you are too familiar with it to do a careful job? Give these guidelines to some oneelse who will proof your work.

Did you spot all five mistakes in that first paragraph? Probably not. You were reading for content, so your mind made some errors seem correct or overlooked them entirely. Proofreading is very difficult!

● Read material one element at a time. Do all the body copy, then all the headlines, then all the extra material such as page numbers.

● Check for spelling. And just because headlines are big, don't assume they are spelled correctly.

● Check for consistency. Agree on rules about capitalization, grammar and punctuation, then stick with them throughout.

● After everything else is done, read for content. Look especially for ideas which seem left out, signaling a sentence or paragraph overlooked.

You probably read the Doonesbury cartoon first, but are you certain you saw every typo on the page? There is one very easy to miss.

Proofread Everyting!

DOONESBURY   by Garry Trudeau

Pasteup

When your layout is done, you are ready for pasteup: creation of camera-ready copy by precise placement of each element on each page, then using adhesive to keep everything in place.

In suggesting you print exclusively from pasteups, I am urging you to make camera-ready copy regardless of your printing process. You need camera-ready copy for either offset or photocopy, and you should use it for a mimeograph as well. Thus, pasteup techniques apply to any production process you are likely to use.

Editors often feel pasteup should be left to the printer. Doing it themselves seems too complicated. While it is true pasteup requires some unfamiliar materials and techniques, it is actually one of the easiest parts of newsletter production.

Pasteup is no more complicated than cooking, sewing or carpentry. Your layout is a guide like a recipe, pattern or drawing; your tools as simple and inexpensive as a rolling pin, hem marker or level; your techniques as easy as simmering, tacking or mitering.

There are three reasons why you should do your own pasteup.

- ▶ **You control the finished product.** Because you can see how each printed page will look, you are the final judge when it comes to positioning copy, cutting or jumping stories, and changing the size of art or photographs. There is no room for misunderstanding or printer error.
- ▶ **You give the printer only finished pages.** Everything is pasted down; nothing is loose and easy to misplace.
- ▶ **You cut your costs.** Pasteup takes time. If your printer does it for you, it can cost as much as the print run itself.

Your goal in pasteup is to make each page look as close as possible to printing. Everything you want printed must be perfectly placed and securely stuck down. Nothing—not one line or speck—should be on the sheet which you do not want in the final printed product. When that job is done, your material is called camera-ready. The pasted-up sheets, sometimes called mechanicals, go directly in front of a printer's camera as the first step in making plates for presses.

Start with your pasteup boards, format specifications and photocopies of all elements. Trim the photocopies, put them in place and lightly tape or glue them down. Does everything fit and look the way you want? If so, use these sheets as a mockup. Trim each element as you did its photocopy, position it carefully using straightedge and triangle, then stick it down.

After you have created mechanicals, make photocopies. On the mechanical itself you tend to see the lines around each piece pasted down. Most of those lines will disappear in the photocopy process, thereby giving you a better idea of how the printed product will look. Equally important, the photocopies serve as your proofs to the printer. Attach a set to your mechanicals and keep a set for yourself. That way there is no argument about how things were intended to look after printing.

Tools and supplies

Necessary

- At least one photocopy of each element: text, art, photographs, headlines, forms and everything else going into the issue. The photocopies are to make a mockup or dummy: the final map showing how the issue will look. The dummy is your guideline and, equally important, your best way to show the printer exactly what you want.

- Adhesive. Rubber cement when used sparingly works well because it does not bond permanently or wrinkle the page. Glue sticks work OK on glossy surfaces for small pieces. Artists spray does fine and is very convenient, but can be messy. Never use mucilage, white paste or tape.

- Supply of borders, screens, letters and other transfer materials you have chosen. Be sure you have everything you need before starting. There's nothing more frustrating than using a pen to finish a line because you ran out of six point border tape.

- Pasteup boards. The "board" is simply a piece of sturdy paper to be the surface on which elements are stuck down. It helps to have a smooth surface to take a clean pen line and to wipe off dirt.

  There's no such thing as the perfect pasteup board, but there are several ways to approach getting the right one for your work. One is to buy a commercial blue-line board such as those shown on page 59. These are usually on stock too thick to use at a light table, but plenty heavy to protect your pasteup at the printer's. They are printed in useful grids with light blue ink which will not reproduce in offset printing (but may reproduce on a photocopy machine).

  Ordinary graph paper is another approach to blue-line boards. You can paste up directly on graph paper and can see through it when taped to a light table. Because it's fairly lightweight stock, you might want to glue it to a heavier board when you have finished pasting

  Still another approach to blue-line boards is to make your own. Get a supply of index sheets or 10 point bookcover paper and draw your own format lines in non-repro blue. You'll save lots of money at the cost of ten minutes work for each issue.

Blue-line boards are handy, but not imperative. You can pasteup just fine on ordinary white paper, especially if it's aligned on a light table over a thin sheet showing your format. And if your format includes borders or rules, you can paste up on preprinted white sheets. Create a master sheet showing only the lines, then make a supply either by printing or high quality photocopy. Use them as your pasteup boards.

- Two straight edges. A plastic see-through ruler or triangle work best for positioning copy, but you also need a metal edge for cutting with your art knife.

- A right triangle.

- Templates, pens and other equipment for drawing lines, arrows and curves.

- An edge on your working surface which you can be certain is perfectly aligned with your copy. Ideally this edge is made slightly raised so a T square can be moved up and down the working surface. A line drawn along the T square goes at a 90 degree angle to your pasteup. The triangle and T square also form a perfect right angle.

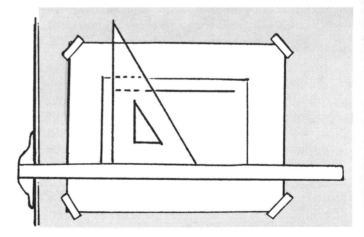

- White typing correction fluid or tempura paint to eliminate small mistakes and shadow lines.
- A knife with a very sharp tip to position and pick up copy, trim screens and border tape.
- A non-reproduction blue pencil or pen for drawing lines and writing instructions directly on pasteup sheets.
- Good pair of scissors.
- A clean, uncluttered surface. (Well, at least uncluttered when you start.)

- Drafting tape to hold down pasteup boards. Masking tape will do.
- A burnishing tool to rub down transfer lettering and art. The flexible plastic kind is OK; the rubber roller kind is better.

Convenient

- Light table. When your working surface is lit from underneath, the light shines through your blueline sheets and allows copy to be easily aligned.

   A light table works on the same principle as a table for viewing slides or scoring stencils. It is nothing but fluorescent tubes placed eight or ten inches away from an acetate surface. The tubes give a soft light evenly diffused by the plastic.
- Hand waxer. Printer's wax is a much better adhesive than rubber cement. Wax goes on quickly and evenly: no lumps or bubbles. Wax is clean: no smudges or sticky spots at the edges of copy. Wax allows you easily to pick up and reposition copy.

   A hand waxer costs about the same as six reams of paper or a bulk rate postage permit. Available from most art supply stores, it is an item which will make your job easier, more fun and more professional.
- Acrylic spray. Once you have pasted up your newsletter, there is always a chance of getting copy dirty. Final copy sometimes acts as a magnet for fingerprints and smudges. Spray your finished pasteup with dull or mat (not glossy) acrylic to insure a surface easy to wipe clean.

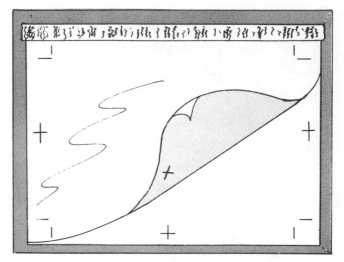

Overlays should have register marks which perfectly align with identical marks on the pasteup board beneath. Lines at corners are crop marks showing trim size.

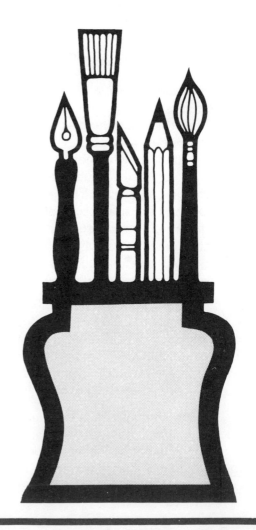

Pasteup check list

"I can laugh now, but it sure wasn't funny at the time. We were doing a six page issue instead of our usual four—two more pages to cover the convention. I got everything done just right, then hurried over to the printer.

"When I picked up my 400 copies, there were the usual four pages. The extra two were still in pasteup—taped neatly to the light table in my basement. I had them printed, then pulled my first all-nighter since college to get them folded and stapled in with the rest. The last straw was having to mail first class to be sure everything arrived on time."

✔ Does each page have everything: text, headlines, graphics, photographs? How about borders, gutter lines or page numbers?
✔ Is each page clean—completely free from finger prints, smudges, bits of glue or wax, or stray lines?
✔ Are there any edges which might yield shadow lines?
✔ Are there corner marks to show exactly how you want printed pages trimmed?
✔ Does each page have your name and the job name somewhere outside the area to be printed?
✔ Do you have everything the printer needs—every page plus any art or photographs to be added at the print shop?
✔ Have you attached a copy of your specifications sheet or other page with review of information about stock, number of copies, deadlines and other instructions?

Production

When it is time actually to print a newsletter, most editors choose from among three processes: mimeograph, photocopy and offset. Often the choice has already been made. Equipment purchases, printing contracts or simply habits and special opportunities may lead to continuing old arrangements. Nevertheless, the twin goals of high quality and low cost may mean previous decisions should be reviewed. One of the processes you are not now using might serve you better than your current production method.

Criteria

There are four criteria to keep in mind when selecting a print process. Which criteria you find most important depend on your preferences and circumstances. For any publication, all the processes have both plus and minus aspects. The choice is highly individual.

Cost

Each process involves direct costs for paper, printing and perhaps services such as collating, stapling and folding. Each also involves indirect costs which may equal or even exceed direct ones. Indirect costs include such things as postage (affected by the weight of paper), mileage (for delivery or pickup of the job), staff time, and (if you own equipment) machine maintenance and depreciation.

Cost is heavily influenced by what kind of equipment, supplies and services your group has available. For example, you may already own a mimeograph or photocopy machine or have access to one you can "borrow." You may be able to get free mimeo paper, but not free offset paper. Your free mimeo paper may be balanced by the fact that you can get free offset if you supply paper.

Time

Your time is your newsletter's most valuable resource. Each print process requires different amounts of time, again depending on your circumstances. If there is a low cost print shop around the corner, money spent there may be worth time cut from driving across town and waiting to use a free photocopy machine. If it takes all night to get the old mimeo machine working right, the increase in both efficiency and quality from commercial offset may be worth the money it costs.

A print process usually involves a time lag as well as time investment from you. Only you can judge what your turn-around time must be: how quickly you must get from camera-ready copy to printed product. For example, if you have a mimeo machine but must go elsewhere to cut electronic stencils, the travel and waiting time might add a day to your production schedule. Perhaps in the same day you could have the whole job done offset.

Quality

There are three stages of making your newsletter in which you have control over quality: developing content, doing layout and pasteup, and printing. How well you handle each stage depends partly on time and money and partly on the image you want. A mimeograph newsletter, for example, no matter how well done, looks homemade. An offset product, even if done only moderately well, seems professional. The mimeo says, "We do it ourselves," the offset, "We can afford to pay for printing." Photocopied newsletters usually fall somewhere in between.

Flexibility

How often will you want to make last minute changes? Do you want some art or copy in color? If you do your own work at a mimeo or photocopy machine, you keep "in house" control over the entire production process. With mimeo you can also do your own color work. If you must take copy elsewhere to leave for a day or two, it will be cumbersome and costly to make a change.

Mimeograph

Perhaps you share the common stereotype of mimeograph as a slow, messy operation yielding inferior copies. Thinking about mimeo may lead to visions of torn stencils, agonizing proofreading, acrid correction fluid and smudged ink.

These visions need not be true. For starters, most mimeo companies and equipment suppliers can now make low cost electronic stencils for your machine. You simply create camera-ready copy as you would for photocopy or offset. The stencil cutter (scanner) translates your copy into a stencil ready to print. Electronic stencil cutting also means you can easily do headlines, line art and even photographs by mimeograph—all without ever rolling a stencil into your typewriter.

Newer mimeo machines also offer flexibility with colors previously available only at high cost through offset. Relatively easy changes of inks, rollers and pads mean you can do nameplates and art in eyecatching displays. Using the color options of mimeo requires accurate registration: perfect alignment of sheets as they go through the machine a second or third time. It does take some practice to get the technique, but it may well be worth your time.

Mimeo paper is highly porous so it will absorb ink quickly. Thus colors tend toward pastel tones rather than the vivid tones of offset. Deep ink absorption also means printing on both sides of a sheet can result in a problem of see-through. Slightly heavier paper is one solution. Twenty pound paper is most common, but twenty-four pound will give better results. Color stock offers another solution, although it should be selected very carefully. It is easy to choose colored paper too dark to provide good contrast between print and paper. Colored paper may also look gimmicky.

The mimeograph process offers two features which might cut your costs. First, mimeo machines are much less complicated than equipment for either photocopy or offset. As a result, they cost less to buy, lease and maintain. Second, mimeographs produce less expensive copies than offset and far less expensive copies than photocopy.

From the standpoint of cost, mimeo is especially attractive when compared to photocopy. There are three reasons:

- mimeo paper is usually cheaper than photocopy paper.
- the average mimeo machine makes considerably more copies per minute than the average photocopy machine.
- photocopy charges per page are about the same for the 10th, 100th or 1000th page, while mimeo costs per page decrease sharply as the run becomes longer.

Manufacturers of mimeo equipment and their sale representatives are very interested in staying competitive with photocopy and offset. Turn that interest to your advantage by asking a person representing your brand of machine to teach you how to get the most of it. A short course in cleaning, new inks and papers, and electronic stenciling may do wonders for the quality of your newsletter.

Photocopy

If you have access to free or greatly reduced photocopying, you should consider using that process. Usually you will get satisfactory quality at modest cost in time and money.

Early photocopy machines were not well suited to newsletter production. They often gave rather light copy, especially with blocks of black such as headline letters. Furthermore, they were slow, printed on only one side of the sheet, and required special and usually expensive paper.

Most newer machines have overcome these problems. They can yield crisp copy fairly quickly and printed on both sides of fairly inexpensive stock. Both quality control and time efficiency are high because the editor is usually running the machine personally. While even newer machines may yield shadow lines from pasteups, their overall quality can be quite close to that available from offset.

Photocopy machines offer two features which make them attractive. From the standpoint of quality, they can produce blacks on paper which has been previously run offset for color. Thus your nameplate or logo could be done in color offset to make a large stock on which page one of each issue would be completed photocopy. From the standpoint of cost, many photocopy machines can reduce. Thus, for example, you could type your copy with a pica typewriter edge to edge on 8½ by 11 sheets, then reduce each sheet to 75 percent. The result would be type size and margins similar to elite typing, a result giving about 20 percent more copy per page than pica.

Some photocopy machines have features which should lead you to caution. Fine tuning is one. Like cars, photocopiers need maintenance to give good results. Like some cars, some copiers need constant attention. Also watch for the occasional copy machine which runs hot on the glass. Newly printed logos or letterheads may smear.

There is a good chance you can get free or very low cost photocopy service. Most large institutions, agencies and businesses have sophisticated equipment often inactive during noon hours, evenings or weekends. Access to one of those machines is a good form of donated support for your organization. The pricing structure of photocopy equipment is so complicated that people who control machines think they can let you do your newsletter virtually for free. Even if they know it's not free, letting you produce a few hundred newsletters may be an easier way for them to contribute to your organization than writing you a check.

Even if you must pay by the copy for photocopy, don't rule it out. Prices from one quick print shop to the next vary tremendously depending on type of equipment and number of copies. Once you know the size, length and number of your issue, it is well worth an hour on the phone to compare costs. You might be pleasantly surprised at how inexpensive it can be.

> *"Every time I throw away some newsletter just after opening it, I ask myself why I didn't read it. My answer always helps me do a better job with Signposts. I don't want our newsletter to be just another piece of junk mail."*

Offset

Regardless of how hard you try with mimeo or photocopy, you will not get the quality available through offset printing. Offset simply yields sharper letters in higher contrast than either of the other methods. Offset also gives better registration and page alignment and can produce fine color work.

While offset offers top quality, it usually costs more than mimeograph and takes longer than photocopy. Few editors have offset presses available or would know how to run them if they did. Thus, copy goes into a shop and comes out a day or two later, taking control from your hands.

Quick print vs. commercial

Most so-called quick print shops and in-house printing departments use offset. So do most commercial printers. What's the difference and which should you use?

Quick or instant printers and in-house shops have roughly comparable capabilities. Both typically use paper masters to give good quality for short runs: three or four thousand. These shops are geared for low volume, fast turnaround using standard papers, folds and drills. Photo halftones are acceptable with 85 or 100 line screened PMTs.

Commercial printers use metal plates (masters) for good quality over long runs. These shops are geared for medium to high volume, week or two week turnarounds, and use a variety of papers and folds. Photo halftones are good to superior, using 120 or 133 line screened negatives.

Press size is an important difference between quick and commercial printers. Instant presses use 8½ by 11 sheets and sometimes 11 by 17. Commercial presses use 11 by 17 as the smallest and more commonly multiples such as 17 by 22 or 23 by 35. This is important because time on the press forms a large part of the cost of printing. Large presses cost more per hour to run than small ones, but can do your newsletter in far less time.

Press quality is also important. Instant presses are fine for most newsletters, but are not suited to tight registrations, precise page alignments and fine screens. If you want this superior work, look for a commercial printer.

How do you know which printers are which grade? Obviously the differences are not always clear and depend on an individual shop's equipment and—equally important—attitude toward quality

Coast to Coast Books

2934 Northeast Sixteenth Avenue
Portland, OR 97212

Request for printing costs

Name of newsletter _____

Name, address and _____

  phone of editor _____

Quote needed by (date) _____

Specifications

- Copy camera ready to printer specifications

- Paper stock _____.lb or equivalent

- Trim size ___ by ___ inches and printed both sides

- Ink color _____ first side and _____ second side

- # pages per issue _____   - # copies per issue _____

- Other (halftones, screens, binding, drilling, folding):

Cost per issue: you supply paper $_____

                        we supply paper _____

At ____ issues per year,
cost per year: you supply paper _____

                    we supply paper _____

Payment terms _____

Printer name, address and phone _____

_____

Quote given by _____
                           signature

work. As a general rule, however, the chains and national name printers take the instant approach, while the local and usually larger shops take the commercial approach.

Whichever type of printer you choose, always, ALWAYS, make a precise mock-up showing **exactly** how you want pagination, folding, stapling, drilling and anything else you can think of. Write screen sizes, colors and other instructions directly on the mock-up in a very bold hand. Give the mock-up to the printer along with your camera-ready copy. That way both sides of the counter know who is responsible if you end up unhappy with the job.

Costs

Printing is a labor intensive business, so cost estimates vary greatly from one shop to the next. Fifty percent variations are common; one hundred percent occasional.

For any print job costing more than a figure you consider modest, get quotations. Use the form on page 109 or make your own similar to it. And note this form doesn't yield the full cost of your newsletter but only the cost of printing. To compute the full cost, use the form on page 117.

The cost analysis forms I urge you to use point in the direction of long-term relationships with printers. Take plenty of time to find a shop whose prices, quality and reliability you like, then stick with them on at least a yearly basis. Once the printer sees you as a regular customer, you'll start getting tips to save time and money and turn out better work. Printers thrive on repeat business, so the initial price list—or quotation form—isn't necessarily the entire answer to who does good work at reasonable cost.

Many print shops belong to the National Association of Printers and Lithographers. The Association issues a list of trade customs covering matters such as printer and customer liability, proofing systems and acceptances, production schedules and payment terms. Not all of these customs are relevant to newsletter work and not all printers go by these rules. Ask your printer for the list of trade customs used at that shop, read it, and be sure you understand any items you think apply to your newsletter.

Papers

Paper costs typically represent somewhere between thirty and fifty percent of a print job. To save money and get good quality, it pays to know about paper and how it fits in with other aspects of production.

Paper has eight characteristics which affect costs and quality.

Size. Most newsletters are 8½ by 11. That's the finished size, known to printers as the trim size. Your printer may put 8½ by 11 sheets on the press, but may also run larger sheets. An 11 by 17 sheet printed both sides folds into a four page newsletter. Two 11 by 17 sheets or one 17 by 22 would produce an eight page issue.

Most parent sheets are multiples of 8½ by 11, thus give greatest cost efficiency when trimmed to standard sizes after printing. Four 8½ by 11 pages fit on a 17 by 22 sheet and eight on a 23 by 35. That's called printing four up or eight up and is why longer newsletters (over four pages) should be in multiples of four.

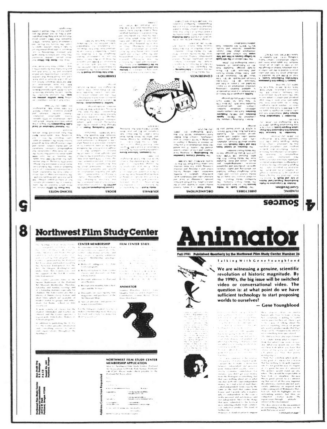

Four-up printing on a 17 by 22 sheet will fold and trim to an eight page, 8½ by 11 newsletter.

Weight. Basis weights are figured on the poundage of large quantities of large sheets. The formulas date from centuries-old ways of making paper. Most modern printers don't understand them and you don't need to try.

Spend a few minutes in a print shop or stationery store comparing papers of different weights. You'll soon get a sense of how one compares to another. And if you mail your newsletter, you are interested in ounces, not pounds. Weigh two or three sheets to be sure their combined weight, when in the form of your newsletter, does not take you over your postage budget.

Grade. You'll hear printers refer to book, text, cover, index, bond and perhaps other names. Ask for samples. All you really need to specify is stock suitable for your newsletter process: mimeo, photocopy or offset.

Bulk. Papers with the same basis weights can still have different bulks. Mimeo paper, for example, is bulkier—thicker—than offset. Bulky paper might give your newsletter a more substantial feel than lighter stock.

Opacity. Paper is opaque when print on one side does not show through to the other. Heavy papers are generally more opaque than light ones; color more opaque than white. A bulky paper, although thick, may cost some opacity because it's also porous; ink soaks through easily.

Opacity is a matter of taste. If you run photos or heavy lines on both sides of a sheet, how much show-through is acceptable? Instead of paying for very opaque paper, can you design your newsletter so heavy inking doesn't back up? If large solids must back up, how about screening them to lighten ink coverage?

Finish. Opacity can be improved by coating papers so they absorb ink more slowly. Coated papers also yield brighter colors and better halftones than uncoated. The coating, of course, costs more because of the extra steps in manufacturing and the reduced press speed at which they are sometimes run. Instant printers especially have trouble with coated papers unless they have a powder spray attachment.

Finish also refers to smoothness. Just as with photographs, you can get papers that are glossy, silky or textured. The finishes have industry names such as wove, laid and vellum. As with basis weights, the best way to learn is to compare various sheets.

Color. Although some editors use colored stock, it's best to stick with some variant of white. Pure white, however, isn't necessarily best. An off-white tone such as ivory, natural or sand is more readable and may seem richer. On the other hand, off-whites make photos less contrasty.

Grain. Paper has grain much like the wood from which it is made. If fibers run up and down, it's called grain long; across the sheets, grain short. Grain affects how easily and neatly paper folds, especially with heavy stocks. Most newsletters have one or two folds, so should be properly aligned on the parent sheets.

Buying paper

Printers buy paper from wholesalers, distributors and similar suppliers. Because they buy at wholesale in large lots, they get prices quite a bit lower than what you see on the shelves of a stationery store. Most printers mark up paper fifteen or twenty percent—a perfectly legitimate practice as part of running their business.

You might cut costs by buying paper separately and supplying your printer. Not all printers welcome that approach, for it cuts their profits. It can also lead to problems: you have to know exactly what you are doing to be sure the paper you buy will work on the particular presses at your printer. You also must know details such as that printers routinely figure ten percent paper waste per job or that certain printers may not have equipment to trim large parent sheets. Finally, there is no guarantee you'll get better prices, even considering printer mark-up. Quantity buying power and professional contacts count for a lot.

Shopping for paper yourself, however, may lead to significant savings. If you buy parent sheets at wholesale in quantities to last a year or more, you might cut your paper costs by forty or fifty percent. You'll do even better if you keep your paper options open and look for bargains. Paper distributors, like every business, have sales and special offers. Look up addresses under "paper distributors" in your local classified directory. If you get lucky, you might cut your paper costs by as much as eighty percent.

Paper in this book

This book is printed on two kinds of paper to produce good quality and give readers examples. This page and most others are 60 lb. natural vellum: 60 lb. is the basis weight; natural is the color; vellum is the finish.

Pages 59 thru 74 are printed on 70 lb. white matte. Coated paper is slightly less bulky than uncoated, so I specified one weight unit increase for consistent feel. Matte coat means the sheet has one coating, something like the primer coat on wood before painting. The white, coated pages show colors better for the section on nameplates. The section on photographs was planned for printing partly on matte and partly on uncoated so you could compare halftones on each stock.

Editors who want good photo reproduction and/or strong colors use coated stock. The paper costs more, but reflects the overall effort to put out a quality newsletter. Quality, however, does not require expensive paper. It stems also from thoughtful writing, creative design and careful printing.

Cost cutting tips

1. Decide whether your newsletter is really necessary. If not, stop publishing; cut costs by 100%.
2. Consider publishing less often or having fewer pages or printing fewer copies.
3. Use standard paper sizes, colors and weights.
4. Shop and compare prices for major services such as design, typesetting, paper and printing. Look for bargains, especially in paper.
5. Work from quotes on your specifications for all jobs costing more than what you consider a modest sum.
6. Plan, plan, then plan some more. Anticipate your needs, make a schedule, and stick to it.
7. Do your own paste up.
8. Keep up with local technology: learn about such things as computer graphics, optical character readers, word processors and web presses.
9. Pool buying supplies; coordinate buying services.
10. Buy paper in quantity; contract services for long periods.
11. Use lighter weight paper.
12. Use house sheets or other alternate papers.
13. Do your own photography and darkroom work.
14. Learn to size and print clip art and display type in your darkroom. Make your own PMTs.
15. Think gang. Cluster orders for photostats, PMTs, halftones and especially print runs.
16. Learn to overlap screens; cut four-color printing to two.
17. Avoid bleeds, tight registrations and other tricky printing. Build quality into design and content in preference to printing.
18. Always have a proof copy: photocopy duplicate of dummy you gave printer or printer's blue line. Don't waste time arguing when the proof would settle the issue.
19. Stick to your plan: every change costs money.
20. Don't accept or pay for bad work.
21. Edit! Cut words, therefore costs for typesetting, paper, printing, postage.
22. Pay bills on time: keep your credit good. Printers quotes are estimates: don't encourage them to build in a penalty for expected late payment.
23. Be dependable. Deliver work on time.
24. Enforce deadlines. Delays cost money.
25. Learn about printers and suppliers in your area. Talk shop with other editors. Get on mailing lists.
26. Look for freebies. Watch for paper or supplies from someone going out of business, changing print processes or trimming off sizes you can use.
27. Ask printers to quote cost of paper separately, then compare your direct cost if you supply.
28. If you go over four pages, keep page counts in multiples of four.
29. Use a typesetting service whose machines have good memories: make small changes in frequently used material rather than starting from scratch each time.
30. Save pasteup time by having typesetting machines do rules and boxes also.

Addressing

Many newsletters are handed out door to door or at meetings. Others are simply left at convenient places to be picked up by interested persons. Most, however, are mailed.

Why mail? Newsletters left to be picked up on impulse or distributed along with other material seldom get careful attention. They seem impersonal, therefore are easy to ignore. The mails, on the other hand, bring the most personal—even intimate—pieces of written communication. Mail seems important so your newsletter is off to a good start before it is even opened.

Mailing a newsletter requires an accurate up-to-date system of maintaining addresses. Ideally, your membership director or secretary will have such a system already developed. An editor should not have to worry about an address file but rather be supplied the information when it comes time to mail.

The least expensive way to address newsletters is to write each address by hand. Hand work also takes the most time and is most subject to error. Address labels offer a far better alternative at only a slight cost. Type sheets of peel off labels (usually 33 labels to a sheet). If an individual address becomes unusable, simply remove the label from the sheet and replace it with one carrying the proper information. When it is time to address newsletters, the master sheets are photocopied on a machine loaded with blank label sheets. The copies can be peeled off and one placed on each newsletter.

Peel off label masters are handy and inexpensive, but not very flexible. As names and addresses change, the labels go out of alphabetical order or zip code order. If that situation proves a problem, you have four options. You could return to hand addressing based on some form of file card system. You could buy supplies and equipment for one of the commercial addressing systems based on press cards or plastic plates. You could contract with a direct-mail or business-services company.

The first choice (hand addressing) is attractive because of its simplicity and flexibility. The second choice (your own specialized equipment) requires a modest investment of time and money, but is well suited to large mailings. It also allows you to maintain full control over mailing. The third choice (commercial service) is most expensive and means your job is scheduled along with dozens of others. It also means, however, that the work is done accurately at high speed, considerations especially important if you mail thousands of copies.

I mentioned four options, but have described only three. The fourth is based upon rapidly growing access to micro computers. List maintenance is exactly the kind of job these machines do best. Individual addresses can be numerically coded, then electronically stored via standard keyboard entry. With proper spacing, addresses are printed out directly on peel-off mailing labels. For lists having thousands of names, addresses are printed four-up on sprocket-feed paper designed for special machinery at direct-mail companies. And because the list is computerized, you can print only selected names. For example, you could mail only to people in certain ZIP codes or categories of membership rather than to the whole list each time.

You need a printer to make micro-computer addressing work. It doesn't have to be letter- quality or handle an 8 1/2 by 11 sheet: peel-off labels are available on one-up rolls. If the system to which you have access doesn't include a printer, perhaps you could use one off-line. If you have disk storage, take your disk to a compatible system with a printer. If not, try a telephone-line read-out into a memory to drive a printer. Make the new technology work for your newsletter.

"What do you do about well-meaning people who ask for your mailing list? Most are members of our own organization. One man wants to advertise his maps. Another wants contributions towards an entry in some race. Then there are environmental groups who think we'll all help lobby the water flow issue.

"I had so many problems I finally got really harsh. I went to the board and laid out the facts. We decided to keep the address list strictly under wraps. Not even someone on the board has access without approval from the others."

Mailing your newsletter

Mary Anderson 429 First Street Anytown, ST 40933	Alan Hamm, Treasurer State Tax Group 42 Anthony Road Anytown, ST 40948
Irwin and Sally Baker 97 Second Street Anytown, ST 40934	Dean Riley, Director Riley Business Forms 9 Union Avenue Anytown, 40950
Doug Belcher 530 Third Street Anytown, ST 40935	Matson and Matson 67372 Eighth Street Anytown, ST 40951
Glenn Chandler 2354 Fourth Street Anytown, ST 40936	Sibling Rivalry, Esq. Family Counseling Ctr 4950 Glower Bldg Anytown, ST 40952
Sarah and Peter Dolan 4956 Fifth Street Anytown, ST 40937	Hon. Kathleen Ryan 21 Senate Office Bldg Capitol, ST 40940
Nancy Forbes 37 Sixth Street Anytown, ST 40938	Dr. Harry Stein Archives and Records 33 State Library Capitol, ST 40941
Dennis Grey 56 Seventh Street Anytown, ST 40939	Peter Irvington Director of Directions 43 Bureaucrat Bldg Capitol, ST 40942

Most organizations have their newsletters distributed by the U.S. Postal Service. If you make that choice, you must consider several factors which influence procedures and costs.

You have two possibilities: first class and third class bulk rate.

First Class. If you mail less than 200 copies, you probably will use first class. (Use first class if each item weighs less than one ounce. Use single piece third class if each piece weighs more than one ounce but less than two ounces.)

Third Class. Third class has two types of bulk rate: **commercial** and **non-profit.**

To use either type of bulk rate, you must do **all** of the following:

- Mail 200 or more copies.
- Pay an annual fee. (The fee is based on a calendar year only and is not pro-rated.)
- Have all the pieces you mail at any one time be identical in size, shape, weight, and number of content items. (There may be variations in the text.)

- Sort and bundle all pieces by zip code. (No less than ten items per bundle, but some bundles may contain more than one zip code.)
- Identify each bundle with the proper Postal Service color code sticker.
- Take the bundles directly to the proper area of your post office.

There are four ways to pay bulk rate postage: meter, precancelled stamps, precancelled envelopes and permit imprint.

If you use meter, stamps, or envelopes, you do not need a permit number. If you use a permit imprint, you need a permit number. The number is assigned by the Postal Service upon payment of a once-only fee. (Each time the permit number is used it automatically renews for one year. If you do not use the number for a year, it will lapse. You have to pay the fee again.)

A **commercial** permit

(with the substitution of your city and state names and addition of your permit number):

> Bulk Rate
> U.S. Postage
> PAID
> Yourtown, State
> Permit #

A **non-profit** permit

(with the substitution of your city and state names and addition of your permit number):

> Non-profit Org.
> U.S. Postage
> PAID
> Yourtown, State
> Permit #

"Was I angry—mostly at myself! My first issue was all done and ready to mail—sorted by zip code, bundled, and at the post office an hour before the deadline. Then a postal inspector glanced at the first copy and rejected the whole batch. I had left the city name out of the indicia box.

"I had to type a correct bulk rate imprint 20 times on a sheet of address labels, get six copies of my master, cut them all to size, and place one of the "stamps" on every newsletter.

"Proofread EVERYTHING."

Qualifying for non-profit rate.

Non-profit bulk rate costs less than half of commercial bulk rate. To use non-profit bulk rate, you must file an application and have it approved by the proper postal official. Your chances for success are best if you

- first consult informally with your postmaster or postal imprint officer.
- submit with your application clear copies of documents such as your constitution, by-laws, articles of incorporation, financial reports, and minutes of annual meetings.
- submit a copy of an Internal Revenue Service letter of determination or certificate of income tax exemption for your organization. The letter or certificate should refer to section 501 (c) of the Tax Code.

Note: You might qualify without an IRS certificate, and you might be disqualified even though you have a tax exemption. The Postal Service makes its own decision and does not automatically use the IRS status.

Forwarding and returning

Bulk rates do not include all the forwarding and returning services of first class. If you mail bulk rate:

- your newsletter might be forwarded only within your local area.
- your newsletter will be returned only if you print **Return Postage Guaranteed** under your return address.
- you will get an address correction only if you print **Address Correction Requested** under your return address.

There is an extra charge for return and address correction services. Check with your local postal officials for current rates and procedures.

For details, read **Mailing Permits,** a publication of the U.S. Postal Service. Get a copy of this pamphlet from your post office, the Government Printing Office or your public library.

ADDRESS CORRECTION REQUESTED

"Paul Anderson is one of our members who works over at the hospital. He's in the accounting department and has access to all the data processing machines they use to keep track of the money.

"Paul got his boss to agree to a nice arrangement for me and our membership chairman. He went in one Saturday morning and put our whole membership list on punch cards. Every card had holes for name and address, dues status, and special skills and interests. Then every month or so we give him new information and he brings the stack of cards up to date. It only takes him a few minutes during his lunch hour.

"Two days before I mail our newsletter I take Paul a set of blank address label sheets. He tells the machines to do their thing with the cards and labels, and I get three hundred perfectly printed and up to date labels dropped off the next day on his way home from work. Paul says the whole job takes about four minutes of machine time."

Newsletter production schedule

This form is to help set the series of deadlines needed to assure readers get newsletters on time.

As you make your production schedule, remember the basic rule of publishing: Everything takes longer than you think it will and much longer than you think it should.

Item	
Information deadline	
Meetings, publications, dates, events, people, trends, decisions, actions . . .	
Writing deadline	
Stories, ads, captions, credits, forms, letters, editorials, calendars, notices . . .	
Elements deadline	
Typesetting, headlines, art, borders, maps, photographs, nameplate, masthead . . .	
Pasteup deadline	
Copy finished camera-ready.	
Printing deadline	
All pages back from printing.	
Production deadline	
All copies folded, sealed, addressed, bundled and ready to distribute.	
Distribution deadline	
All copies delivered to Post Office or other distribution points.	
Readers have copies	

Newsletter budget form

This form is to help compute the costs of your newsletter. The form is laid out so you can assign dollar amounts to various categories. Use a per/issue, per/year, or any other basis you find convenient.

The dollars actually spent for your publication represent only part of its cost. To compute the full cost, use the column marked **Value of Donated or Allocated.** Write the worth of anything you get for free. Put down your share of machine leases or maintenance. Remember materials you may take from some general source of supplies. Most important, enter the value or cost of your time and the time of others heavily involved in your newsletter.

	Value of Donated or Allocated	Cash Outlay	Subtotals	Totals
Gathering news				
Supplies		+	=	
Services		+	=	
Equipment		+	=	
Making the parts				
Supplies		+	=	
Services		+	=	
Equipment		+	=	
Making the whole				
Supplies		+	=	
Services		+	=	
Equipment		+	=	
Production				
Supplies		+	=	
Services		+	=	
Equipment		+	=	
Distribution				
Supplies		+	=	
Services		+	=	
Equipment		+	=	
			Total	

Recommended reading

The first time I edited a newsletter, I went to my public library for a how-to book. There wasn't one there nor one listed in standard sources. Moreover, the books about graphics and printing seemed complicated or too oriented to advertising design. I was just a volunteer and wanted something simple and related to newsletters.

The book situation improved greatly during the 1970s. With more "do-it-yourselfers" in all fields several authors wrote books about simple graphics. With newsletters becoming a popular medium, the first few books appeared telling how to make them. I had titles to recommend in my workshops and had also decided to join the ranks of authors.

In compiling the list below, I decided to include only books dealing directly with newsletters or simple graphics and production. Libraries and bookstores have good stocks of books about writing and editing, but books just about design and production are harder to find. I've also tried to limit this list to inexpensive books. As of this writing (March 1982), most of the titles below are available in paperback for less than ten dollars.

Publishing Newsletters, by Howard Penn Hudson. Author Hudson's *Newsletter on Newsletters* has for eighteen years put him at the center of activity regarding commercial newsletters. His book is strong on editorial planning, market analysis, building and maintaining subscription lists and using direct mail. No one publishing a newsletter for profit should be without this source of good advice. **ISBN 684–17496–0. 224 pages. Charles Scribner's Sons, 597 Fifth Ave., New York City 10017.**

The Newsletter Editor's Desk Book, by Marvin Arth and Helen Ashmore. These authors edit *Newsletter Forum,* a commercial newsletter strong on aspects of writing and editing. With backgrounds in journalism, their book includes a model style manual and tips for working with reporters. **ISBN 0–938270–02–8. 130 pages. Newsletter Forum, 4700 Roanoke Pkwy. #105, Kansas City MO 64112.**

Studio Tips, by Bill Gray. Lettered and drawn by hand, this practical book is full of tricks for better pasteup and printing. It's also a delight to read. Get one if you are at all serious about graphics. In fact, get the sequels as well: **More Studio Tips** and **Still More Studio Tips,** by the same author. **ISBN 0–442–22819–8. 128 pages. Van Nostrand Reinhold Company, 135 West 50th St., New York City 10020.**

Complete Guide to Pasteup, by Walter Graham. This title means what it says: complete. Text, drawings and photos show every trick of the trade. Even the twenty page glossary is illustrated. Author Graham comes to pasteup from the standpoint of printing rather than design, so the book is strong on production. **ISBN 0–912920–40–8. 216 pages. Dot Pasteup Supply, Box 369, Omaha NB 68101.**

The House Journal Handbook, by Peter Jackson. This fine book is the British counterpart to **Editing Your Newsletter.** The pages are rich with sound advice and clear examples, most drawn from publications in business and industry. Author Jackson left wide margins next to black body copy, then went back through it to print comments and tips in purple. Nicely done! **No ISBN. 196 pages. The Industrial Society, Box 1BQ, Robert Hyde House, 48 Bryanston Square, London W1H 1BQ.**

Manual of Graphic Techniques, by Tom Porter and Bob Greenstreet. When you're ready to move to the next level of graphics, get this book. It covers all the important topics in plenty of detail and with super illustrations (like the sample on page 58 of this book). It's design-oriented and has some four color work, so goes well with other graphics books more oriented to production. **ISBN 0–684–16504–X. 128 pages. Charles Scribner's Sons, 597 Fifth Ave., New York City 10017.**

Graphic Idea Notebook, by Jan White. Another book strong on design, as you can see from the excerpts I used on pages 62 and 63. Author White built his book around concepts such as "combining and joining", "the editorial eye" and "breaking up text." It's also one of the very few graphics books to show how to make maps. Lots of inspiration here to make newsletters look better. **ISBN 0–8230–2149–1. 192 pages. Watson–Guptill Publications, 1515 Broadway, New York City 10036.**

Photography for Student Publications, by Carl Vandermeulen. Don't be put off by the word "student." This book is by far the best about photography for any small publication such as a newsletter. It's full of pictures as examples, technical tips and ways to save money. Rave reviews from magazines in photography and journalism. **ISBN 0–931940–01–X. 164 pages. The Middleberg Press, Box 166, Orange City, IA 51041.**

Pocket Pal, by International Paper Company. This graphic arts production guide has become a classic since its first publication in 1934. Now in its twelfth printing, it still covers everything from history of papers to technology of presses and binding. Two-color printing throughout makes dozens of illustrations especially useful. **No ISBN. 204 pages. International Paper Company, 77 West 45th St., New York City 10036.**

Paper Basics, by David Saltman. Everything you might ever want to know about paper and have been afraid someone would offer to tell you: forestry, manufacture, selection, purchasing, mathematics, and even recycling. Covers papers for products from newsletters to greeting cards through posters. **ISBN 0–442–25121–1. 223 pages. Van Nostrand Reinhold Company, 135 West 50th St., New York City 10020.**

In addition to these fine books, you should know about the huge range of clip art and design books published by Dover Publications, 180 Varick St., New York City 10014. They'll be happy to send you a catalog. For directories of newsletter names, see the list on page seven. Oh yes, one more thing! To get more copies of the book you are reading now, use the order form inside the back cover.

Editors associations

There are probably thousands of organizations which an editor might join for professional companionship. Here are a few of the larger ones. Most have several dozen state and local affiliates.

1. In-plant Print Management Assn., 666 No. Lake Shore Drive-Ste. 513B, Chicago IL 60611.
2. Institute for Graphic Communication, 375 Commonwealth Ave., Boston MA 02115.
3. Natl. Assn. of Government Communicators, Box 2148, Rockville MD 20852.
4. Society for Technical Communication, 815 15th St. NW-Ste. 506, Washington DC 20005.
5. Internatl. Printing and Graphics Communications Union, 1730 Rhode Island Ave. NW, Washington DC 20036.
6. Women in Communications, Box 9561, Austin TX 78766.

7. Internatl. Assn. of Business Communicators, 870 Market St.-Ste. 940, San Francisco CA 94102.
8. Council for the Advancement and Support of Education, One Dupont Circle NW-Ste. 660, Washington DC 20036.
9. Newsletter Assn. of America, 900 17th St. NW-Ste. 504, Washington DC 20006
10. Bank Marketing Assn., 309 W. Washington St., Chicago IL 60606.
11. American Society of Association Executives, 1575 Eye St. NW, Washington DC 20005
12. American Society of Hospital Public Relations, 840 Lake Shore Drive, Chicago IL 60611
13. Towers Club (for entrepreneur editors), P.O. Box 2038, Vancouver WA 98668

Newsletter addresses

Nameplates, front pages or other portions of these sixty newsletters appeared as illustrations in this book.

1. American English Today, P.O. Box 401865, Dallas TX 75240.
2. The Animator, Northwest Film Study Center, 1119 SW Park Ave., Portland OR 97205.
3. APHA Letter, American Printing History Association, Technical College Library, 300 J St., Brooklyn NY 11201
4. As the Wheel Turns, Budget Rent-a-Car Co., 35 E. Wacker Drive, Chicago IL 60601.
5. Barnes Bulletin, Beaverton Schools, P.O. Box 200, Beaverton OR 97002.
6. California Department of Forestry, 1416 Ninth Ave., Sacramento CA 95814.
7. Cedar Hills Happenings, Beaverton Schools, P.O. Box 200, Beaverton OR 97002.
8. Cedar Millrace, Beaverton Schools, P.O. Box 200, Beaverton OR 97002.
9. Communication News, American Society of Association Executives, 1575 Eye St. NW, Washington DC 20005.
10. Congressman Ron Wyden Reports, U.S. House of Representatives, Washington DC 20515.
11. Cooper Mountain News, Beaverton Schools, P.O. Box 200, Beaverton OR 97002.

12. Council Circle, Urban Indian Council, 1364 SW Alder, Portland OR 97205.
13. The Council Newsletter, Council on Foundations, 1828 L St. NW, Washington DC 20036.
14. Currents, Columbia River Cirl Scout Council, 4747 SW Kelly, Portland OR 97201.
15. Daytime PM, Pacific Mutual Insurance Company, 700 Newport Drive, Newport Beach CA 92663.
16. The Delta Hotels Bulletin, 10211 St. Edwards Drive., Richmond BC, Canada V6X 2M8.
17. The DMSO Report, 10149 SW Barbur Blvd. #103, Portland OR 97219.
18. Emphasis, Panned Parenthood Federation of America, 810 Seventh Ave., New York City 10019.
19. En Route Club, Air Canada, 905 W. Georgia, Vancouver BC, Canada.
20. Exchange Networks, National Center for Citizen Involvement, 1214 16th Ave. NW, Washington DC 20036.
21. The Falcon Flier, Five Oaks School, P.O. Box 200, Beaverton OR 97006.
22. Garden Home Gazette, Beaverton Schools, P.O. Box 200, Beaverton OR 97002.
23. Gifted Children Newsletter, P.O. Box 115, Sewell NJ 08080.
24. Grafica, P.O. Box 1435, Beaverton OR 97075.
25. Government Marketing News, Rockford Trust Bldg. 11th floor, Rockford IL 61101.
26. Housing Consultants Inc., TP Management, 11999 Katy Freeway #340, Houston TX 77079.
27. Huenefeld Report, P.O. Box U, Bedford MA 01730.
28. The Image Digest, P.O. Box 1463, Ann Arbor MI 48106.
29. Inside 24J, Salem School District 24J, Salem OR 97302.
30. Intercom, Citizens Bancorporation, 636 Wisconsin Ave., Sheboygan WI 53081.
31. ISCC Executive Report, 20 No. Wacker Drive, Chicago IL 60606.
32. JEMIMA, Japan Electric Assocation, 1910 Toronomon, Minatoku, Tokyo, Japan.
33. Kanata News, One Grant McConochie Way, Vancouver BC, Canada V7B 1V1.
34. The Kerr Report, 601 University Av. 150, Sacramento CA 95825.
35. Kovels, Antiques Inc., P.O. Box 22200, Beachwood OH 44122.
36. Life and Breath PEOPLE, American Lung Association, 10001 W. Lisbon Ave., Milwaukee WI 53222.
37. The Little Red Schoolhouse, 7215 NE 165th Court, Bothell WA 98011.
38. Management Insight, 155 Cottage St. NE, Salem OR 97310.
39. Metroforum, Metropolitan Service District, 527 SW Hall, Portland OR 97201.
40. NAIS Report, 18 Tremont St., Boston MA 02108.
41. Neighbor to Neighbor, City Hall, 1220 SW Fifth, Portland OR 97204.
42. The Newsletter Forum, 4700 Roanoke Pkwy. #105, Kansas City MO 64112.
43. Newsletter on Newsletters, 44 W. Market, Rhinebeck NY 12572.
44. On the Level, Neil Kelly Company, 804 N. Alberta, Portland OR 97217.
45. Open Forum, Fund for an Open Society, 9803 Roosevelt Blvd., Philadelphia PA 19114.
46. Opportunity, Georgia Pacific Co., 900 SW Sixth Ave., Portland OR 97204.
47. Oregon State Parks Quarterly, 525 Trade St. SE, Salem OR 97310.
48. Pathfinder, Center for Free enterprise, Texas A&M University, College Station TX 77843.
49. Portland Meadows Flyer, 1001 N. Schmeer Rd., Portland OR 97217.
50. Portsmouth Biweekly, Port of Portland, 700 NE Multnomah, Portland OR 97212.
51. Que Pasa, Mission Viejo Company, 26137 Christiana, Mission Viejo CA.
52. The RCI Communicator, Reddy Communications Inc., 537 Steamboat Road, Greenwich CT 06830.
53. Real Estate Intelligence Report, 7315 Wisconsin Ave. NW, Washington DC 20014.
54. Reportland, Portland Convention Bureau, 26 SW Salmon, Portland OR 97204.
55. Scholarships, Fellowships and Loans, Bellman Publishing Company, Arlington MA 02174.
56. Shelter Sense, Humane Society of the U.S., 2100 L St. NW, Washington DC 20037.
57. Shipyard Weekly, 600 New Hampshire Ave. NW, Washington DC 20037.
58. The Trader, Chicago Board of Trade, 141 West Jackson Blvd., Chicago IL 60604.
59. UPDATE, Office on Latin America, 110 Maryland Ave. NE, Washington DC 20002.
60. Ways and Means, Conference on Alternative Policies, 2000 Florida Ave. NW, Washington DC 20009.

GEOMETRIC DESIGN AND ORNAMENT

Index